MORE
THAN CAKE

MORE THAN CAKE

100 Baking Recipes Built
for Pleasure and Community

Natasha Pickowicz

PHOTOGRAPHS BY GRAYDON HERRIOTT

Artisan | New York

Library of Congress Cataloging-in-Publication Data

Names: Pickowicz, Natasha, author.
Title: More than cake : 100 baking recipes built for
pleasure and community / by Natasha Pickowicz.
Description: New York : Artisan, [2023] | Includes index.
Identifiers: LCCN 2022027918 | ISBN 9781648290541 (hardcover)
Subjects: LCSH: Baking. | Baked products. | LCGFT: Cookbooks.
Classification: LCC TX765 .P477 2023 | DDC 641.81/5—dc23/eng/20220809
LC record available at https://lccn.loc.gov/2022027918

Design by Giulia Garbin

Artisan books are available at special discounts when purchased in bulk for
premiums and sales promotions as well as for fundraising or educational use.
Special editions or book excerpts also can be created to specification.
For details, please contact specialmarkets@hbgusa.com.

Published by Artisan,
an imprint of Workman Publishing Co., Inc.,
a subsidiary of Hachette Book Group, Inc.
1290 Avenue of the Americas
New York, NY 10104
artisanbooks.com

Artisan is a registered trademark of
Workman Publishing Co., Inc.,
a subsidiary of Hachette Book Group, Inc.

Printed in China on responsibly sourced paper

First printing, March 2023

1 3 5 7 9 10 8 6 4 2

In good company there is a place for you:
a disposition for amusement,
a healthy appetite, an attentive ear,
a capacity for laughter, each is fuel
for celebration's fire.

—PATIENCE GRAY

For my parents

CONTENTS

INTRODUCTION

 A few years ago, I visited the Food and Finance High School, a culinary-focused public school in the Hell's Kitchen neighborhood of Manhattan, where I spoke to a class of ninth graders about my path into pastry. We talked about bake sales, cookie potlucks, and recycling. We talked about leadership, early mornings, and empathy.

The next week, thirty sweet thank-you emails appeared in my in-box. One of the students, who began his letter with "Dear Chef Natasha," observed that I had taught him that being a pastry chef is "so much more than cake." This wise young person nailed it.

Being a pastry chef is so much more than cake—it's the patience and focus to execute it, the hard work and fortitude to continue, and then, finally, the indescribable, euphoric finale of bringing people together over something special that you made.

More Than Cake is not about baking for one. Baking is about reinforcing connections and creating new ones. I was drawn to restaurants because of the exhilarating communal energy so specific to kitchen work. I wanted to work pastry: the corner of the kitchen that is responsible for creating the dishes that symbolize celebration, decadence, romance, and pampering.

I lucked into my first kitchen job, as the baker for a queer, punk luncheonette called Dépanneur Le Pick Up in Montréal. I had just moved to the city and had few friends and even less confidence. The immersion into the exacting physical work, the big personalities, the chatty regulars, and the creative energy left

me exhausted but exhilarated. When I was in the kitchen, hours felt like minutes.

My job wasn't just about baking, either. While I was at Le Pick Up, I created community events that revolved around food. Coworkers' birthdays, pregnancies, and graduations meant there would be fudgy cakes at the end of the shift. Chefs, food writers, and local personalities taught intricate workshops about the basics of canning, pickling, and sausage making. Independent radio stations broadcasted doo-wop live from the gravel-lined backyard. Musicians on tour stopped by to play in front of the beer fridge, and I sent them on their way with slices of carrot cake and potato galettes.

I still had so much to learn about baking, but I felt right away the effect it had: sharing simple treats brought people to our weird little world. Baked goods are part of my commitment to community building. Since then, I've shared those values with every pastry team I've had, through volunteering, field trips, classes, and bake sales. I am my most confident self in a kitchen, but I need to feel tethered to others in order to connect the dots between what comes from my hands and what I feel in my heart.

My confidence in the kitchen didn't happen right away. I didn't attend culinary school, so I don't approach baking the same way that pastry chefs who have do. I've always felt like an outsider in that way, inferior to my colleagues, who pulled sugar, rolled fondant, and tempered chocolate effortlessly. Who was I, if I wasn't that?

Over the years, through exhaustive trial and error, obsessive book reading and video watching, turning to friends and peers, and working in kitchens alongside talented people, I gradually developed my own baking perspective. My love of nature and art, my background in literature and music, my Chinese and Californian heritage—all of it informs my desserts.

It seems like with home cooking (and, honestly, in modern life, too), there is an expectation to see

results immediately. We like to start and finish a dish in one breath; we value "fast" recipes like one-bowl cakes and no-knead breads that pitch a hands-off approach or a quick turnaround. As a baker, I appreciate these types of hacks and tricks, which offer irresistible entry points into the world of pastry.

But what I truly love are the projects that I can examine from a distance, inspect piece by piece, and complete methodically. I approach the kitchen with a plan, timing each mini project around my day and schedule, slowly filling up my fridge and pantry with supporting players waiting for their moment to be put to use. I write out long, detailed lists with a permanent marker before taping them on the wall, which is like stretching before you go for a run—not only does it feel soothing to do it in the moment, but it also really feels necessary once you've hit the pavement.

These recipes are not complicated or hard to execute, but they ask that you be present. "Good cooking is honest, sincere and simple," wrote the legendary Elizabeth David in *A Book of Mediterranean Food*. "And by this I do not mean to imply that you will find in this, or indeed in any other book, the secret of turning out first-class food in a few minutes with no trouble. Good food is always a trouble and its preparation should be regarded as a labor of love."

There is a way to reframe baking not as an overwhelming means to an end but as a meditative process to enjoy in and of itself. Approached with David's wisdom in mind—with an expectation that time is involved, that thoughtfulness will be rewarded, that having a plan physically and mentally feels great—it's possible to cultivate a sense of joy, ease, and pride around a complicated-seeming or involved dish.

I like to call that fizzy, magical feeling "the pride chip." It's the well-earned celebration of a personal accomplishment, like building a teetering cake from scratch or hosting your own bake sale. It's the satisfaction of rolling out a sheet of dough and seeing the speckles of butter evenly encased inside: I did that. I made that happen. It was just flour and butter before I got my hands on it.

Of course, accidents and mistakes will happen—and I have made enough of them to know that they are necessary for growth. What matters is how we respond, how closely we are paying attention, and how we apply logic, intuition, and grace to unexpected circumstances.

A cookbook is your manual for avoiding those mistakes, a critical text with recipes that ask for your trust. Like hitting "repeat" on a great song, I'll often reread a great paragraph, sentence, or page three or four times in a row. I love food writing in particular, because of the way sensual, witty language is deployed side by side with the more clinical, procedural tone of recipe steps. It is in this tension, of the passionate context for the dish next to the technical how-to, that my favorite cookbooks come alive.

This book is designed to provide you with a million ideas for how to delight and honor other people, no matter how big or small the occasion: from the one-on-ones to riotous groups, from baking just for your partner to baking for your entire office, from once-in-a-lifetime celebrations to more ordinary, small moments.

It has been a great honor to write this book, a unique, intense process that synthesized my personal histories, influences, and ideologies. I used to feel that there was no joy greater than feeding other people, until I started to share my recipes instead. Creating recipes is a loving,

community-based act in constant communion with our world. Recipes reference history, acknowledge inspirations, and tell us something about who we are as people. Baking made me a better leader and critical thinker. Baking asks me to work with compassion, kindness, and thrift. Baking brings me closer to my parents, my friends, and my neighbors. Baking is more than cake.

ESSENTIAL TOOLS

Too weak, too strong, too mild, too bitter:
sometimes interesting, never delicious. One night at a party
a painter twice my age said tiredly to me, "It's all in the
measurements. Just measure accurately and I guarantee it will
come out fine." He was right. I learned to measure, and the coffee
misery ended as suddenly as it had begun: as though I had driven
through a patch of fog on a night when visibility is already low.

—VIVIAN GORNICK, *Fierce Attachments*

 You don't need many tools to be a great baker, just the right ones. It took me some time to learn that lesson, since I was so spoiled from my time in professional fine-dining kitchens, with their shiny convection ovens and sharp Japanese knives.

But restrictions bring out our inner resourcefulness, and even if your kitchen is small, like mine, you can still be creative and efficient, and thrive. If you're a beginner, these tools will take your baking to the next level. If you get only one item, please make it a digital scale.

Purchasing these tools piecemeal from specialty stores can get pricey. Look up the local restaurant supply store—the no-frills warehouse where chefs and cooks shop for everything from cutting boards to giant rolls of plastic wrap to cake pans—and make a trip. The prices will be lower, and your kitchen will be stocked with the same tools as your favorite restaurants.

Digital scale: A small scale is the absolute easiest and best way to become a better, more consistent baker. It is indispensable. Baking with a digital scale is like running in sneakers instead of high heels. It's faster and just more enjoyable to bake with a scale instead of fumbling around with cup measurements. You will soar to the finish line of every baking project if you have a scale. I love the small Escali models that can handle weights of up to 5 kilos.

Half-sheet (13-by-18-inch/33 by 45 cm) and quarter-sheet (9-by-13-inch/23 by 33 cm) pans: Aluminum sheet pans can roast fruit, toast nuts and flours, store sheeted doughs, and cool hot candies—in short, pretty much everything. They're preferable when baking thin layer cakes, because the stacked sheet pans take up less space than a wobbly tower of round cake pans.

Silicone spatulas: High-heat silicone spatulas have soft, rounded edges that are crucial for stirring curds, custards, and jams; cleanly scraping the edges of mixing bowls and pots; or spreading out super-hot caramel candies or jellies. Look for commercial Rubbermaid spatulas, which last forever, come in many sizes, and resist absorbing unwanted savory smells.

Offset spatulas: Sometimes I imagine myself as a cowboy, with a holster slung low on my hips. My quick-fire tool of choice? A 4¾-inch (12 cm) offset spatula, which I use for everything from handling delicate cookies and flipping sticky fruits to spreading fillings and swooping buttercream. The long, angled blade makes precise, delicate movements as well as big, efficient gestures, like spreading cake batter in as few strokes as possible. For icing cakes taller than 5 inches (12.5 cm), look for an offset spatula that's 8 or 10 inches (20 or 25 cm) long.

Balloon whisk: The open structure of a bulbous balloon whisk introduces air into dry ingredients like flour, or into wet ingredients like whipped cream, much faster than any other kind of whisk; look for pliant wires that aren't too stiff.

Candy thermometer: A small digital thermometer is like a scale: it provides comfort and ease via precise numerical measurements. Though you could make an Italian buttercream or caramel candy without one, why would you? Use it for checking everything from loaves of bread to wobbly custards.

Immersion blender: If you don't have space for a food processor or blender, a small, handheld immersion blender will ably take on the responsibilities of these larger appliances. Even the smallest ones are great for smoothing out custards and ganaches, whipping cream, and breaking down cooked fruit.

Bench scrapers and bowl scrapers: You'll want the sharp rigid edge of a bench scraper to divide sticky bread doughs quickly and with ease. Then drag the edge of the bench scraper down your work surface to quickly clean up shaggy dough bits and patches of water. The rounded, floppy edges of flexible bowl scrapers quickly transfer doughs from container to counter, cleanly scrape the inside of mixing bowls, and efficiently scoop and lift finely chopped or cooked ingredients.

French-style tapered rolling pin: For rolling any kind of dough, you can use a French-style pin, which is a long, slender piece of wood that gently tapers at the ends (versus the heavier American-style pin, which is a thicker, untapered cylinder of wood with a handle at each end). The ease of use of the French-style pin is a game changer; because it is one solid piece, you can move your hands closer together to target "problem areas" that you want to roll thinner. Your hands are also closer to the dough and can apply more direct pressure.

Pastry brush: For adding a soak to cake layers, a small pastry brush with a 1-inch (2.5 cm) head of natural boar bristles is best. For dusting off excess flour, use a wider 1½- or 2-inch (2.5 to 5 cm) head, and never, ever let it come in contact with anything wet, which can clump the bristles. To prevent shedding, always wash the brushes by hand.

Pastry bags and piping tips: For piping decorative patterns, portioning choux, or filling baked goods, pastry bags give sharp, clean results. Assorted piping tips aren't essential but are extremely fun to play around with.

Ice cream scoop: A 2-ounce trigger ice cream scoop is a speedy way to portion batches of dough for cookies or biscuits before baking. It's perfect for when you're scaling up your baking for the holidays or bake sales, or don't have a scale handy.

Revolving cake stand: If you want to improve the finished look of your layer cakes, a 12-inch-diameter (30 cm) revolving cake stand, or turntable, is the best way to achieve polished, fluid lines. Using one is a bit like patting your head and rubbing your stomach at the same time: slowly rotate the stand with one hand while icing the cake with the other, gradually speeding up to get that clean, elegant exterior. Look for a grippy, heavy base made of cast iron.

Silicone baking mats: Heatproof silicone baking mats have a slippery, nonstick surface that is great for handling boiling-hot candy, rolling out cookie or tart dough, or dehydrating sticky fruits or candied herbs.

Fish spatula: This indispensable tool is not just for cooking seafood! Its wide, slightly flexible slotted blade is ideal for handling delicate pastry or fruits held in syrup.

Notebook, tape, and Sharpie: Most professional bakers keep their own notebooks, which they use to copy down recipes, make annotations and observations, and draw diagrams of desserts. Keeping your own notes will let you retain information in a different, deeper way than just following along on a computer screen or in a cookbook. And always keep a roll of masking tape and a fresh Sharpie on hand to label and date everything.

What follows are the tools and materials you likely own already, and that are used regularly throughout these recipes as well:

Nonstick spray: I named my sourdough starter after my kitchen guilty pleasure, PAM spray. Besides using it to lightly coat baking surfaces like cake molds and sheet pans, you can spray it in measuring cups when working with sticky liquids like honey or on your hands when handling wet dough like focaccia.

Parchment paper: It's a necessary evil for even baking. At least you can buy recycled paper versions for more eco-friendly options, and most parchment can be rolled up to be used again.

Aluminum foil: If handled gently, a sheet of foil can be used many times, as it softens like a well-worn dish towel. Very handy for oven-steaming projects, like cheesecake, flan, or crème brûlée.

Foodservice film: For protecting everything from proofing doughs to baked loaves, there's no denying that plastic film is incredibly useful. Skip the pathetic, flimsy grocery store rolls of plastic wrap, and invest in at least 2,000 feet of "foodservice"-style film that comes in a big box with a sharp blade. (Reynolds manufactures the sturdiest boxes; these also make excellent unexpected presents.)

Mixing bowls: One set of stackable metal bowls is vital to your mise en place, the process of measuring each ingredient out before mixing. Use them for everything: as part of a double boiler, for whisking up

sabayons or melting chocolate, as a home for rising doughs or cooling curds, or as a sturdy container for building a bombe parfait or dome-shaped layer cake.

Forms for baking: For this book, you'll need a standard 12-cup muffin tin, 8-inch (20 cm) and 10-inch (25 cm) round cake pans, and an 8-inch (20 cm) Pullman loaf pan. Though glass is a popular material for baking dishes and pie plates, aluminized steel or anodized aluminum has superior versatility and grip and a more even heating style. Though nonstick pans will work, voluminous cakes like a chiffon or genoise sponge won't climb as high against a nonstick surface. Cast-iron skillets look great on the table, especially if holding single-layer cakes, dinner rolls, or scones.

Knives: You don't need a fancy chef's knife to make anything in this book. A nimble 5-inch-long (12.5 cm) petty knife is engineered to handle delicate pastry techniques like slicing citrus, peeling fruit, cutting herbs, and cubing butter. For a cheaper everyday option, stock up on small serrated knives with a 3½-inch (9 cm) blade—they can do everything a petty knife does, but for about $6. And, finally, a larger serrated knife (look for a blade at least 8 inches/20 cm long) slices sharp-looking cross sections of bread, a frozen slab of parfait, or a creamy, vertiginous layer cake.

Timer: Use your cell phone, built-in oven timer, computer timer, whatever—it takes 2 seconds to implement crucial insurance for your bake. When experimenting with new recipes, it's tough to guess when something is ready, so take an extra moment to get the alarm set for proofing doughs, chill times, and oven work.

Sieves: Tea strainers are great for sifting small amounts of baking leaveners or cocoa powder, while a larger sieve can strain liquids, de-clump powdered sugar, or aerate flour in a matter of moments. For the smoothest, silkiest curds, fruit purees, and pastry creams, you might want to invest in an 8-inch (20 cm) chinois, which is a conical sieve with extremely fine stainless steel mesh.

Coffee filters: For clarifying flavored oils, syrups, stocks, or juices with any particulate matter, pass the liquid through a coffee filter; it will strain slowly but result in a clear, vivid liquid, as in the crystalline Herb Oil (page 189).

Round cookie cutter set: Even if you aren't a fan of novelty cookie cutter shapes, you'll need perfectly circular shapes, for punching out scones, biscuits, or sheet cookies like linzer sandwiches (see page 39) and gingerbread (see page 47). For the best bang for your buck, look for sets of between 8 and 12 stainless steel round cutters, which come nestled in a case like Russian dolls.

 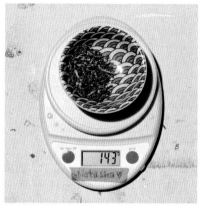 

  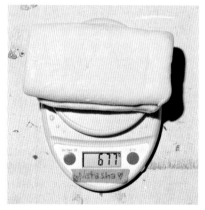

NEVER-ENDING

COOKIES

Cookies are the easiest place to start baking, which is great because everyone loves cookies. They have a universal, timeless appeal; infinite variations; and a pocket-size scale perfect for sharing.

We all love to gift cookie boxes during the holiday season, but why not make them ubiquitous year-round? Cookies are such a direct and unpretentious way to express gratitude and love. Instead of an email, a tip, or a bottle of wine, cookies tell the receiver that you spent time and care making them. (In my family, a box of Nubby Granola Shortbread, page 25, and a Sharpie doodle are far more precious than any delivered flowers.)

A cookie box doesn't have to feature an ambitious assortment of six or eight kinds of cookies, which can be a drag to execute. I'd like to normalize the single-variety cookie box, accented with some in-season fruit; even better, an elegant duet of two contrasting cookies. The moment a baking project fills you with dread instead of excitement, it's time to scale back.

Another way to share these cookies throughout the year is simple: spend an afternoon mixing batches of your three favorite cookies, then freeze them portioned and unbaked. Bake a few sheet pans next time you plan to walk past your local community fridge or pantry. If you volunteer at a local organization, bring a dozen cookies to your next scheduled shift. Fancy restaurants send guests home with pastries for the next morning; bring the same energy to your next dinner party or bake sale (see How to Bake Sale, page 35).

For casual everyday surprises that feel surprisingly personal, wrap up a few cookies (only three or four at a time!), enough for a person to share with a friend, or nibble over two days. The beloved people you see regularly—teachers, baristas, cat sitters, health-care workers, a roommate having a bad week—wouldn't they all love an extra treat for no reason at all? These days, I rarely leave the house without a tiny bundle of cookies tucked into my bag, just in case I run into someone.

My hope is that you will make your favorite classics—like chocolate chip cookies, chewy macaroons, and crisp biscotti—and go crazy for the unexpected twists and deep flavor I've engineered into each bite.

CITRUSY MACAROONS

American-style coconut macaroons are a captivating study in opposing textures. Clusters of honeyed coconut bake with a crunchy, spiky exterior and a soft, taffy-like center. Coconut gets the spotlight, but the sticky sweet-and-sour citrus peel is a funky, bright second player.

Like pâte à choux (as for the Mocha Latte Puffs, page 303) or the Seeded Rye Dough (page 205), this cookie dough is cooked in a pot over steady heat. Rely on your senses for consistent execution: important visual cues (film gathering on the bottom of the pot) and olfactory triggers (a toasty and sweet steam) will guide you to the finish line. Err on the side of undercooking the macaroon slurry; a tight, dry batter will result in a brittle, disappointing cookie. (Though I do have an easy fix; see tip #1.)

1. PREHEAT THE OVEN AND PREP THE PANS. Preheat the oven to 350°F (175°C). To bake in batches, top two half-sheet pans with parchment paper lightly misted with cooking spray.

2. MIX THE INGREDIENTS. In a wide bowl, combine the coconut flakes, egg whites, coconut sugar, honey, kosher salt, and white rice flour and stir until well mixed and goopy.

3. COOK THE DOUGH. Gently heat a large skillet (at least 10 inches/25 cm wide) over low heat. Add the coconut mixture to the pan all at once. Stir constantly with a silicone spatula or wooden spoon; the mixture should lightly coat the bottom of the pan with a fine film. After 6 to 8 minutes, the mixture should appear glossy and wet but not runny, nor parched or scorched-looking. Off the heat, stir in the vanilla and chopped candied grapefruit peel.

4. REST THE DOUGH. Transfer the mixture to a bowl and press plastic wrap on top. Let the dough cool slightly, 15 to 20 minutes.

→

MAKES 20 TO 24 MACAROONS

20 MINUTES ACTIVE TIME
1 HOUR INACTIVE TIME

2½ cups (200 g) unsweetened coconut flakes
4 egg whites (120 g) (see tip #2)
1 cup (200 g) coconut sugar
3 tablespoons (60 g) honey
1 teaspoon kosher salt
¼ cup (30 g) white rice flour
1 teaspoon vanilla extract
¾ cup (about 200 g) Candied Grapefruit Peel (page 131), roughly chopped
Flaky sea salt

TIP 1 —— *Overcook your macaroon dough? Don't throw it away! Stir in 1 large egg white after the mixture has cooled to reintroduce moisture and lift, and you'll be able to bake as normal.*

TIP 2 —— *Save the extra egg yolks for the crumbly-crisp cookies in this chapter, like the Coffee-Hazelnut Linzers (page 39) or Pine Nut Sablés with Taleggio (page 37). Freeze the yolks in a small container if you won't use them in the next few days.*

5. SHAPE THE COOKIES. Transfer 2-tablespoon mounds of the dough to the prepared sheet pans, spaced 2 inches (5 cm) apart; you should be able to fit 10 to 12 per pan. Sprinkle the tops with a bit of flaky sea salt.

6. BAKE THE COOKIES. Bake the cookies until golden brown all over and glossy and crisp on the edges but soft and tender in the center, 18 to 20 minutes. Let cool completely on the pan. (The macaroons will continue to crisp up as they cool; you should be able to easily press a finger into the top of a hot macaroon.) The macaroons will stay chewy for up to 4 days if tightly wrapped and stored at room temperature.

NUBBY GRANOLA SHORTBREAD

This breakfast-inspired shortbread is a special way to utilize the last serving of your favorite granola, which adds a mysterious crunch to the buttery cookie. Sandy ultrafine rice flour enhances this cookie's naturally melt-in-your-mouth texture. Cold cubed butter is worked into the dry ingredients using a food processor, before the dough is pressed into a pan with your knuckles. The final flurry of powdered sugar is essential.

Because of its impressive life span after being baked, a pan of this shortbread, scored but not cut, is an exceptional, easy gift—it stays fresh for over a week and will survive even the bumpiest journey.

1. **PREHEAT THE OVEN AND PREP THE PAN.** Preheat the oven to 350°F (175°C). Tuck a sheet of parchment paper into a quarter-sheet pan (9 by 13 inches/13 by 33 cm). Lightly mist the parchment with cooking spray.

2. **COMBINE THE DRY INGREDIENTS.** In a food processor, combine the granola, walnut pieces, white rice flour, granulated sugar, and kosher salt and pulse until the mixture is pebbly and fine.

3. **ADD THE COLD BUTTER.** Add the butter and pulse another 8 to 10 times, until the mixture feels like damp, coarse bread crumbs. The butter should almost disappear into the dry ingredients but not be taken so far that the dough is clumping and gathering around the blade.

4. **PRESS INTO THE PAN.** Scatter the dough evenly in the prepared sheet pan. Use your knuckles to lightly press the crumb into an even layer. It should be about 1/2 inch (1.25 cm) thick. Do not apply too much pressure, as this would make the shortbread dense and gummy. (The pan of shortbread can also be held in the freezer for up to 1 month and baked from frozen.)

$\rightarrow$

MAKES TWENTY-FOUR 1½-IINCH (4 CM) BARS

15 MINUTES ACTIVE TIME
2 HOURS INACTIVE TIME

2 cups (200 g) your favorite granola
¾ cup (85 g) walnut pieces
2 cups (300 g) white rice flour
¾ cup (150 g) granulated sugar
1 teaspoon kosher salt
8 ounces (225 g) unsalted butter, cut into ½-inch (1.25 cm) cubes, well chilled
Flaky sea salt
Powdered sugar, for dusting

TIP——*It's tricky to tell when an unfamiliar recipe is done in your oven. Never throw away a seemingly botched batch of anything—there's always another purpose for it. If the baked shortbread tastes undercooked or feels gummy, invert the shortbread onto a clean sheet pan, so the crumbs spill out. Break it up with your fingers and bake again at 325°F (165°C) for 10 minutes. Now you have instant streusel for the Millet, Parsnip, and Chocolate Chunk Muffins (page 282) or a crunchy addition to the Panna Cotta with Grated Melon (page 223). Is the shortbread overbaked and dry? Tip the crumbs into a food processor and blend until fine. Fold these crumbs into the Caramel Chocolate Chip Bombe (page 225), or add big handfuls to your next layer cake and generously brush it with the Maple and Vanilla Milk Soak (page 121).*

5. BAKE AND THEN SCORE. Bake until the edges of the shortbread are lightly browned and the center feels soft but cooked through, 35 to 40 minutes (see tip). Remove the pan from the oven and sprinkle the surface with flaky sea salt. While the shortbread is still hot, use a small knife to score it into 24 squares. Let cool completely, then cut the cookies, still in the pan, along the scored lines and dust with powdered sugar. The shortbread can be stored, tightly wrapped at room temperature, for up to 1 week.

FENNEL, CHOCOLATE, AND HAZELNUT SPEARS

Some of my most memorable recipe breakthroughs are a result of error, mistakes, and happenstance. I try to reframe even the most upsetting accidents as a potential victory or chance for growth: Does it help me examine a recipe or dish from another angle? Is there something I can learn from my failure? Can I repurpose my mistake in some way? The answer is yes!

In the process of revising my favorite biscotti recipe, I accidentally doubled the amount of butter and sugar. Butter isn't even a traditional ingredient in biscotti, so what happens when you add twice as much? In the oven, the log spreads like inching lava, finally settling into a flat, bronzed disc. Once the disk is cooled, sliced into thin spears, and baked again, the result is a super-crisp cookie, studded with toasted fennel seeds, dark chocolate, and whole hazelnuts.

A small tumbler of vin santo or espresso for dunking would be a heavenly accompaniment. Cheers to happy accidents and faux biscotti.

1. **SEPARATE ONE OF THE EGGS.** Set the white aside to be used for brushing on the cookies later.

2. **CREAM THE WET INGREDIENTS.** In a stand mixer fitted with the paddle (or in a large bowl using a handheld mixer), beat the butter, sugar, and fennel seeds until fluffy and pale, about 3 minutes. Scrape the mixer bowl with a spatula. Drop in the whole egg, the yolk, and the vanilla and beat to combine, another minute.

3. **INCORPORATE THE DRY INGREDIENTS.** In a small bowl, whisk together the all-purpose flour, almond flour, baking powder, and kosher salt. Tip the mixture into the stand mixer and beat on the lowest speed until the ingredients are halfway combined and the flour looks streaky, 8 to 10 seconds. Remove the bowl from the mixer stand, add the hazelnuts and chocolate chunks, and stir in by hand. Transfer the dough to the fridge to chill for at least 1 hour (or up to 4 days).

$\rightarrow$

MAKES TWENTY-FIVE TO THIRTY 5-INCH (12.5 CM) COOKIES

30 MINUTES ACTIVE TIME
2 HOURS INACTIVE TIME

2 eggs (100 g), at room temperature
8 tablespoons (4 ounces/115 g) unsalted butter, cubed, at room temperature
¾ cup (150 g) sugar
1 tablespoon (6 g) fennel seeds
1 teaspoon vanilla extract
¾ cup plus 1 tablespoon (100 g) all-purpose flour
¼ cup (25 g) almond flour
½ teaspoon baking powder
½ teaspoon kosher salt

(ingredients continue)

1 cup (130 g) hazelnuts
5 ounces (140 g) dark chocolate,
   roughly chopped (about 1 cup)
Flaky sea salt

4. PREHEAT THE OVEN AND PREP THE PAN. Preheat the oven to 350°F (175°C). Top a half-sheet pan with a piece of parchment paper and lightly mist the paper with cooking spray.

5. BAKE THE COOKIES. Lightly coat your hands with cooking spray. Place the dough on the prepared sheet pan and shape into a 12-by-3-inch (30 by 7.5 cm) rectangle 1 inch (2.5 cm) thick. Brush the surface of the dough with the lightly beaten reserved egg white and sprinkle the surface with flaky sea salt. Bake the mound until the edges are deeply browned and the center is slightly puffed but baked through, 35 to 40 minutes (the dough will spread quite a bit). Let the cookie cool completely.

6. CUT AND BAKE THE COOKIES A SECOND TIME. Using a serrated bread knife, slice the cookie, on a diagonal, into batons 6 inches (15 cm) long and about ¾ inch (3 cm) wide. Arrange the batons, cut side up, on the pan, tightly packed together. Return to the oven and bake until lightly golden on the surface, about 10 minutes. Let cool completely and store, tightly covered, at room temperature for up to 2 weeks.

VARIATIONS

Like granola, these spears are a great pantry-cleaner. Play around with inclusions to create your own custom riff. Add ½ teaspoon each of two different extracts (like almond or coconut); substitute polenta or rice flour for the almond flour; trade whole almonds or walnuts for the hazelnuts; incorporate dried fruits and citrus zest instead of chocolate; or sprinkle the cookies with sesame seeds or powdered sugar.

SHOYU PEANUT COOKIES

Crisp, crackling edges; a chewy, truffle-like core; and a dotted outer shell of skin-on roasted peanuts are just a few of this sweet-and-salty cookie's delights. Vacuum-sealed roasted Chinese peanuts, a nostalgic childhood favorite of mine, are sweeter, crunchier, and less greasy than Western supermarket varieties, so try to use those. No matter what, keep the peanuts in their papery skins, which crisp up in the oven into sugary, flaky shards.

A glug of shoyu—slightly sweet Japanese-style soy sauce—enhances the natural savory qualities of the peanut butter and adds a crucial umami underpinning to this classic American cookie.

MAKES 12 LARGE COOKIES

20 MINUTES ACTIVE TIME
3 HOURS INACTIVE TIME

8 ounces (225 g) unsalted butter, cubed, at room temperature
¾ cup (150 g) granulated sugar
½ cup (100 g) dark brown sugar
1 cup plus 3 tablespoons (285 g) Shoyu Peanut Butter (recipe follows)
1 egg (50 g), at room temperature
1 teaspoon vanilla extract
2 cups (240 g) all-purpose flour
2 tablespoons (15 g) rye flour
1½ teaspoons baking soda
½ teaspoon kosher salt
2 cups (150 g) unsalted skin-on roasted peanuts
½ cup (60 g) powdered sugar or snow sugar (doughnut sugar)
Flaky sea salt

1. **CREAM THE WET INGREDIENTS.** In a stand mixer fitted with the paddle (or in a large bowl using a handheld mixer), combine the butter, granulated sugar, and dark brown sugar and beat until fluffy and lightened in color, about 3 minutes. Add the shoyu peanut butter and paddle to combine. Scrape the mixer bowl with a spatula so the mixture combines evenly. Drop in the egg and vanilla and paddle for 1 minute to combine.

2. **INCORPORATE THE DRY INGREDIENTS.** In a small bowl, whisk together the all-purpose flour, rye flour, baking soda, and kosher salt. Tip the mixture into the stand mixer and paddle on the lowest speed until the ingredients are halfway combined and the flour looks streaky, about 8 seconds. Use a spatula to finish mixing by hand. Transfer the dough to an airtight container and refrigerate for at least 3 hours to chill (or up to 5 days).

3. **PREHEAT THE OVEN AND PREP THE PANS.** Preheat the oven to 350°F (175°C). To bake in batches, top two half-sheet pans with parchment paper and lightly mist the paper with cooking spray.

4. **SHAPE THE COOKIES.** Put the roasted peanuts in a shallow bowl; put the powdered sugar in another shallow bowl. Using an ice cream scoop or bench scraper, divide the dough into 12 equal portions (each should weigh between 75 and 85 g).

Lightly coat your hands with cooking spray and roll each portion into a ball. Dunk the top half of each dough ball into the roasted peanuts and press firmly so the peanuts stick. Then roll the cookie in the powdered sugar. Place 5 or 6 cookies, peanut side up, at least 4 inches (10 cm) apart on each prepared sheet pan and press gently with the heel of your hand to flatten. Sprinkle with flaky sea salt.

5. BAKE THE COOKIES. Bake until the edges are beginning to crackle and the centers look souffléed and puffy, 14 to 15 minutes. Let cool completely on the sheet pan. Store, covered, at room temperature, for up to 2 days.

VARIATIONS

This cookie dough can be easily made peanut-free. Some combinations that you'll love just as much: 1 cup (255 g) almond butter plus 3 tablespoons (45 g) tahini, with the cookies rolled in sliced almonds, or 1 cup (255 g) pistachio butter plus ½ cup (60 g) finely ground pistachios, with the cookies rolled in a blend of whole pistachios and cacao nibs.

Shoyu Peanut Butter

IN A FOOD PROCESSOR, process the peanuts until a paste forms, 3 to 4 minutes. With the machine running, stream in the oil, honey, and shoyu and continue to blend until smooth, another 3 minutes.

MAKES 1½ CUPS (300 G)

5 MINUTES ACTIVE TIME

2 cups (300 g) unsalted peanuts
2 tablespoons (30 g) grapeseed oil
2 tablespoons (40 g) honey
2 tablespoons (30 g) shoyu

TIP ——*If you aren't able to make your own peanut butter, use 1 cup (260 g) of your favorite unsweetened creamy peanut butter and add 1 tablespoon (20 g) honey and 2 tablespoons (30 g) shoyu.*

BROWN BUTTER, BUCKWHEAT, AND CHOCOLATE CHUNK COOKIES

Chocolate chip cookies get their chewy, toffee-like texture from a mixture of white and brown sugars. The sugars dissolve as they are whipped with the eggs, which is the same technique that gives great brownies a satin, crackly finish (you get that with these cookies, too). Think of sugar less as a singular "flavor" and more of a seasoning or enhancer, like salt. A little sugar nudges butter and flour into bolder, more vibrant versions of themselves. It can soften the edges of bitter, acidic chocolates. Use too much, though, and it mutes and dulls other ingredients.

The butter is browned until nutty and fragrant. Toasting wheat and buckwheat flours coaxes out their natural, earthen sweetness. Both the dark chocolate and the creamy semisweet chocolate are chopped into boulder-like chunks. Buy the best single-origin, ethically sourced vanilla extract you can find for the cookie's characteristic caramel undertones.

MAKES ABOUT 15 LARGE COOKIES

30 MINUTES ACTIVE TIME
1 DAY INACTIVE TIME

8 ounces (225 g) unsalted butter
1 cup plus 3 tablespoons (145 g)
    all-purpose flour
½ cup plus 2 tablespoons (75 g)
    buckwheat flour
½ cup plus 3 tablespoons (140 g)
    granulated sugar
½ cup plus 1 tablespoon (135 g)
    dark brown sugar
2 eggs (100 g), at room temperature

(ingredients continue)

1. **MAKE THE BROWN BUTTER.** In a small pot, bring the butter to a boil over medium-high heat. As the milk solids begin to settle to the bottom of the pot, the foam will burn off. Reduce the heat to low. Once the milk solids are a deep mahogany hue, another 4 to 5 minutes, and the air smells nutty and sweet, remove the pan from the heat. Carefully pour the liquid into a small bowl, scraping up all the browned milk solids on the bottom of the pot. Transfer to the refrigerator to resolidify, about 2 hours.

2. **TOAST THE FLOURS.** Preheat the oven to 300°F (150°C). Spread the all-purpose and buckwheat flours in a large ovenproof skillet or on a sheet pan and toast for 10 to 15 minutes. Set aside to cool completely. (This can be done up to 2 weeks in advance and stored until ready to use.)

3. **CREAM THE BUTTER.** When the brown butter feels softened but not greasy, add 145 g (about ⅔ cup; see tip #1) of it to a stand mixer fitted with the paddle (or a large bowl for using a handheld mixer). Cream the butter on medium-high speed until it is fluffy, smooth, and white in color, about 2 minutes. Scrape the butter into a small bowl and set aside.

→

2 teaspoons vanilla extract

½ teaspoon baking soda

1 teaspoon kosher salt

3½ ounces (100 g) dark chocolate, roughly chopped into chunks (about ¾ cup)

2½ ounces (70 g) semisweet chocolate, roughly chopped into chunks (about ½ cup)

One 2.1-ounce (60 g) dark chocolate bar

Flaky sea salt

TIP 1 —*You will have about 3 tablespoons of brown butter left over. Save it for another use, such as dazzling the Italian Espresso Buttercream (page 135) or Sunflower Seed Frangipane (page 175).*

TIP 2 — *Cookie doughs rich in butter and sugar need at least 1 or 2 days (and up to 4 days) to "age" in the refrigerator, otherwise they spread too much and taste greasy. As any dough rests, it hydrates, meaning the flour soaks up the moisture from the butter and eggs. That translates into a superior cookie with crisp edges and tender insides.*

4. DISSOLVE THE SUGAR IN THE EGGS. Switch to the whisk attachment (or continue to use a handheld mixer). In the same bowl (no need to wash it), combine the granulated sugar, dark brown sugar, and eggs and whip until the mixture is lightened in color and doubled in volume, 4 to 5 minutes. Swap the whisk out for the paddle, add the brown butter and vanilla, and mix on medium-low speed to combine, about 1 minute.

5. PREPARE THE DRY INGREDIENTS. In a medium bowl, whisk together the toasted flours, baking soda, and kosher salt. Tip the dry ingredients into the mixer bowl and paddle on low speed until they are halfway combined, about 10 seconds. When the dough looks streaky, add both chopped chocolates and paddle to combine.

6. AGE THE DOUGH. Transfer the dough to an airtight container. Refrigerate for 24 hours before baking (see tip #2).

7. PREHEAT THE OVEN AND PREP THE PANS. Preheat the oven to 350°F (175°C). To bake in batches, top two or three half-sheet pans with parchment paper and lightly mist the paper with cooking spray.

8. SHAPE THE COOKIES. Scoop the chilled dough into plump tangerine-size balls (aim for 65 g to 70 g each); you should get about 15 cookies. Transfer the cookies to the pans, spacing them about 4 inches (10 cm) apart. Break the chocolate bar into 12 to 15 inch-long (2.5 cm) shards and press a couple of them onto the surface of each ball. Sprinkle generously with flaky sea salt.

9. BAKE THE COOKIES. Bake until the cookies are golden and puffy in the center, 17 to 19 minutes. Remove from the oven and firmly rap the sheet pans on top of the counter to force the cookies to fall. Let the cookies cool completely on the sheet pans. Store the cookies wrapped at room temperature for 1 to 2 days or in the freezer for up to 3 weeks.

HOW TO BAKE SALE

I may have arrived at professional baking after many career twists and turns, but the first time I hosted a bake sale, I realized that those other seemingly unrelated jobs and passions were secretly preparing me all along. Running my first bake sale, in 2017, felt like I was finally connecting all the dots. My years of community organizing, curating concerts, and producing workshops and fundraisers had given me the tools to bring people together with joy, energy, and purpose. I was able to look at my past and be grateful for those odd jobs, instead of dismissive or ashamed of them.

Once I viewed my own skills and history with compassion, I was ready to begin the transformative work of giving back. Volunteering is an act of communal love. There is something very liberating about working toward something greater and more complicated than your own feelings and ego. Bake sales are my way of accessing that communal love, outside society's traps of chasing so-called success.

You have secret tools, too. You do not have to be a baking pro to host a bake sale. You don't have to *be* anything, except yourself—curious, open, excited, and ready to work. The pastries don't have to look perfect. You don't have to raise $50,000. You don't have to promote the sale with a slick advertising graphic or conform to what we normally think of as "cool" or trendy. Just bake something you love, doodle a simple poster, set manageable goals, and ask for plenty of help.

If you don't have access to a commercial kitchen, bake sales are still within your grasp. In fact, the majority of bake sales I've witnessed have happened on someone's front stoop, in a shady park, on a wide stretch of sidewalk, all coordinated by home bakers who have never worked in restaurants or bakeries. Working without mainstream resources and clout is what gives bake sales their sense of urgency and immediacy—to me, it feels very punk and DIY.

Bake sales, at their core, prioritize equity and inclusive communal practices, not the "top-down charity" found in splashy fundraisers. Anybody can organize a bake sale, and anybody can come. After many years of working fancy galas, selling $5 pastries feels radical to me. I want to create an event for the people I actually spend time with—my friends, co-workers, family, and neighbors—and affordable pastries are accessible for everybody.

Let your bake sales grow organically, through your community, as you learn and get feedback and listen. Once I started accepting the imperfections of my baking, or the ways in which I felt, in my head, that I was somehow falling short, I was able to be more present and in the moment, to truly feel the love of the people around me, and to better articulate my commitment to shaping a different future.

The strength of the bake sale is in its specificity. The premise is beautifully simple: you bake a few things, some people show up and buy those things, and at the end of the day you've raised some money, or brought some awareness to a community issue you care about, or just had a really special time working alongside people you like and trust. It's not about how much money you raise. It's about redefining your relationship to pastry and reaffirming your commitment to social justice, one small table of cookies at a time.

My mom drew this for me in 2019, after I organized a giant bake sale for Planned Parenthood that raised more than $125,000. I still feel so proud of that day.

PINE NUT SABLÉS WITH TALEGGIO

It's hard to beat the simple, divine pleasures of a buttery sablé, a beloved cookie that traces its origins to Normandy, on the northwestern coast of France. Yet a cobbled topping of pine nuts and a smear of Taleggio transform this cookie into a mini explosion of savory flavors; it's a fully composed dish in one bite.

Taleggio's funky, creamy meatiness is a mouthwatering foil for these nutty cookies, but there are plenty of alternatives that pair well, too. Look for either a semisoft, washed-rind style of cheese, like Brie or raclette, or a firmer, slightly pungent cheese like fontina or Havarti.

1. **CREAM THE WET INGREDIENTS.** In a stand mixer fitted with the paddle (or in a large bowl using a handheld mixer), beat the butter, granulated sugar, and powdered sugar until just combined, 1 to 2 minutes. Scrape the mixer bowl with a spatula so all the ingredients are mixed evenly, then paddle for 10 seconds. Drop in the egg yolks and vanilla and paddle to combine, another minute.

2. **INCORPORATE THE DRY INGREDIENTS.** Add the all-purpose flour, buckwheat flour, and kosher salt to the mixer bowl. Paddle on the lowest speed until the ingredients are just combined, 8 to 10 seconds.

3. **ROLL AND REST THE DOUGH.** Cut two 12-by-16-inch (30 by 40 cm) pieces of parchment paper (about the size of a half-sheet pan). Place the dough in the middle of one piece of parchment and gently shape it into a square. Place the other piece of parchment on top. Use a rolling pin to firmly press the dough down. Using strong, forceful motions radiating out from the center, roll the dough out until it's 3/8 inch (1 cm) thick (see tip #1)—it should end up about the size of the pieces of parchment. Transfer the parchment pack to a half-sheet pan and set in the refrigerator to thoroughly chill, at least 1 hour.

4. **PORTION THE DOUGH.** Remove the parchment-sandwiched dough from the refrigerator. Carefully peel the

MAKES FORTY 3-INCH-LONG (7.5 CM) COOKIES

30 MINUTES ACTIVE TIME
1 HOUR INACTIVE TIME

8 ounces (225 g) unsalted butter, cubed, at room temperature
½ cup (100 g) granulated sugar
½ cup (60 g) powdered sugar
2 large egg yolks (40 g), at room temperature
2 teaspoons vanilla extract
1¾ cups (210 g) all-purpose flour
⅓ cup (45 g) buckwheat flour
1 teaspoon kosher salt
⅓ cup (40 g) pine nuts
Flaky sea salt
2 ounces (60 g) Taleggio cheese, at room temperature

TIP 1 ——*Engage all of your senses to inform your movements and technique. If you're rolling out a cookie dough between sheets of parchment, it can be tricky to actually see how thin it's getting, or if it's uneven. Think of your index finger and thumb as your personal caliper—pinch the dough in the center and edges to see if you're rolling the pastry to an even thickness.*

TIP 2 ——*Most rolled and cut cookies bake neatly if the dough is frozen, or at least very chilled, before going into the oven. Freeze the unbaked sablés on a sheet pan before stacking and consolidating in an airtight container. If the sablés spread into lopsided rectangles in the oven, you still can attain a precise, professional finish by carefully trimming the edges with a sharp knife or bench scraper while the cookies are still warm and soft, but I think the soft, organic shapes are pretty, too.*

top sheet of parchment off (if it sticks at all, the dough is not chilled enough; try freezing it for 20 more minutes) and lay the parchment flat on the counter. Sprinkle the pine nuts on top of the dough and press gently with a rolling pin so they adhere to the surface. Use a sharp knife to cut the dough into batons 3 inches (7.5 cm) long and 1 inch (2.5 cm) wide. Let the cookies firm back up in the freezer for 15 minutes before baking (see tip #2).

5. PREHEAT THE OVEN AND PREP THE PANS. Preheat the oven to 350°F (175°C). To bake in batches, top two half-sheet pans with parchment paper and lightly mist the paper with cooking spray.

6. BAKE THE COOKIES. Arrange 20 cookies in four rows of 5 on each sheet pan, leaving at least 1 inch (2.5 cm) of space between them. Add a pinch of flaky sea salt to the top of each cookie. Bake until the edges are slightly darkened and the centers are soft but not raw, 16 to 18 minutes. Let cool completely on the pan.

7. SERVE. Add a thick smear of Taleggio cheese to the top of each cookie, and eat immediately. If baking in advance, store the cookies in an airtight container and add the cheese right before serving.

VARIATIONS

Skip the pine nuts and cheese for a more classic, streamlined French-style butter cookie. Dip the edges of the cookies in egg white and then again in turbinado sugar, then bake as directed. Or add a tablespoon of fragrant seeds, like fennel, lavender, or caraway, while the sugar and butter are creaming.

COFFEE-HAZELNUT LINZERS

Yolk-heavy cookies, like these nutty linzers, bake with a controlled, even spread and a tight, compact crumb. Similar to the buttery sablés (see page 37), linzer dough can be rolled out, punched with cookie cutters or cut by hand, and baked into neat, tidy shapes. Additionally, this cookie contains no baking powder or baking soda, which give pastries rise and puffiness, and so these bake to a satisfying crispness.

A spoonful of sunny kumquat preserves, pressed between two cookies, softens the sandwich just slightly. Even if you don't live in a tropical part of the world, it's become much easier to source kumquats during the winter months. If you can source (or grow) kumquats in abundance, lucky you! Double or triple the kumquat amounts; it's an instant mood-booster spooned over oatmeal, served on a cheese board, or smeared on toast.

1. **CREAM THE WET INGREDIENTS.** In a stand mixer fitted with the paddle (or in a large bowl using a handheld mixer), combine the butter, granulated sugar, and dark brown sugar and paddle until blended, 1 to 2 minutes. Scrape the mixer bowl with a spatula, then paddle again for 10 seconds (see tip #1). Drop in the egg yolks and vanilla and paddle to combine, another minute.

2. **INCORPORATE THE DRY INGREDIENTS.** In a food processor or spice grinder, process the hazelnuts into fine crumbs. In a small bowl, whisk together the flour, ground hazelnuts, coffee grounds, and kosher salt. Tip the mixture into the stand mixer and paddle on the lowest speed until the ingredients are nearly combined and the dough looks streaky, 8 to 10 seconds. Turn the mixture out onto the counter and gently knead until the dough looks smooth.

3. **ROLL AND REST THE DOUGH.** Cut four 12-by-16-inch (30 by 40 cm) pieces of parchment (about the size of a half-sheet pan). Divide the dough in half. Place one dough half in the middle of a piece of parchment and gently shape it into a square. Place another piece of parchment on top. Use a rolling pin to firmly

MAKES TWELVE 3-INCH (7.5 CM) SANDWICH COOKIES

40 MINUTES ACTIVE TIME
2 HOURS INACTIVE TIME

8 ounces (225 g) unsalted butter, cubed, at room temperature
¼ cup (50 g) granulated sugar
½ cup (120 g) dark brown sugar
2 large egg yolks (40 g), at room temperature
1 teaspoon vanilla extract
1¼ cups (140 g) hazelnuts, toasted and cooled
2 cups (240 g) all-purpose flour
2 teaspoons finely ground coffee
1 teaspoon kosher salt
1 cup (320 g) Kumquat Preserves (recipe follows)
Powdered sugar, for dusting
Flaky sea salt

TIP 1 —— *The butter creaming method for rolled cookie doughs like this hazelnut linzer and the pine nut sablés (see page 37) is shorter than the process of making fluffy cake, where you're aiming to aerate the butter and sugar as much as possible. To achieve the crumbly, delicate texture of a punched cookie, paddle the butter and sugar until just combined, no more.*

TIP 2 —— *Sandwiching sticky cookie dough between two sheets of parchment paper makes cleanup easier, renders mistakes nonexistent (no shaggy, torn dough sticking to the countertop or your pin!), and yields a more consistent cookie (no added flour sprinkled on the rolling pin before rolling).*

TIP 3 —— *"YORO." I learned that rule from Marc Cohen, co-owner of the Montréal restaurant Lawrence, where I used to work. It stands for You Only Reroll Once. You can save every scrap from rolling dough, but every subsequent reroll toughens the cookies. (Or, do as we did after a long dinner service: bake the irregular scraps as is, and eat all the pieces.)*

press the dough down, sandwiching it between the parchment (see tip #2). Using strong, forceful motions radiating out from the center, roll the dough out to the size of the parchment paper. (The dough will be quite thin.) Repeat with the second dough half. Transfer the parchment packs to a half-sheet pan and refrigerate for at least 1 hour.

4. **PORTION THE DOUGH WITH A COOKIE CUTTER.** Remove the dough sheets from the refrigerator. Carefully peel one piece of the parchment off one sheet of dough (if it sticks at all, the dough is not chilled enough; try freezing it for 20 minutes). Using a 3-inch (7.5 cm) round cookie cutter, punch out as many rounds as will fit on one half-sheet pan; you want 12 per sheet. Repeat with the second sheet of cookie dough. (The scraps can be pressed together, rerolled thinly, and punched again for more cookies; see tip #3.) If the dough begins to soften, return to the fridge to chill before attempting to punch out more. At this point, the punched cookies can be frozen until ready to bake.

5. **PREHEAT THE OVEN AND PREP THE PANS.** Preheat the oven to 350°F (175°C). To bake in batches, top two half-sheet pans with parchment paper and lightly mist the paper with cooking spray.

6. **BAKE THE COOKIES.** Arrange 12 cookies on each sheet pan, leaving at least 2 inches (5 cm) of space between them. Bake until the edges are darkened but the centers are slightly soft, 12 to 14 minutes.

7. **PUNCH OUT THE DESIGN.** While the cookies are still hot, use a metal drinking straw, a #5 or 6 plain piping tip, or a small round cookie cutter no more than 1 inch (2.5 cm) wide to punch out holes in half of the cookies. These are the cookie tops. The uncut cookies are the cookie bottoms. Save the little cookie buttons for decor. Let the cookies cool on the sheet pan so they can gently crisp up.

8. **ASSEMBLE THE SANDWICHES.** Attach the little cookie buttons by dabbing a bit of kumquat preserves on the bottom of each one and gluing one or two to each cookie top. Using a tea strainer, sift powdered sugar over the cookie tops. Add a small pinch of flaky sea salt to each, too. With a piping bag or a small spoon, spread 1½ to 2 teaspoons kumquat puree on each cookie bottom. Gently press a sugar-topped cookie on top of each one. Add another small spoonful of kumquat puree directly into the punched-out openings as well, so the puree looks flush with the surface. The cookies are most delicious within a few hours.

→

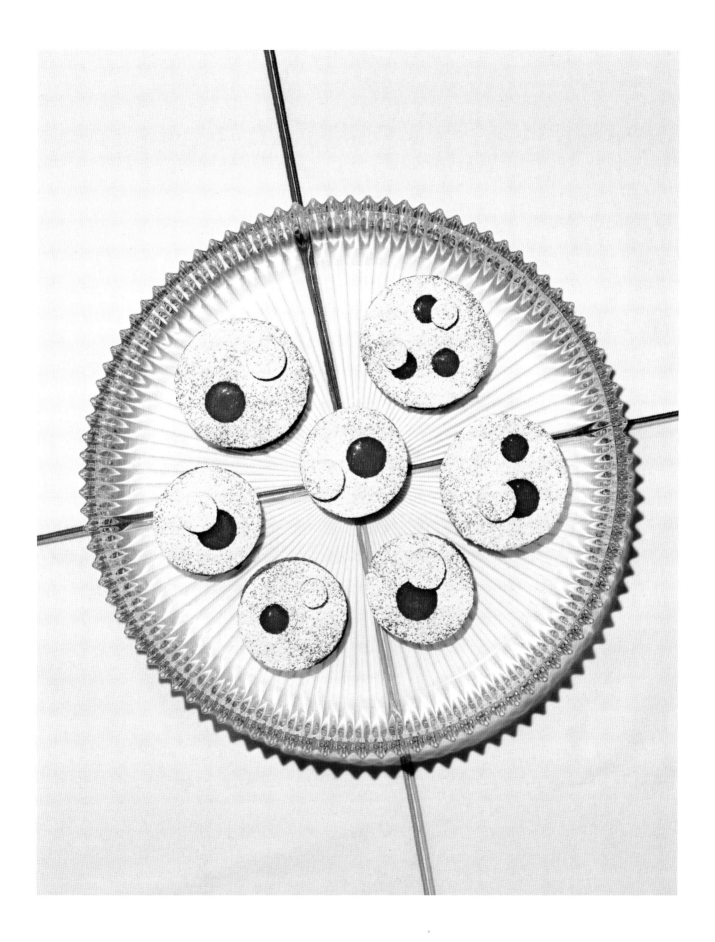

Kumquat Preserves

MAKES 1½ CUPS (480 G)

40 MINUTES ACTIVE TIME

1 pint (about 350 g) kumquats
1 cup (200 g) sugar

HALVE THE KUMQUATS lengthwise. Pluck out the seeds and discard. Bring a small pot of water to a boil, enough so that the kumquat halves can float freely. Add the fruit and simmer until tender and cooked through but not falling apart, about 10 minutes. Remove the pot from the heat and drain off the water. Fill the same pot with 1 cup (240 g) of fresh water and add the sugar and blanched kumquats. Bring back to a gentle simmer over medium-low heat. Cook, stirring periodically, until the kumquats are glossy and translucent, 25 to 30 minutes. Immediately transfer the mixture, while hot, to a food processor or blender and puree until as smooth as possible. Set aside to cool completely; the puree can be stored in an airtight container in the fridge for up to 3 weeks.

VARIATIONS

Mix and match your linzers with imaginative spreads inside. Hazelnut and kumquat provide just the right amount of acid and rich notes, but the possibilities are endless: pecans and cranberry jelly, almonds and blackberry jam, pistachios and strawberry jam, sesame seeds and yuzu curd. Try "auditioning" the flavor combo by eating a spoonful of nuts and jam mixed together before you commit to the recipe.

BLACK SESAME
FORTUNE COOKIES

Who doesn't appreciate the astral and culinary collision of a fortune cookie—your future, as determined by a crunchy treat! When I was growing up, my mother and I would crack open cookie after cookie, cackling at the fortunes inside but always tossing aside the stale, sugary cookie shards. Determined to make a tastier cookie, I've added nutty black sesame paste to this take-out classic.

A fortune cookie requires a series of simple, origami-like folds to create its signature dimpled shape. Save all the broken accidents for sprinkling over big bowls of ice cream.

1. **PREPARE THE FORTUNES.** Cut a piece of paper into 25 strips that measure 2½ inches by ½ inch (6 by 1.25 cm). Write or draw whatever you like—it can be a funny quote, piece of trivia, or inside joke (see tip #1). Set aside.

2. **WHISK THE WET INGREDIENTS TOGETHER.** In a small pot, melt the butter over low heat; remove from the heat. In a medium bowl, whisk together the sugar, egg whites, black sesame paste, vanilla, and melted butter until smooth and shiny.

3. **ADD THE DRY INGREDIENTS.** Stir the flour and salt into the liquid mixture. The batter should drop off a spatula in thick, runny sheets. Refrigerate for at least 1 hour (and up to 1 week) before baking.

4. **PREHEAT THE OVEN AND PREP THE PAN.** Preheat the oven to 350°F (175°C). Mist a half-sheet pan with cooking spray and add a piece of parchment paper. You'll need to bake these in batches, so prepare multiple sheet pans.

5. **BAKE THE COOKIES.** Scoop tablespoons of batter onto the sheet pan, leaving at least 5 inches (12.5 cm) between them. Use a small offset spatula to smooth and spread the batter into 4-inch (10 cm) rounds about 1 inch (2.5 cm) apart from one another. (It's okay if the batter thickness isn't perfectly even or the shape perfectly circular.) Sprinkle black sesame seeds on top. Bake until

MAKES 2 CUPS (450 G) BATTER, ENOUGH FOR 20 TO 25 FORTUNE COOKIES

10 MINUTES ACTIVE TIME
1 HOUR INACTIVE TIME

8 tablespoons (4 ounces/115 g) unsalted butter
¾ cup (150 g) sugar
3 large egg whites (90 g)
2 tablespoons (30 g) black sesame paste
1 teaspoon vanilla extract
½ cup (60 g) all-purpose flour
½ teaspoon kosher salt
2 tablespoons (30 g) black sesame seeds

the edges are beginning to brown and the cookies are pocked with small, spongy holes, 8 to 10 minutes.

6. SHAPE THE COOKIES. Have a water glass and a muffin tin ready. Remove the pan from the oven and let the cookies rest for 10 seconds. While the cookies are still hot and pliable but beginning to set up, flip each cookie over. Place one fortune in the lower half of a cookie, bisecting the cookie (see tip #2). Fold the cookie in half along the fortune like you'd fold a taco. Gently press the edges together, leaving an open pocket of air inside. Transfer the cookie to the rim of the glass and press the center of the cookie onto the glass's rim. Tug the ends of the half-moon downward, crimping it into the signature fortune cookie shape. Transfer the cookie to the well of a muffin tin to set the shape. Repeat with the remaining cookies and batter. Eat immediately or store in a tightly sealed container for up to 1 week.

Clockwise from top left: (1) Place the fortune in the lower half of the warm cookie. (2) Fold the cookie in half, pressing the edges together so they stick. (3) Press the cookie onto the glass rim, tugging the ends downward. (4) Transfer the cookie to a muffin tin to cool.

Never-Ending Cookies

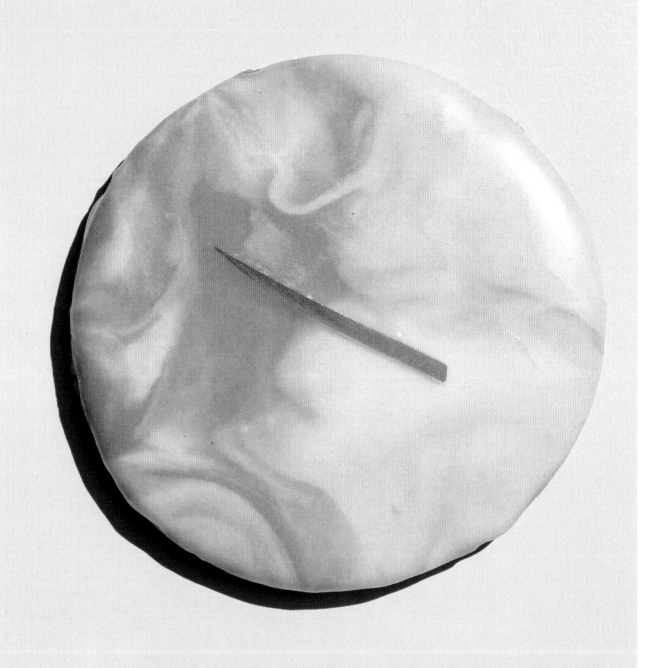

SOUR GLAZE MAPLE GINGERBREAD

Decorating cookies is an easy activity that puts your artistic muscles in the spotlight. Crisp, not-too-sweet gingerbread—gently flavored with maple syrup and coconut oil—is your blank canvas. Eschewing fussy piping techniques, these cookies are coated in thin, delicate glazes that swirl and ripple into impressionistic marbled pools.

A kit of baked gingerbread with small jars of the premixed vinegar icings and a pouch of dried fruit toppings is an incredible gift for anyone who claims they don't bake. My mom may shy away from baking, but I know she'd make masterpieces out of these.

1. MIX THE DOUGH. In a large bowl, whisk the coconut oil, coconut sugar, maple syrup, egg, and vanilla together until smooth. In another bowl, whisk together the all-purpose flour, whole wheat pastry flour, baking soda, baking powder, ginger, cinnamon, salt, pepper, and nutmeg. Add the dry ingredients to the bowl of wet ingredients and stir until combined.

2. ROLL OUT THE DOUGH. Cut four 12-by-16 inch (30 by 40 cm) pieces of parchment paper. Divide the dough in half and sandwich each piece of dough between two pieces of parchment. Use a rolling pin to gently press out the dough to the size of the piece of parchment. (The dough will be thin.) Transfer to a half-sheet pan, stacking the dough packages, and refrigerate until chilled completely, about 1 hour.

3. PREHEAT THE OVEN AND PREP THE PANS. Preheat the oven to 350°F (175°C). To bake in batches, line three half-sheet pans with parchment paper and lightly mist the paper with cooking spray. (If you don't have three baking sheets, let cool after baking before adding new unbaked cookies, or freeze the cookies until ready to bake.)

4. PUNCH AND BAKE. Peel off the parchment and punch out cookies with a 3-inch (7.5 cm) round cookie cutter, aiming for 12 cookies per sheet. Reroll the scraps to get another 4 to 6 cookies, for about 30 cookies total. Transfer 10 to 12 cookies to each of the lined sheet pans, spacing them 2 inches (5 cm) apart. Bake until

MAKES ABOUT THIRTY 3-INCH (7.5 CM) COOKIES

30 MINUTES ACTIVE TIME
1 HOUR INACTIVE TIME

½ cup (110 g) coconut oil, melted
½ cup (80 g) coconut sugar
½ cup (135 g) maple syrup
1 egg (50 g), at room temperature
1 teaspoon vanilla extract
2 cups (240 g) all-purpose flour
1 cup (120 g) whole wheat pastry flour
½ teaspoon baking soda
¼ teaspoon baking powder
2 teaspoons ground ginger
1 teaspoon ground cinnamon
1 teaspoon kosher salt
1 teaspoon freshly ground black pepper
¼ teaspoon ground nutmeg
Vinegar Icing (recipe follows)
⅓ cup (3 ounces/85 g) dried fruit, such as dried blueberries or chopped dried papaya

TIP —*This icing technique is so forgiving. If you don't like your design, you can always scrape off the wet icing with a small offset spatula and start over.*

the edges are slightly darkened, 10 to 12 minutes. The cookies will continue to crisp up as they cool on the sheet pan.

5. GLAZE AND DECORATE. Spoon small dabs of the icings on top of the cooled cookies, creating an abstract pattern (see tip). Tilt the cookie in all directions to allow the excess icing to drip off, warping the shapes into marbled swirls. Scatter the dried fruit on top. Let the cookies air-dry for 10 minutes to set. If not eating immediately, transfer to an airtight container and store for up to 5 days.

Vinegar Icing

The dyes in traditional supermarket food colors are packed with scary chemicals, but plenty of your pantry staples will provide more natural coloring as well as subtle flavor. Wine vinegars and fruit-based vinegars aren't just for salads; they add a beguiling tartness, too, an ideal foil to the powdered sugar.

If you'd prefer a more intense hue, add a few drops of all-natural food coloring; I love the plant-based food dyes by Supernatural Kitchen.

MAKES 1½ CUPS (360 G)

5 MINUTES ACTIVE TIME

2½ cups (300 g) powdered sugar
2 tablespoons (30 g) fruit vinegar, like cherry or raspberry (see headnote)
2 tablespoons (30 g) balsamic vinegar

DIVIDE THE POWDERED SUGAR between two small bowls. Stir the fruit vinegar into one bowl until smooth and no lumps remain. The icing should be runny and sheer. Repeat with the other half of the powdered sugar and the balsamic vinegar. The icings can be refrigerated in airtight containers for up to 1 week.

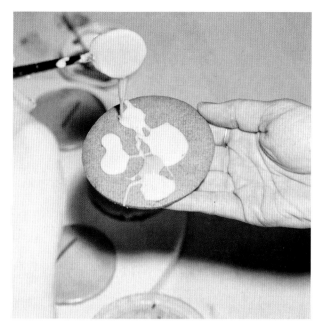

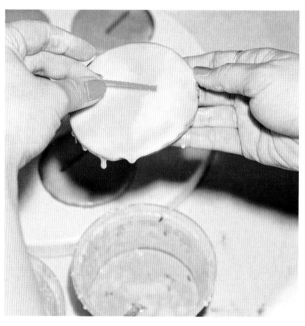

Clockwise from top left: (1) Spoon the icing on top of the cookie. (2) Tilt the cookie in all directions to allow the excess icing to drip off. (3) Gently place the dried fruit garnish on top. (4) Let the cookies air-dry until set.

Never-Ending Cookies

SWEET

AND SALTY

SNACKS

As a constant nibbler, I have strong opinions about snacks. The perfect snack should be an easy-to-prepare bookend to a grander meal, like a plate of cheese and crackers or an after-dinner hunk of chocolate. Snacks are as memorable as an elaborate meal (if not more so!) because they create unique, mellow opportunities to stretch time. The hours magically lengthen at the moment you need it, like when the final course of dinner is cleared but you aren't ready to stand up and say goodnight just yet.

When I was growing up, "dessert" was never a big deal in our house, as it's not an emphasized aspect of Chinese home cooking. But there was *always* something extra to look forward to at the end of dinner, which we simply called "D." D could be anything, as long as it was a treat. It could be a small bowl of crunchy, spicy peanuts. It could be a handful of kettle corn or Ferrero Rocher chocolates. It could be a tangerine or a few sticky dates. It wasn't cakes, cookies, or ice cream. It was a snack.

The perfect snack should be deeply flavorful but not too filling, since it's either anticipating or punctuating a larger meal. Maybe it's a baggie of flaky crackers packed for a long walk with a new friend, a stack of oatcakes paired with a few hands of cards, or a small dish of brittle to chase with hot tea after brunch. Crunchy, wobbly, flaky, or chewy, the crucial element is texture. Snacks are our currency to continue the conversation during these "in-between" mealtimes.

PASSION FRUIT JELLIES

Agar-agar, a stabilizing substance that comes from red algae (which means it's vegan), lends a unique, crumbly-bouncy texture to fruit preserves, ice cream custards, and jellies. Unlike gelatin, which sets to an unsteady, fleshy wobble, agar-agar solidifies swiftly, even at room temperature. For this reason, I love transforming fresh fruit purees and juices into candies with agar-agar, which won't cloud the syrups with any flavor or hue. Hollowed-out passion fruit shells are handy vessels for an easy jelly; save the seeds to sprinkle on top for crunch. This is a fun project for kids, too—give them a small jug or spout to transfer the juice into the cups.

MAKES 12 JELLIES
SERVES 3 OR 4

10 MINUTES ACTIVE TIME
1 HOUR INACTIVE TIME

6 fresh passion fruits
1 cup (240 g) unsweetened
   passion fruit juice
1½ teaspoons agar-agar powder
¼ cup (50 g) sugar
¼ teaspoon kosher salt

TIP 1 —*Taste the passion fruit juice before you begin; boxed passion fruit juice sometimes contains additional ingredients like pear juice and can be sweeter than fresh pulp. If the juice tastes sweet, add ¼ teaspoon of citric acid to the pot.*

TIP 2 —*If your passion fruit shells are on the small side, you may have some jelly base left over. Pour the extra syrup into a clean, dry ice cube tray to set.*

1. PREP THE CUPS. Cut each passion fruit in half crosswise and scoop out the seeds with a small spoon, so only the white inner shell remains. Strain the juice through a small sieve into a bowl; reserve the seeds. Use the fresh juice as part of the 1 cup (240 g) needed to make the jelly. Set the shells in an empty egg carton or muffin tin so they sit upright.

2. COOK THE JELLY. In a small pot, combine the passion fruit juice (see tip #1), agar-agar, sugar, and salt and whisk well over medium heat until the agar-agar has dissolved into the syrup and the mixture is simmering, 5 to 6 minutes. (If you see any clumps, strain the mixture before portioning.) Transfer the mixture to a small pitcher or glass and carefully pour some into each passion fruit cup, stopping short of filling it completely (see tip #2). Add ½ teaspoon reserved passion fruit seeds to the top of each. Carefully transfer the container holding the shells to the refrigerator and chill, uncovered, until the jelly is completely set, about 1 hour. Serve chilled. Held in an airtight container, the jellies are good for up to 5 days.

CARAMELIZED WHITE CHOCOLATE AND COCONUT TRUFFLES

Good white chocolate is a wonderful thing. Not the chalky, saccharine "white morsels" found in supermarket baking aisles, but the snappy, milky, all–cocoa butter varieties made by fair trade and organic manufacturers like Valrhona and Guittard (see Resources, page 311). But even proper white chocolate can get cloying, especially in a rich truffle—unless it is caramelized first.

The transformation occurs in the low, slow heat of an oven, where white chocolate slumps and darkens. (You'll be grateful for the long bake time, which will perfume your kitchen with the most intensely delicious, nutty aroma.) What emerges is something altogether new: a soft, rich paste with butterscotch and toasted graham cracker notes that you'll want to eat by the spoonful. A chewy hand-rolled truffle shows off this special ganache; the dunk into toasted coconut flakes adds a crucial spike of texture.

MAKES 20 TO 24 TRUFFLES
SERVES 6 TO 8

30 MINUTES ACTIVE TIME
3 HOURS INACTIVE TIME

2 cups (340 g) roughly chopped white chocolate or white chocolate chips
3 tablespoons (45 g) heavy cream
½ teaspoon vanilla extract
3 tablespoons (1½ ounces/45 g) unsalted butter, cubed, at room temperature
½ teaspoon kosher salt, plus more to taste
1½ cups (150 g) unsweetened coconut flakes
¼ cup (30 g) powdered sugar
Flaky sea salt

1. CARAMELIZE THE WHITE CHOCOLATE. Preheat the oven to 275°F (135°C). Spread the white chocolate on a half-sheet pan lined with parchment paper and bake until the white chocolate deepens in color and smells like butterscotch, 30 to 45 minutes, stirring with a silicone spatula every 10 minutes. The mixture may look chalky and grainy; it will smooth out in the blender!

2. MIX THE GANACHE. Transfer the caramelized white chocolate to a blender or food processor and puree on high speed for 1 minute. Add the cream, vanilla, butter, and kosher salt and continue to blend until smooth and silky, another 4 minutes. Taste the mixture; it should be sweet, toasty, and a little salty. Add a pinch or two more of kosher salt until the balance is achieved. (You can't perceive the salt, but it helps to offset the sweetness.) Transfer the ganache to a small bowl and refrigerate until solid, 3 to 4 hours (see tip). This can be done up to 2 weeks in advance.

3. TOAST THE COCONUT. In a large skillet, slowly toast the coconut flakes over medium-low heat, stirring occasionally, until beginning to color around the edges, 6 to 7 minutes. Transfer to a bowl and let cool completely.

4. **SHAPE THE TRUFFLES.** Remove the ganache from the fridge and let warm at room temperature briefly, about 30 minutes, before trying to roll truffles. Use a small spoon to portion the chilled ganache into 1-tablespoon chunks; transfer to a small pan or plate. Do this all at once, then lightly coat your hands with cooking spray and roll each chunk between the palms of your hands until smooth and round. If the ganache gets greasy, let it chill for 15 to 30 minutes, until it feels easier to shape. Press each truffle into the cooled toasted coconut flakes, rolling the truffles around to coat. Refrigerate the truffles for 1 hour to chill before serving, then dust with powdered sugar and sprinkle with flaky sea salt.

TIP —— *The caramelized white chocolate ganache can be used in a variety of ways beyond these truffles. Fold ½ cup (95 g) room-temperature ganache into 2 cups (240 g) whipped cream for a silky, rich layer cake filling.*

Sweet and Salty Snacks

MALTED COCOA FUDGE

Chocolate "salami" is a popular treat found across Europe, particularly in Italy, Portugal, and Poland. From the powdered sugar posing as the musty mold to the broken biscuits and nuts that resemble the fatty pork farce, this candy looks just like a dry-cured salami.

Here, a chewy fudge, studded with crumbled butter cookies, is pressed into a small pan, rather than the traditional sausage shape. One batch yields a bounty of tiny cubes that look striking as a gift, piled high into a box, or scattered on a plate, alongside fruit and nuts. Their crunchy-chewy centers are easy to customize with your favorite extras, like chopped chocolate, toasted nuts, or candied orange peel.

Snow sugar (aka doughnut sugar) is much better than regular powdered sugar for this; it's less sweet, for one, and it also won't melt once in contact with the fudge, which makes this treat ideal for gifting and shipping.

1. PREP THE PAN. Line an 8-inch (20 cm) square baking pan or similar size sheet pan with plastic wrap, with plenty of overhang. Set aside.

2. MIX THE FUDGE. In a stand mixer fitted with the paddle (or in a large bowl using a handheld mixer), cream the softened butter, cocoa powder, and malted milk powder until smooth, dense, and thick, about 3 minutes. Add the whole egg and egg yolk and beat to combine, another 2 minutes. Scrape the bowl well with a spatula after each addition.

3. ADD THE SYRUP. In a small pot, combine the granulated sugar and water. Heat over medium heat, swirling occasionally, until the sugar melts and the syrup reaches a simmer. With the stand mixer running on medium speed, slowly stream in the hot syrup and beat until combined, about 3 minutes. The mixture should look glossy and black. (The heat of the sugar syrup will cook the raw egg.) Add the vanilla and salt and beat to combine, another minute. Turn the mixer off and scatter in the broken butter cookies and chopped chocolate. Gently fold with a spatula to combine.

$\rightarrow$

MAKES ABOUT 50 BITE-SIZE FUDGE SQUARES

15 MINUTES ACTIVE TIME
3 HOURS INACTIVE TIME

12 tablespoons (6 ounces/170 g) unsalted butter, cubed, at room temperature
1½ cups (150 g) Dutch process cocoa powder
½ cup (60 g) malted milk powder
1 egg (50 g), at room temperature
1 large egg yolk (20 g), at room temperature
1 cup (200 g) granulated sugar
3 tablespoons (45 g) water
1 teaspoon vanilla extract
1 teaspoon kosher salt

(ingredients continue)

4 cups (about 400 g) roughly crumbled thin butter cookies (like the Pine Nut Sablés with Taleggio, page 37)

5 ounces (140 g) dark chocolate, roughly chopped (about 1 cup)

¼ cup (30 g) snow sugar (doughnut sugar)

Flaky sea salt

4. SHAPE AND CHILL THE FUDGE. Transfer the mixture to the plastic wrap–lined pan, pressing it into the pan with a small offset spatula to smooth the surface as best as you can. Transfer to the refrigerator and chill until completely firm, 2 to 3 hours.

5. PORTION THE FUDGE. Flip the chilled pan over onto a large cutting board. Remove the pan, then carefully peel off the plastic wrap. Heavily dust both sides of the fudge with the snow sugar, using a small tea strainer.

Use a large clean knife to trim the four sides, then measure the thickness of the fudge. For perfect cubes, cut the slab into strips the same width as the thickness of the fudge (it should be about ¾ inch/ 2 cm thick). Then cut each strip into cubes. Keep refrigerated in an airtight container for up to 2 weeks. Sprinkle the cubes with flaky sea salt before eating.

GOLDEN SESAME CANDY

Tidy rectangles of sesame brittle, a ubiquitous East Asian snack, are my mom's all-time favorite treat. I used to covet those little crunchy shingles, which my mom bought at the Asian supermarket 99 Ranch and then squirreled away in cupboards, drawers, and bags at home. Sesame brittle can be a bit of a jaw workout, so I've added some peanuts and baking soda to lighten the crunch, a pat of butter for richness, and vanilla extract and ground turmeric for a lingering warmth. Wrapped up in wax paper and stored in an airtight container, these candies will stay fresh for ages—slip a few into your bag for emergency snacking, just like Mom does.

1. **PREP THE PAN.** Lightly mist two 12-by-16-inch (30 by 40 cm) sheets of parchment paper with cooking spray and set aside. Have a rolling pin at the ready.

2. **COOK THE CARAMEL BASE.** In a small pot, combine the sugar, honey, and water. Set over medium-high heat and tilt the pot gently to swirl the water around. Bring the mixture up to a simmer, about 3 minutes.

3. **ADD THE NUTS AND SEEDS.** Stir in the peanuts and sesame seeds and continue to cook over medium heat, stirring occasionally, until the mixture turns golden yellow, 5 to 10 minutes. The mixture will smell super nutty and bubble and pop along the surface. (Always make sure you have a good light source while cooking caramel so you can accurately judge the color of the syrup!) If you have a candy thermometer, cook the syrup to 300°F (150°C), or the "hard crack" stage.

4. **FINISH OFF THE HEAT.** Once the syrup is the color of a rich, bronzed butterscotch, remove from the heat and stir in the turmeric, salt, vanilla, and butter. Whisk well to combine. Add the baking soda and very gently stir to combine, being careful not to deflate the foam.

5. **ROLL THE CANDY.** Carefully pour the mixture onto one of the greased sheets of parchment. Cover the candy with the

MAKES 45 TO 50 SMALL CANDIES

20 MINUTES ACTIVE TIME
30 MINUTES INACTIVE TIME

1 cup (200 g) sugar
⅓ cup (110 g) honey or rice syrup
2 tablespoons (30 g) water
1 cup (150 g) unsalted roasted peanuts
1 cup (130 g) white or black sesame seeds
2 teaspoons ground turmeric
1 teaspoon kosher salt
2 teaspoons vanilla extract
2 tablespoons (1 ounce/30 g) unsalted butter
½ teaspoon baking soda

second sheet of greased parchment and use a rolling pin to quickly roll the candy out to a thickness of about ⅓ inch (9 mm). While it is still warm, use a dull knife to lightly score the brittle, which will make it easier to cut cleanly later, into batons 2 inches (5 cm) long and ¾ inch (2 cm) wide. Let the candy cool completely, then peel off both pieces of parchment and chop the brittle apart along the scored indentations. Transfer to an airtight container and store in the fridge or freezer for up to 3 weeks.

PIZZA CRACKERS

Baking crackers isn't as fiddly as you'd think, especially when you make them large with ruffly, irregular edges. Two sheets of parchment paper sandwich the stretchy dough, preventing it from snapping back and shrinking, so you can roll the crackers quickly by hand. Generous quantities of tomato powder, dried oregano, and red pepper flakes infuse the crackers with a tang not unlike that of the marinara sauce spread on a pizza crust. If you can, stock your spice drawer with small-batch, single-origin spices, like the high-octane varieties from importer Burlap & Barrel— their vermilion sun-dried tomato powder (see Resources, page 311) is derived from a tomato variety grown along Turkey's Aegean Sea coastline. Serve the crackers with a creamy dip and crisp vegetables.

1. **MIX THE DOUGH.** In a stand mixer fitted with the dough hook, combine the all-purpose flour, rye flour, kosher salt, tomato powder, oregano, and pepper flakes. Separate the egg, reserving the egg white in a small dish, and add the yolk to the mixer bowl. With the mixer running, stream in the olive oil and water and mix on medium speed until the dough is smooth and forms a ball around the hook, about 5 minutes. (To make this dough by hand, combine all the ingredients except the flaky sea salt in a wide bowl, then knead by hand until smooth, about 8 minutes.) Shape the dough into a smooth ball, wrap in plastic wrap, and refrigerate for 30 minutes to rest.

2. **ROLL OUT THE DOUGH.** Cut six 12-by-16-inch (30 by 40 cm) pieces of parchment paper. Unwrap the chilled dough and divide into 3 portions. Transfer one portion to a piece of parchment and press parchment on top. Roll out the dough, pressed between the parchment, as thin as possible, about the thickness of a manila envelope. Continue to roll the remaining dough, stacking and chilling the dough as you go.

$\rightarrow$

MAKES 12 LARGE CRACKERS

25 MINUTES ACTIVE TIME
1 HOUR INACTIVE TIME

3 cups (360 g) all-purpose flour
1/3 cup (50 g) rye or whole wheat flour
1 teaspoon kosher salt
3 tablespoons (30 g) tomato powder
3 tablespoons (15 g) dried oregano
2 teaspoons red pepper flakes
1 egg (50 g), at room temperature
2 tablespoons (30 g) olive oil
1/3 cup (80 g) warm water
Flaky sea salt

3. PREHEAT THE OVEN. Preheat the oven to 375°F (190°C).

4. BAKE THE CRACKERS. Peel off the top piece of parchment from one portion of dough and save for another use. Transfer the bottom piece of parchment, with the cracker dough on it, to a half-sheet pan. Prick all over with a fork or knife. Brush the surface of the cracker with some of the reserved egg white and sprinkle with flaky sea salt. Repeat with the remaining crackers on two additional half-sheet pans. Bake until the surface is bubbly and light, about 20 minutes. Let cool completely, then break into large shards (see tip). Store in an airtight container at room temperature for up to 1 week.

TIP —— *If parts of your crackers emerge from the oven chewy, not crisp, don't fret; let the crackers cool completely, then "flash" (or quickly re-crisp) the baked crackers in a 300°F (150°C) oven for 10 minutes, or until fully dried out.*

FLAKY POPPY SEED CRACKERS WITH WHIPPED FETA

If you bake as many fruit and vegetable tarts as I do, you'll find you always have a bit of leftover dough after trimming the edges. I stopped throwing away these scraps (or, honestly, snacking on them raw) once I realized that the texture of the dough changed dramatically upon the reroll. Because of the way the butter is incorporated into the flour for pâte brisée, the pastry has more of a nubby, crisp, and short texture; so when the dough is rolled out a second time, it creates dramatic flaky layers, like those in puff pastry. These crackers are buttery little morsels, perfect with cool, creamy cheese, like whipped feta, laced with honey.

MAKES 12 LARGE CRACKERS

20 MINUTES ACTIVE TIME
40 MINUTES INACTIVE TIME

1 cup (150 g) crumbled feta cheese
½ cup (125 g) ricotta cheese,
    preferably whole-milk
1 tablespoon (20 g) honey
1 pound (455 g) Pâte Brisée
    (page 164) scraps (see tip #1) or
    fresh pâte brisée (see tip #2)
1 large egg white (30 g)
¼ cup (35 g) poppy seeds
Flaky sea salt

TIP 1 ——*The best way to store dough scraps is to gather all the trimmings with your hands and press and shape them into a round to remove the air. Wrap in plastic wrap and store in the freezer.*

1. **MAKE THE WHIPPED FETA.** In a food processor, combine the feta, ricotta, and honey and puree on high speed until glossy and smooth. Scrape this mixture into a bowl and keep covered and refrigerated until ready to serve.

2. **ROLL OUT THE DOUGH.** Press the pâte brisée scraps together to form a ball. Set it on a piece of parchment lightly sprinkled with flour and roll it into a rectangle about 15 inches (38 cm) long and ⅛ inch (3 mm) thick. Slide the dough, on its parchment, onto a half-sheet pan. Refrigerate for 15 minutes before baking.

3. **PREHEAT THE OVEN.** Preheat the oven to 400°F (200°C).

4. **PORTION AND WEIGHT THE CRACKERS.** Portion the chilled dough into 6 large squares with a knife. Prick the dough all over with a fork and brush the surface with the egg white. Sprinkle the poppy seeds on top to coat. Place a second sheet of parchment and then another half-sheet pan on top to weight the crackers down. (If you don't have a second half-sheet pan, use the removable bottom of a springform pan or a silicone baking mat.) The weight of the extra sheet pan helps the crackers bake evenly and keeps the dough from shrinking or warping in the oven.

→

More Than Cake

TIP 2 ——*If using freshly made pâte brisée, set 455 g of dough on a sheet of parchment paper lightly sprinkled with flour and roll into a rectangle 15 by 10 inches (38 by 25 cm) and ⅛ inch (3 mm) thick. With a long side facing you, lift the right third of the dough up and over to fall on top of the middle third. Repeat with the left third of the dough, bringing it up and over to fall on top of the middle section. Fold this bar in half crosswise so you have a 5-inch (12.5 cm) square. Refrigerate for 10 minutes, then roll out again to a thickness of about ⅛ inch (3 mm) on a piece of parchment lightly sprinkled with flour.*

5. **BAKE THE CRACKERS.** Bake for 15 minutes. Remove the top sheet pan and top piece of parchment paper, exposing the crackers to the air. Continue to bake until deeply golden, 6 to 8 minutes longer. Sprinkle the crackers with flaky sea salt. Let cool completely on the pan.

6. **SERVE.** Break the crackers into large, flaky shards and serve with the chilled whipped feta.

CHEDDAR OATCAKES

Traditional oatcakes, a popular biscuit found all over Scotland and England, have a hearty, not-too-sweet crumb. When I was a student living abroad in Edinburgh, I bought sleeve after sleeve of supermarket oatcakes, having never experienced their unique, sturdy texture at home in the States. Later, as a pastry cook at the English restaurant Lawrence, I baked hundreds of tiny round oatcakes, which we paired with fancy cheeses and house-made pickles.

Though it seems a simple thing, an oatcake can range from crisp to chewy, from big as a cell phone to as petite as a coin, baked in a hot oven or on a stovetop griddle. Here, curls of salty cheddar cheese are pressed right into the oatcakes, which gives them an irresistible sharp finish. They're wonderful with even more cheese, or just on their own, as a nourishing snack for a long walk or a work break. Serve with sliced cheddar, crunchy pickles, or Apple Butter (page 169).

1. **PREPARE THE TOPPING.** In a small bowl, combine ½ cup (50 g) of the oats and the cheddar. Set aside in the freezer to chill.

2. **MAKE THE OAT FLOUR.** In a food processor, pulse the remaining 2 cups (200 g) oats until coarse. Dump into a small bowl and whisk in the all-purpose flour, baking soda, and kosher salt.

3. **MIX THE DOUGH.** In the food processor bowl (or in a bowl using a handheld mixer), pulse the butter and dark brown sugar until just combined, about 1 minute. Scrape the bowl well and add the yogurt. Pulse until combined, another minute. Scrape well and add the dry ingredients. Pulse until the dough is nearly combined but still streaky, about 15 seconds.

4. **ROLL THE DOUGH OUT.** Transfer it to a piece of parchment paper and lightly press into a ball. Drape another piece of parchment paper on top and press down with a rolling pin to flatten. Gently push and roll the dough until it is an even ¼-inch (6 mm) thickness. Peel off the top layer of parchment and scatter the whole oat and cheddar mixture on top. Press gently with your

MAKES FORTY TO FORTY-FIVE
1-INCH (2.5 CM) OATCAKES

30 MINUTES ACTIVE TIME
1 HOUR INACTIVE TIME

2½ cups (250 g) old-fashioned
    rolled oats
½ cup (60 g) grated sharp cheddar
    cheese
1 cup (120 g) all-purpose flour
1 teaspoon baking soda
1 teaspoon kosher salt
8 tablespoons (4 ounces/115 g)
    unsalted butter, cubed, at room
    temperature
⅓ cup (65 g) dark brown sugar
½ cup (120 g) yogurt, preferably
    whole-milk
Flaky sea salt

fingertips to adhere the topping to the dough. Refrigerate for at least 30 minutes before baking.

5. **PREHEAT THE OVEN AND PREP THE PAN.** Preheat the oven to 350°F (175°C). Top a half-sheet pan with parchment paper and lightly mist the paper with cooking spray.

6. **PORTION AND TOP THE OATCAKES.** Remove the dough from the refrigerator and peel off the parchment. Use a 1-inch (2.5 cm) square cookie cutter or a sharp knife to portion the dough into squares (see tip). Transfer the oatcakes to the prepared sheet pan, spacing them at least 1 inch (2.5 cm) apart; you should be able to fit them all on one sheet. Add a small sprinkling of flaky sea salt.

7. **BAKE THE OATCAKES.** Bake until the edges are set and the centers feel puffy and soft but are baked through, 15 to 17 minutes. Let cool completely on the tray before serving.

TIP ——*The unbaked, portioned oatcakes can be stored in an airtight container in the freezer for up to 1 month.*

FENNEL SEED SQUIGGLES

Puff pastry forms the base for many delicious desserts, like the Nectarine and Miso Tarte Tatin (page 176) and the Still Life Tart (page 180), but it's also a divine treat on its own. Here, crunchy turbinado sugar and fragrant fennel seeds are sprinkled onto a puff parcel, like a piece of ribbon spooling out onto the counter. Baked until sizzling, golden and crisp, these glittering, buttery treats are an elegant conclusion to a simple meal.

MAKES SIXTEEN TO EIGHTEEN
3-INCH (7.5 CM) SQUIGGLES

20 MINUTES ACTIVE TIME
30 MINUTES INACTIVE TIME

½ cup (100 g) turbinado sugar
2 tablespoons (12 g) fennel seeds
½ teaspoon flaky sea salt
All-purpose flour, for rolling the puff
340 g Rough Puff Pastry
    (page 178), chilled
1 large egg white (30 g), lightly
    whisked

VARIATION

For a savory variation, omit the fennel sugar. Combine ½ cup (45 g) grated Parmesan, 1 teaspoon smoked paprika, 1 teaspoon freshly ground black pepper, and ½ teaspoon flaky sea salt and sprinkle that all over your squiggles before and then again halfway through baking.

1. PREHEAT THE OVEN AND PREP THE PANS. Preheat the oven to 400°F (200°C). To bake in batches, top two half-sheet pans with parchment paper.

2. MAKE THE CRUNCHY SUGAR TOPPING. In a small dish, combine the turbinado sugar, fennel seeds, and flaky sea salt. Set aside.

3. PREPARE THE PUFF. Sprinkle a large piece of parchment paper with flour and place the chilled puff pastry on top. Roll the puff to a rectangle about 10 by 14 inches (25 by 35 cm). Use a sharp knife to trim any jagged, uneven edges, then cut the puff pastry crosswise into strips 10 inches (25 cm) long and about ¾ inch (2 cm) wide. Each strip should weigh about 30 g.

Brush the strips with the egg white and sprinkle half of the sugar mixture on top. Return the puff pastry strips to the refrigerator for 15 minutes to re-chill.

4. SHAPE THE SQUIGGLES. Pick up one strip and drape it into a curvy S shape. As you shape them, divide the squiggles between the two parchment-lined pans, spacing them 3 inches (7.5 cm) apart.

5. BAKE THE SQUIGGLES. Bake until lightly golden and sizzling, about 6 minutes. Remove from the oven and carefully flip each one over. Sprinkle the remaining fennel sugar on top. Continue to bake until the squiggles are golden all over and crisp, 6 to 7 minutes longer. Transfer the squiggles to a cooling rack. Store in an airtight container at room temperature for up to 4 days.

More Than Cake

SINGLE-

LAYER

CAKES

Towering wedding cakes festooned with frosting garlands, layered birthday cakes glowing with candles, fruited Christmas cakes moist and dark—all are symbols of celebration. So, on a less magnificent scale, is a seedcake baked for an afternoon tea, or a cupcake shaped to please a small child. Cakes, in sum, are a festive food, and the techniques for making them constitute one of the happier culinary arts.

—RICHARD OLNEY, *The Good Cook: Cakes*

A single-layer cake—in the form of a hearty loaf, glazed sheet cake, or streusel-topped coffee cake—satisfies a different kind of desire than an elaborate layer cake does. These are sturdy, shaggy, not-too-sweet cakes that should be eaten at any moment of the day or night and can mark occasions both everyday and extraordinary. They have unusual twists built right into their crumb, like shreds of rutabaga or bits of chewy pineapple. They look striking and architectural, like the dappled surface of an upside-down date cake, or the spiky almonds topping a marzipan cake. They have all the personality of a layer cake but are easier and faster to execute.

Because these cakes require little adornment or supplemental garnishes, their batters are more motley than those for my layer cakes, which are engineered to be absorbent, simple, and neutral tasting. These single-layer cakes, by contrast, have longer ingredient lists, and they emerge from the oven studded with dried fruit or almond paste, ribboned with jam, or dotted with seeds, coconut, nuts, or vegetables, and more. They feel self-actualized and independent and need to be accented with little more than a sticky caramel sauce, cocoa glaze, or squiggle of whipped cream.

These cakes welcome your own interpretation, circumstances, and creativity. One cake batter can be used in so many ways—as a sheer topping for a fruit cobbler, for individual cupcakes or petits fours, or for a shapely Bundt cake. That's for you to decide. Depending on what you have available, the cake batter can be poured into a cast-iron pan, half-sheet pans, a baking dish, stout loaf pans, fluted tart forms, or a Dutch oven. Fruit fillings can be altered to fit the season, flavorful flours like rice or corn can be swapped in, nuts and chocolate can be sprinkled into the batter at the last moment.

Because these recipes are easygoing, they make great gifts. If I get invited to a party, I don't wait for the host to ask me to bring cake—I offer right away, which is a relief to my friend and a pleasure for me.

CARROT AND COCONUT CAKE

I know every carrot cake aficionado will say this, but I promise that my version, while not traditional, is truly the very best. You'll find no warming spices like cinnamon or nutmeg. And there are definitely no chewy raisins or walnut rubble complicating its plush texture. Instead, the natural, earthy sweetness of carrots gets the spotlight all to itself.

For a little tiki-inspired oomph, the cake contains both unsweetened coconut flakes and finely cubed pineapple (even better, mix in the Pineapple and Lime Marmalade, page 128). And while I think that this cake rolled in sugar is absolutely perfect, a dramatic swoosh of Black Sesame and Cream Cheese Frosting (page 133) tips it into pure bliss (if you go this route, skip the snow sugar or powdered sugar).

1. **PREHEAT THE OVEN AND PREP THE CAKE PAN.** Preheat the oven to 350°F (175°C). If using a round cake pan, cut out a round of parchment paper to fit and adhere with cooking spray. If using a loaf pan, drape a saddle of parchment paper inside and add cooking spray.

2. **DISSOLVE THE SUGAR IN THE EGGS.** In a stand mixer fitted with the whisk (or in a large bowl using a handheld mixer), whip the eggs on high speed until foamy, about 20 seconds. Slowly stream in the granulated and dark brown sugars and continue to whip until the mixture is lightened in color and doubled in volume, 5 to 6 minutes (see tip #1).

3. **PREPARE THE DRY INGREDIENTS AND MIX-INS.** In a small bowl, whisk together both flours, the baking powder, baking soda, and kosher salt. Set aside. In a medium bowl, stir together the pineapple, carrots, and coconut flakes.

4. **STREAM IN THE LIQUIDS.** With the mixer running on medium speed, stream in the grapeseed oil and vanilla and whip for 1 minute. The whipped eggs will appear to slightly fall; this is okay!

→

MAKES ONE 10-INCH (25 CM)
ROUND CAKE OR ONE 10-INCH
(25 CM) LOAF
SERVES 8 TO 10

30 MINUTES ACTIVE TIME
3 HOURS INACTIVE TIME

3 eggs (150 g), at room temperature
¾ cup (150 g) granulated sugar
¼ cup (60 g) dark brown sugar
1½ cups (180 g) all-purpose flour
¼ cup (35 g) whole wheat flour
1 teaspoon baking powder
¾ teaspoon baking soda
1 teaspoon kosher salt
½ cup (120 g) finely diced fresh
    pineapple
2 cups (250 g) grated peeled
    carrots (about 6 medium)
2 cups (160 g) unsweetened
    coconut flakes

(ingredients continue)

1 cup (225 g) grapeseed oil

1 teaspoon vanilla extract

½ cup (60 g) snow sugar
(see tip #2) or powdered
sugar

TIP 1 —— *Some oil-based cakes can feel greasy and dense. Whipping the eggs with sugar on high speed dissolves the sugar, incorporating airy volume into the cake. The result? A lighter, melt-in-your-mouth crumb.*

TIP 2 —— *Snow sugar (see Resources, page 311) is one of my favorite pastry chef discoveries. Though it looks and feels just like traditional powdered sugar, snow sugar (also called doughnut sugar) doesn't melt on moist surfaces or on still-warm or slightly oily pastries.*

5. STIR IN THE REMAINING INGREDIENTS. Turn the mixer off and remove the bowl. Using a spatula or wooden spoon, stir in the flour mixture halfway, so it still looks streaky. Add the mix-ins all at once and continue to stir until combined.

6. BAKE THE CAKE. Pour the mixture into the prepared pan and immediately place in the oven. Bake until a cake tester inserted in the center comes out clean, with a crumb or two attached, 50 to 55 minutes. Let the cake sit for 5 minutes. If it's a loaf cake, lift it out of the pan, rest it on a cooling rack, and peel off the parchment liner. If the cake was baked in a round pan, invert the cake onto a cooling rack, remove the pan, and peel off the parchment liner. Allow the cake to cool completely, about 2 hours.

7. ROLL IN SUGAR TO COAT. Spread the snow sugar in a wide dish or baking dish. Carefully dredge all sides of the cake in the sugar, pressing the powder in with your fingertips to adhere, until the cake is completely coated and opaque. Slice into portions 1 inch (2.5 cm) wide and eat, or wrap well in plastic wrap and hold at room temperature for up to 4 days, or in the freezer for up to 1 month.

COCOA AND CHICORY SHEET CAKE

I like to brew a hot mug of ground roasted chicory root in the evenings. The penetrating, caramel aromas—quite similar to those of my morning cup of coffee—are soothing after a heavy meal (especially when the drink is paired with a buttery cookie or a juicy orange). And it's even better stirred into a moist chocolate cake, a perennial crowd-pleaser.

This is a wonderfully forgiving recipe to scale up and down—you can halve the batch here to make a dozen cupcakes, or double it to make four 6-inch (15 cm) loaves to give to neighbors.

1. **PREHEAT THE OVEN AND PREP THE PAN.** Preheat the oven to 350°F (175°C). Drape a saddle of parchment paper inside a 9-by-13-inch (23 by 33 cm) baking dish and coat with cooking spray.

2. **MAKE THE CHICORY COFFEE.** In a saucepan, combine the water and chicory grounds over low heat, 3 to 4 minutes. Pour the mixture through a tea strainer into a small cup to remove the grounds.

3. **DISSOLVE THE SUGAR IN THE EGG.** In a stand mixer fitted with the whisk (or in a large bowl using a handheld mixer), whip the egg on high speed until foamy, about 20 seconds. Slowly stream in both sugars and continue to whip until the sugar is dissolved and the mixture has doubled in volume, 4 to 5 minutes.

4. **PREPARE THE DRY INGREDIENTS.** In a medium bowl, combine the flour, baking soda, baking powder, and kosher salt. Sift the cocoa powder over the mixture and whisk.

5. **STREAM IN THE LIQUIDS.** With the mixer running on medium speed, stream in the buttermilk, grapeseed oil, vanilla, and brewed chicory, 1 to 2 minutes.

→

MAKES ONE 9-BY-13-INCH (23 BY 33 CM) SHEET CAKE
SERVES 10 TO 12

20 MINUTES ACTIVE TIME
40 MINUTES INACTIVE TIME

½ cup (120 g) water
¼ cup (30 g) ground roasted chicory root
1 egg (50 g), at room temperature
¼ cup plus 1 tablespoon (75 g) granulated sugar
¼ cup (50 g) light brown sugar
1 cup (120 g) all-purpose flour
1½ teaspoons baking soda
½ teaspoon baking powder
1 teaspoon kosher salt
½ cup plus 2 tablespoons (50 g) cocoa powder
½ cup (120 g) buttermilk or kefir, at room temperature
¼ cup (55 g) grapeseed oil
1 teaspoon vanilla extract

(ingredients continue)

Cocoa Gloss (recipe follows)

¼ cup (about 50 g) cacao nibs or
   sprinkles

Flaky sea salt

TIP —— *Because of their moist, super-hydrated crumb, you can store oil-based cakes in the freezer, where they'll never dry out. This is an ideal cake for frozen desserts: try it as the base for the Caramel Chocolate Chip Bombe (page 225).*

6. WHISK IN THE DRY INGREDIENTS. Add the flour mixture all at once and whisk vigorously until just combined. The mixture will be slightly lumpy, but do not whisk until smooth.

7. BAKE THE CAKE. Scrape the batter into the prepared baking dish. Bake until a cake tester inserted in the center comes out clean, about 30 minutes. Let cool slightly, then place a cutting board on top of the pan. Flip the pan over. Remove the pan and peel off the parchment.

8. GLAZE THE CAKE. Pour the cooled cocoa gloss on top of the inverted cake and smooth it to coat every corner. Sprinkle with the cacao nibs or sprinkles and flaky sea salt. Let rest at room temperature for at least 10 to 15 minutes before slicing. (Alternatively, the cake, still in its pan, can be wrapped and stored in the fridge for up to 4 days before eating—see tip.)

Cocoa Gloss

Instead of using a fluffy, buttery frosting, top this cake with a lacquered, barely sweet cocoa sauce—the kind you'd drizzle over an ice cream sundae—inspired by the mirrored, glossy surfaces of Viennese tortes. It gets its sheen and viscous texture from the addition of glucose, a prized ingredient among pastry chefs. Corn syrup is an easy swap.

MAKES 1 CUP (250 G)

10 MINUTES ACTIVE TIME
30 MINUTES INACTIVE TIME

¼ cup (30 g) ground roasted
   chicory root

½ cup (40 g) cocoa powder

⅓ cup (100 g) glucose or light corn
   syrup

2 tablespoons (25 g) sugar

½ teaspoon kosher salt

1 teaspoon vanilla extract

¼ cup plus 2 tablespoons (85 g)
   water

IN A SMALL POT, combine the ground chicory, cocoa powder, glucose, sugar, salt, vanilla, and water and whisk well to break up the clumps of cocoa powder. Bring the sauce up to a simmer over medium-low heat and let simmer gently, whisking occasionally, until thickened, 8 to 10 minutes. Pour the sauce through a tea strainer into a small jar to remove the chicory grounds. Allow the gloss to cool for 30 minutes as it will continue to thicken. The gloss can be made up to 2 weeks in advance and stored in an airtight container in the refrigerator. Rewarm before using.

DAPPLED DATE CAKE

An upside-down cake is my very favorite way of incorporating dried or fresh fruit into a batter. It's like having two desserts in one—a triumphant fruit tart on top and a golden cake underneath. Here, torn dates, scattered into the bottom of a coconut sugar–crusted cake pan, create a dappled, sticky camouflage on the surface, while the ring of sesame seeds adds crunch and structure to each slice. It's as special as an ambitious layer cake, but with a fraction of the work.

MAKES ONE 8-INCH (20 CM)
ROUND CAKE
SERVES 8

20 MINUTES ACTIVE TIME
30 MINUTES INACTIVE TIME

3 tablespoons (25 g) white and black sesame seeds
½ cup plus 1 tablespoon (115 g) coconut sugar or granulated sugar
1 pound (450 g) unpitted dates (about 2 cups)
1 egg (50 g), at room temperature
3 tablespoons (45 g) fresh lemon juice
¾ cup (175 g) canned unsweetened full-fat coconut milk, at room temperature
¼ cup plus 2 tablespoons (85 g) coconut oil, melted
2 teaspoons vanilla extract
¾ cup (90 g) all-purpose flour
¼ cup (35 g) cornmeal
½ teaspoon baking powder
½ teaspoon baking soda
½ teaspoon kosher salt
Flaky sea salt

1. PREHEAT THE OVEN AND PREP THE CAKE PAN. Preheat the oven to 350°F (175°C). Coat an 8-inch (20 cm) round cake pan with cooking spray and press a round of parchment paper into the pan. Tilt the cake pan on its side and sprinkle the sesame seeds on the walls of the pan, slowly rotating the pan to coat the sides evenly.

2. ARRANGE THE DATES IN THE PAN. Scatter 1 tablespoon of the coconut sugar all over the parchment. Tear the dates in half lengthwise and remove the pits. Arrange the dates all over the parchment round.

3. COMBINE THE WET INGREDIENTS. In a medium bowl, whisk together the remaining ½ cup (100 g) coconut sugar, the egg, lemon juice, ½ cup (115 g) of the coconut milk, the coconut oil, and 1 teaspoon of the vanilla. In a small glass, combine the remaining ¼ cup (60 g) coconut milk and remaining 1 teaspoon vanilla and set aside for soaking the cake later.

4. COMBINE THE DRY INGREDIENTS. In a small bowl, whisk together the flour, cornmeal, baking powder, baking soda, and kosher salt. Dump the dry ingredients into the liquid ingredients bowl and gently whisk to combine.

5. BAKE THE CAKE. Scrape the batter into the cake pan over the dates. Bake until a fork inserted into the center comes out clean.

6. SOAK THE CAKE AND LET COOL. Remove the cake from the oven and let cool slightly. Using a small brush or spoon, drizzle the reserved coconut milk mixture over the surface of the cake. Set a platter on top of the cake pan. Slowly flip both the pan and platter over. Carefully remove the cake pan and peel off the parchment paper. Sprinkle with flaky sea salt and use a serrated knife to portion the cake into 8 slices.

VARIATION

To make this upside-down cake with fresh fruit, try 1 thinly sliced apple, 3 cubed stalks rhubarb, 2 cubed peaches or nectarines, or 2 cups (200 g) cranberries or pitted sour cherries. I find citrus to be too watery and fibrous for this treatment, and more muted fruits like pears tend to get lost in the cake.

CRUNCHY ALMOND CAKE

As a child, I lusted after the artful, heavily lacquered marzipan miniatures sold in European patisseries and shops, sculpted into cherries and garlic cloves. It never occurred to me that I could make my own marzipan until I joined the staff at Lawrence, in Montréal, where the pastry cooks knead almond paste by hand before draping the fragrant sheets over checkered Battenberg cakes.

As it turns out, marzipan is very easy to make by hand and requires just a few ingredients. Rather than buying a roll or tube of marzipan, you can mix your own, using either fresh almond meal or whole almonds, ground into a fine crumb. Here, a thick rope of homemade marzipan runs through the core of the cake, like a rich, chewy surprise.

The irresistible crunchy topping is a nod to one of Lawrence's most popular desserts, the Queen Elizabeth cake. Instead of using shredded coconut to provide the lacy topping, I like to use thinly sliced almonds, which are stirred into an amber-colored toffee sauce. As the cake broils, the topping bubbles and pops, forming a toasty, caramel crust better than any frosting or glaze.

This cake is best eaten the day it is made, when the topping is crisp. It's still delicious on the second, third, and fourth days, but the almond topping may get a bit sticky.

MAKES ONE 10-INCH (25 CM)
LOAF CAKE
SERVES 6 TO 8

40 MINUTES ACTIVE TIME
1 HOUR INACTIVE TIME

6½ ounces (180 g) marzipan, homemade (recipe follows) or store-bought

(ingredients continue)

1. **PREHEAT THE OVEN AND PREP THE LOAF PAN.** Preheat the oven to 350°F (175°C). Mist a 10-inch (25 cm) loaf pan with cooking spray and drape a sheet of parchment inside, like a saddle, so that it comes up the long sides of the pan.

2. **DIVIDE THE MARZIPAN.** Using a knife or bench scraper, pinch off one-third (60 g) of the marzipan and set aside. Dust your fingertips with powdered sugar and gently roll and shape the remaining marzipan into a rope 10 inches (25 cm) long. It's okay if it looks a little misshapen and lumpy, or breaks into pieces, as it can be patched later. Drape a tea towel on top and set aside.

$\rightarrow$

Powdered sugar, for dusting

8 tablespoons (4 ounces/115 g) unsalted butter, cubed, at room temperature

½ cup plus 2 tablespoons (130 g) granulated sugar

3 eggs (150 g), at room temperature

1 teaspoon vanilla extract

1 teaspoon almond extract

¾ cup (90 g) all-purpose flour

3 tablespoons (20 g) blanched almond flour

1 teaspoon baking powder

1 teaspoon kosher salt

Toffee Almond Topping (recipe follows)

Flaky sea salt

3. COMBINE THE WET INGREDIENTS. In a stand mixer fitted with the paddle, combine the reserved piece of marzipan, the butter, and granulated sugar and paddle on high speed until fluffy, aerated, and pale in color, 5 to 6 minutes. With the stand mixer running on low speed, drop in the eggs one at a time, waiting until each egg is incorporated before adding the next. Add both extracts and paddle to combine.

4. ADD THE DRY INGREDIENTS. In a small bowl, whisk together the all-purpose flour, almond flour, baking powder, and kosher salt. Turn off the stand mixer and add the dry ingredients. On the lowest speed, paddle until just combined, 10 to 15 seconds.

5. BAKE THE CAKE. Scrape the cake batter into the prepared loaf pan and gently smooth the surface. Drape the marzipan rope lengthwise down the center of the pan. Transfer to the oven and bake until the top springs back to the touch, 40 to 45 minutes.

6. BROIL THE TOP. Remove the cake from the oven. Move one of the oven racks to the highest position, so it's right underneath the broiler element. Switch the oven to its broiler setting. Pour the almond topping on top of the cake, spreading it evenly to cover the whole surface. Broil, watching the cake closely and pulling it out after a minute or two to nudge the almonds around so they toast evenly. Once the topping is deeply golden and bubbling, 3 to 4 minutes total, remove from the oven.

7. COOL AND SERVE. Let the cake cool in the pan for about 30 minutes before slicing. Cut into slices 1 inch (2.5 cm) thick and add a pinch of flaky sea salt to each. (If not serving right away, leave the cake in the loaf pan, wrap tightly with plastic wrap and refrigerate.)

Easy Marzipan

IN A SMALL BOWL, combine the almond flour, powdered sugar, egg white, almond extract, and salt and work with a spatula until a soft, pliable dough forms, about 2 minutes. (Alternatively, combine all the ingredients in a food processor and pulse until a dough forms.) Wrap the marzipan tightly in plastic wrap and refrigerate until ready to use. The marzipan can be made up to 2 weeks in advance and stored in an airtight container in the fridge.

MAKES 6½ OUNCES (180 G)

10 MINUTES ACTIVE TIME

¾ cup (75 g) blanched almond flour
¾ cup (90 g) powdered sugar
1 tablespoon (15 g) lightly whisked egg white
1 teaspoon almond extract
½ teaspoon kosher salt

Toffee Almond Topping

IN A SMALL POT, combine the cream, butter, and brown sugar and boil rapidly over medium-high heat until bubbling, richly caramel-colored, and glossy, about 4 minutes. Remove from the heat and stir in the almonds, vanilla, and a big pinch of flaky sea salt. Set aside to cool slightly before using.

MAKES 2 CUPS (260 G)

5 MINUTES ACTIVE TIME
5 MINUTES INACTIVE TIME

3 tablespoons (45 g) heavy cream
3 tablespoons (1½ ounces/45 g) unsalted butter
¼ cup plus 2 tablespoons (90 g) light brown sugar
1 cup (100 g) sliced almonds
½ teaspoon vanilla extract
Flaky sea salt

JAMMY COFFEE CAKE

A classic coffee cake has two essential components: a fluffy cake and a decadent crumb topping. My coffee cake adds a sticky ribbon of raspberries racing through the center. In the oven, the macerated berries thicken, and the sweet-and-salty oat topping collapses into the fruit, forming a buttery, crisp crust. Try playing around with equal amounts of other fruits, depending on the season—finely diced rhubarb or sour cherries in the spring, or roughly chopped cranberries in the winter. Just look for a tart, barely sweet fruit for the proper amount of acidity.

1. PREHEAT THE OVEN AND PREP THE PAN. Preheat the oven to 350°F (175°C). Mist a 10-inch (25 cm) loaf pan with cooking spray and drape a sheet of parchment inside, like a saddle, so that it comes up the long sides of the pan.

2. MACERATE THE BERRIES. In a small bowl, combine the raspberries and 1 tablespoon of the granulated sugar. Use your fingers to crush the raspberries, pressing in the sugar and releasing the fruit's juices.

3. CREAM THE BUTTER AND SUGARS. In a stand mixer fitted with the paddle (or in a large bowl using a handheld mixer), cream together the butter, the remaining granulated sugar, and the brown sugar on medium speed until fluffy and lightened in color and inching up the sides of the bowl, 4 to 5 minutes.

4. ADD THE EGG, VANILLA, AND SOUR CREAM. Add the egg and paddle for 2 minutes. Add the vanilla and sour cream and paddle until smooth, another minute (the mixture may look curdled, but this is fine).

5. ADD THE DRY INGREDIENTS. In a small bowl, combine the all-purpose flour, spelt flour, cinnamon, and kosher salt. Sift the cocoa powder and baking soda through a tea strainer into the bowl and whisk well to combine. Turn the mixer off and gently tip in the dry ingredients all at once. Using the lowest speed on the mixer, mix until the ingredients are halfway combined, about 10 seconds.

$\rightarrow$

MAKES ONE 10-INCH (25 CM) LOAF COFFEE CAKE SERVES 6 TO 8

35 MINUTES ACTIVE TIME
1 HOUR INACTIVE TIME

1 pint (about 150 g) raspberries
¼ cup plus 2 tablespoons (75 g) granulated sugar
8 tablespoons (4 ounces/115 g) unsalted butter, cubed, at room temperature
¼ cup (60 g) light brown sugar
1 egg (50 g), at room temperature
½ teaspoon vanilla extract
¼ cup plus 1 tablespoon (75 g) sour cream or yogurt
¾ cup plus 1 tablespoon (100 g) all-purpose flour
2 tablespoons (20 g) spelt or whole wheat flour
¼ teaspoon ground cinnamon
½ teaspoon kosher salt
1 teaspoon cocoa powder
¼ teaspoon baking soda
Sweet-and-Salty Oat Crumbs (recipe follows)
Flaky sea salt

TIP —— *It can be tricky to test a cake for doneness when the top layer is a sticky, wet jam. Try sliding the knife in at a sharp sideways angle, count to three, and then remove the knife. If it's dry, the cake is done.*

Turn the mixer off, remove the bowl from the stand, and finish folding by hand, with a spatula.

6. ADD THE TOPPINGS. Spread the cake batter in the prepared pan. Spoon the macerated raspberries over the surface of the cake. Scatter the sweet-and-salty oat crumbs on top.

7. BAKE THE CAKE. Transfer the pan to the oven and bake until a small knife inserted in the center (see tip) comes out clean, 40 to 45 minutes. Let cool before slicing. Cut into thick slices and sprinkle with flaky sea salt.

Sweet-and-Salty Oat Crumbs

You can keep a pint container of raw oat crumbs stored in the refrigerator; a spoonful pressed into a cookie or a scoop of muffin batter before baking is an easy, tasty upgrade.

MAKES 1½ CUPS (205 G)

5 MINUTES ACTIVE TIME
20 MINUTES INACTIVE TIME

½ cup (100 g) light brown sugar
　(see tip)
¾ cup (90 g) rolled oats
¼ cup (30 g) all-purpose flour
⅛ teaspoon baking soda
½ teaspoon kosher salt
3 tablespoons (45 g) unsalted
　butter, cubed

TIP —— *One cut-up apple magically rehydrates rock-hard sugar. Bury the apple chunks in the sugar, cover tightly, and wait. It will be plush and damp the next day.*

IN A SMALL BOWL, combine the light brown sugar, oats, flour, baking soda, and salt. Pinch in the butter until it has disappeared into the crumbs and the mixture feels slightly damp. Refrigerate for 20 minutes to chill. The crumbs, held in an airtight container, can be stored in the freezer for up to 3 weeks.

OLIVE OIL CAKE WITH CRISPY CAPERS

This olive oil cake, with its coarse, amber crumb, glows as if lit from within. Use your everyday workhorse cooking olive oils for the cake batter (see tip). Your fanciest finishing olive oil—the kind you'd dress a salad with, or drizzle over fresh fish—is best saved for the final soak after the cake is baked. For that, you want straight-up fireworks: you can't go wrong with *olio nuovo*–style olive oils, which are the super-intense verdant oils made with the first pressing of just-harvested olives. A special cake soak "vinaigrette," made from whisking orange juice, fancy olive oil, and fortified wine together, further underlines this cake's subtle savoriness, as does a flurry of crispy capers, which add an addictive crunch and surprisingly mellow flavor.

1. **PREHEAT THE OVEN AND PREP THE CAKE PAN.** Preheat the oven to 350°F (175°C). Cut out a round of parchment paper to fit a 10-inch (25 cm) round cake pan and secure with cooking spray.

2. **PROCESS THE ORANGE.** Grate the zest from the orange; you want about 1 tablespoon zest. Juice the orange and measure out ⅓ cup (80 g) juice for the cake batter. Then measure out another 2 tablespoons (30 g) for the vinaigrette and set aside.

3. **DISSOLVE THE SUGAR IN THE EGGS.** In a stand mixer fitted with the whisk (or in a large bowl using a handheld mixer), whip the eggs on high speed until foamy, about 20 seconds. Slowly stream in 1 cup (200 g) of the sugar and continue to whip until the mixture is lightened in color and doubled in volume, 5 to 6 minutes.

4. **COMBINE THE DRY INGREDIENTS.** Sift the baking soda and baking powder through a small tea strainer into a small bowl. Add the flour and kosher salt and whisk to combine.

5. **INCORPORATE THE REMAINING INGREDIENTS.** With the mixer running on low speed, stream in the ⅓ cup (80 g) orange juice, the orange zest, milk, olive oil, and almond extract and mix to combine. Add the dry ingredients. Mix until just combined

MAKES ONE 10-INCH (25 CM)
ROUND CAKE
SERVES 8

40 MINUTES ACTIVE TIME
1 HOUR INACTIVE TIME

1 large orange
2 eggs (100 g), at room temperature
1 cup (200 g) sugar, plus
    2 tablespoons (30 g) for
    sprinkling
½ teaspoon baking soda
1¼ teaspoons baking powder
2 cups (240 g) all-purpose flour
1 teaspoon kosher salt
¾ cup (185 g) whole milk, at room
    temperature
½ cup plus 2 tablespoons (150 g)
    olive oil
½ teaspoon almond extract
3 tablespoons (20 g) capers
3 tablespoons (45 g) grapeseed oil

(ingredients continue)

Single-Layer Cakes

¼ cup (60 g) finishing olive oil
2 tablespoons (30 g) Marsala wine
   or sherry
Flaky sea salt

TIP —— *Delicious, affordable choices include the cold pressed oils from Partanna, Campagna, and Palermo in Southern Italy and Arbequina olive oils from Catalonia, Spain, and Capay Valley, California. (Look for high-end brands sold by the gallon for more affordable options.)*

VARIATIONS

Cake soaks should have a balance of tart, sweet, and savory notes—just like a vinaigrette for your favorite salad. Try adding champagne or balsamic vinegar to the soak, a spoonful of jam, or a grind of black pepper.

Oil-based cakes don't mind lots of ingredient substitutions. Try Meyer lemon or lime in place of the orange. Sub out 3 tablespoons of flour for cornmeal for cake with a heartier texture. Add 2 tablespoons (18 g) poppy seeds for a slight crunch. Sprinkle 2 teaspoons finely diced rosemary into the flour for an herbal note. The whole milk can be replaced by nondairy alternatives like coconut milk or almond milk. You can truly make this recipe your own!

(the batter will be thin with some lumps; do not whip until the batter is totally smooth, as that would make the cake tough).

6. BAKE THE CAKE. Scrape the batter into the prepared cake pan and sprinkle the surface with the 2 tablespoons sugar. Bake until the cake springs back when poked with a finger, 35 to 40 minutes.

7. MEANWHILE, FRY THE CAPERS. Spread the capers out on a tea towel and gently pat dry. In a small saucepan, heat the grapeseed oil over medium heat. (A thermometer inserted in the oil should read around 350°F/175°C.) Add the capers all at once and fry, stirring constantly, until they have lightened in color and the flower buds are beginning to open up, about 2 minutes. With a slotted spoon, remove the capers to a paper towel and let drain completely.

8. MIX THE CAKE-SOAK VINAIGRETTE. In a small bowl, whisk together the reserved 2 tablespoons (30 g) orange juice, the finishing olive oil, and the Marsala.

9. SOAK THE OLIVE OIL CAKE. Run a small offset spatula around the edges of the pan and gently tug the cake out and onto a platter to cool completely. Gently lift the cake up to peel off the parchment and discard. When ready to serve, gently dab the vinaigrette onto the cake with a small pastry brush. Sprinkle with flaky sea salt. Slice into wedges and serve with a scattering of crispy capers.

More Than Cake

PASSION FRUIT ROLL-UP CAKE

A simple tea towel trick and a single jelly-roll twist instantly elevate this sheet-pan sponge into retro showstopper territory. Technically a *roulade*, a French word that describes the circular spiral made from twisting up a cake like a scroll, this passion fruit roll-up is inspired both by the traditional Yule log, or bûche de Noël, as well as the pull-apart spiral of a cinnamon bun.

Roulades offer the alternating textural delights of a layer cake, but with none of the multiple-day assembly. I adore a roll-up because of the infinite aesthetic possibilities it affords, including a chance to bust out my collection of star tips to make the playful mascarpone whip squiggle.

1. **PREHEAT THE OVEN AND PREP THE CAKE PAN.** Preheat the oven to 350°F (175°C). Mist a 9-by-13-inch (23 by 33 cm) quarter-sheet pan with cooking spray, press a rectangle of parchment onto the bottom, and mist the paper.

2. **HARVEST THE COCONUT CREAM.** Open the can of coconut milk. Use a spoon to carefully remove the solidified coconut cream on the top. In a small saucepan, gently melt the coconut cream until it is smooth and runny; set aside at room temperature for the whipped cream. Measure out ¼ cup plus 2 tablespoons (100 g) of the remaining coconut milk for the batter. Measure out a second ¼ cup plus 2 tablespoons (100 g) for the soak and set aside.

3. **DISSOLVE THE SUGAR IN THE EGG.** In a stand mixer fitted with the whisk (or in a large bowl using a handheld mixer), whip the egg on high speed until foamy, about 20 seconds. Slowly stream in the granulated sugar and continue to whip until the mixture has doubled in volume, 5 to 6 minutes.

4. **COMBINE THE DRY INGREDIENTS.** Using a small tea strainer set over a medium bowl, sift the baking powder and baking soda to remove clumps. Add the flour and kosher salt to the bowl and whisk to combine.

→

MAKES ONE 10-INCH (25 CM) ROLLED CAKE
SERVES 10 TO 12

40 MINUTES ACTIVE TIME
2 HOURS INACTIVE TIME

One 13.5-ounce (400 g) can unsweetened full-fat coconut milk
1 egg (50 g)
½ cup (100 g) granulated sugar
½ teaspoon baking powder
½ teaspoon baking soda
1 cup (120 g) all-purpose flour
½ teaspoon kosher salt
3 tablespoons (45 g) fresh lemon juice
¼ cup plus 2 tablespoons (85 g) grapeseed oil
2 teaspoons vanilla extract
1½ cups (360 g) cold heavy cream
3 tablespoons (20 g) powdered sugar

(ingredients continue)

¾ cup (180 g) mascarpone
1 cup (270 g) Passion Fruit and
Olive Oil Curd (see page 127),
at room temperature
Seeds from 1 passion fruit

TIP 1 —*Try not to overbake the sponge! Any kind of "crispness" on the cake will cause it to crack more easily. In any case, the coconut milk soak gives the cake a pliability that makes it easy to roll up.*

TIP 2 —*Rescue a chunky overwhipped cream by stirring in a tablespoon of heavy cream or coconut milk. You'll get a silky, perfectly glossy whip instantly.*

5. INCORPORATE THE REMAINING INGREDIENTS. Add the ¼ cup plus 2 tablespoons (100 g) coconut milk, the lemon juice, grapeseed oil, and 1 teaspoon of the vanilla to the mixer bowl and whip for 2 to 3 minutes. Turn the mixer off and add the dry ingredients all at once. Mix on low speed for 5 seconds, or until the ingredients are halfway combined. Then turn the mixer off and finish mixing by hand with a spatula.

6. BAKE THE CAKE. Scrape the batter into the prepared sheet pan. Bake until the cake springs back when poked with a finger, 14 to 15 minutes (see tip #1). Let cool completely in the pan.

7. SOAK THE CAKE. Run a knife around the edges of the pan and invert the cake onto a cutting board. Remove the pan and peel off the parchment paper. Flip the cake back over so it is right side up. Trim the long edges of the cake with a small knife and discard (or snack on) the scraps. Slide the cake onto a clean kitchen towel lined with plastic wrap. With a clean pastry brush, brush the cake with the reserved ¼ cup plus 2 tablespoons (100 g) coconut milk soak.

8. WHIP THE CREAM. In a stand mixer fitted with the whisk (or in a large bowl using a handheld mixer), whip the heavy cream, powdered sugar, and mascarpone on high speed until thick and fluffy, 3 to 4 minutes. Add the reserved melted coconut cream and the remaining 1 teaspoon vanilla and beat until smooth, another minute. The whipped cream should be super stiff but not turning into butter (see tip #2).

9. FILL AND ROLL UP THE CAKE. Spread the passion fruit curd over the entire surface of the cake with a small offset spatula. Dollop on half of the whipped cream and gently smooth to coat. Starting on a long side, roll up the sponge. Trim the ends for a neater look. Cup the ends of the cake with your hands and transfer it to a platter.

10. PIPE THE WHIPPED CREAM ON TOP. Transfer the remaining whipped cream to a pastry bag fitted with a star tip. Pipe squiggles down the top of the roll-up. Refrigerate the cake for at least 1 hour to chill before serving. Sprinkle the cake with the passion fruit seeds and cut the cake into 1-inch (2.5 cm) slices.

More Than Cake

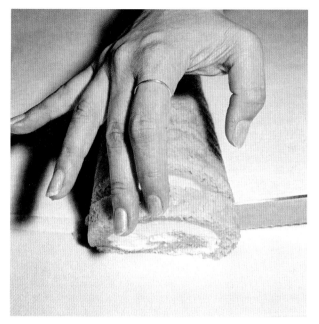 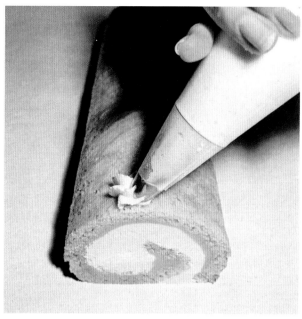

Clockwise from top left: (1) Trim the ends of the sponge for a neat look. (2) Fill a piping bag with whipped cream and pipe squiggles down the length of the roll-up (3). (4) Refrigerate the roll for one hour, then sprinkle passion fruit seeds on top and serve.

Single-Layer Cakes

STICKY FIG CAKE

Steaming a cake in a water bath, similar to what is used for a cheesecake or flan, is a common technique in traditional British pudding recipes like fruitcake. The gentle low-temperature bake yields a soft cake with no browned edges or bottom, and it is a great method for stodgier recipes that are heavy with fruit, like dates, figs, or bananas.

The combination of dried figs and vin santo, a sweet dessert wine made in Tuscany, is a favorite of mine, and the fig seeds in the cake add an unexpected crunch. (The vin santo and fig puree, on its own, is delicious paired with salty, creamy cheeses, too.) A silken, slightly savory toffee sauce, also spiked with vin santo, adds another layer of richness. Top it all off with a dollop of crème fraîche.

MAKES ONE 10-INCH (25 CM)
ROUND CAKE
SERVES 8

20 MINUTES ACTIVE TIME
45 MINUTES INACTIVE TIME

2 cups (225 g) whole dried figs
1¼ cups (300 g) vin santo (see tip)
1 teaspoon baking soda
4 tablespoons (2 ounces/60 g)
    unsalted butter, at room
    temperature
½ cup (100 g) sugar
2 eggs (100 g)
1 teaspoon vanilla extract
⅔ cup (65 g) almond flour
1 teaspoon baking powder
1 teaspoon kosher salt
¼ cup plus 1 tablespoon (40 g)
    tapioca starch or cornstarch
1 cup (120 g) whole wheat flour
Vin Santo Toffee Sauce (recipe
    follows)
Flaky sea salt

1. **PREHEAT THE OVEN AND PREP THE CAKE PAN.** Preheat the oven to 350°F (175°C). Mist a 10-inch (25 cm) round cake pan with cooking spray and press in a round of parchment paper. You'll also need a lidded Dutch oven with at least 1 inch (2.5 cm) clearance around the sides and 1 inch (2.5 cm) above the top of the cake pan. (If you don't have a Dutch oven, you can use a large roasting pan or deep cast-iron skillet as long as it can provide the clearances listed.)

2. **SOFTEN THE FIGS.** Remove the dried fig stems with a small knife. Slice the figs in half and place in a small pot. Add the vin santo and simmer over medium-low heat until the figs are softened by the wine, 7 to 8 minutes. Stir in the baking soda. Transfer to a food processor (or use an immersion blender) and puree until creamy.

3. **CREAM THE BUTTER AND SUGAR.** In a stand mixer fitted with the paddle (or in a large bowl using a handheld mixer), cream the butter and sugar on medium speed until the mixture is smooth and fluffy, 3 to 4 minutes.

4. **ADD THE REST OF THE INGREDIENTS.** Drop in the eggs one at a time, beating well after each addition. Add

the vanilla and paddle until combined. In a medium bowl, whisk together the almond flour, baking powder, kosher salt, tapioca starch, and whole wheat flour. Turn the mixer off, remove the bowl from the stand, and add the dry ingredients all at once to the bowl. Stir in by hand until halfway mixed and streaky. Fold in the warm pureed figs with a spatula until combined.

5. PREPARE THE WATER BATH. In a pot or teakettle, heat 4 cups (1 L) water until steaming hot. Scrape the batter into the prepared cake pan and nestle it into the Dutch oven (or other steaming pan). Slide the Dutch oven into the preheated oven and add the hot water to the pan, being careful not to splash the water into the cake batter, until the water comes up about ½ inch (1.25 cm). Set the lid on the Dutch oven and close the oven door. (If using another steaming pan, crimp a piece of foil over the top to seal.)

6. STEAM THE CAKE. Steam the cake until a skewer inserted in the center comes out clean, with a crumb or two attached, 40 to 45 minutes. Remove the Dutch oven and carefully lift the cake pan out. Allow the cake to rest for 10 minutes, then invert onto a serving platter and peel off the parchment round.

Brush ¼ cup (60 g) of the toffee sauce all over the surface and sides of the cake. Slice into 8 wedges, arrange on plates, and spoon the remaining warmed toffee sauce on top. Add a big pinch of flaky sea salt to each slice and eat while warm and sticky. Store the cake in an airtight container, chilled, for up to 4 days.

Vin Santo Toffee Sauce

MAKES 1 CUP (240 G)

10 MINUTES ACTIVE TIME

½ cup (90 g) dark brown sugar
⅓ cup (80 g) heavy cream
4 tablespoons (2 ounces/60 g) unsalted butter
2 tablespoons (30 g) vin santo
1 teaspoon vanilla extract
½ teaspoon kosher salt

IN A SMALL POT, combine the dark brown sugar, cream, and butter and bring to a boil over medium-high heat. Reduce to a simmer and cook, whisking occasionally, for 3 to 4 minutes. Remove from the heat and stir in the vin santo, vanilla, and salt. Whisk until smooth. The toffee sauce can be made and stored in the refrigerator for up to 3 weeks in advance; gently warm before serving.

TOASTED VANILLA BEAN POUND CAKE

Elevating a pound cake from ordinary to sublime requires a careful hand and a few simple techniques. Controlling the temperature of your ingredients before you begin mixing is one key to a perfectly executed cake. A stand mixer will most efficiently beat air into the butter, so the final cake tastes delicate, not dense.

Your stand mixer has just spent 5 minutes creaming air into your cake, so use a superlight touch when incorporating the dry ingredients at the end. Overmixing is the easiest way to deflate a butter-based batter, leading to an unappetizing gummy texture. I radically undermix—you should see powdery streaks in your batter as you go—and then finish by hand.

Resist the urge to open your oven until at least halfway through your bake. The first 30 minutes of a "closed oven" are crucial for a dense cake batter to "jump," giving it spring and lift. An open oven door can drop your oven temperature dramatically, which can lead to sad-looking cakes.

This pound cake, with its sweet-and-salty crust and fragrant vanilla bean crumb, is extraordinary on its own, but individually toasted slices truly catapult it into your special-occasion repertoire.

1. PREHEAT THE OVEN AND PREP THE LOAF PAN. Position a rack in the center of the oven and preheat the oven to 350°F (175°C). Mist an 8-inch (20 cm) loaf pan with cooking spray. Drape a sheet of parchment inside, like a saddle, so that it comes up the long sides of the pan, and lightly mist the paper with cooking spray. Sprinkle 2 tablespoons of the turbinado sugar into the pan and shake the pan gently so that the sugar sticks to the sides of the parchment (see tip #1).

2. MAKE THE VANILLA SUGAR. Use a small sharp knife to halve the vanilla bean lengthwise, pry open the two halves, and scrape the vanilla seeds out. Add the vanilla caviar and granulated sugar to the bowl and massage until damp and fragrant. (Don't toss the vanilla pod; see tip #2.)

→

MAKES ONE 8-INCH (20 CM) LOAF
SERVES 8

20 MINUTES ACTIVE TIME
5 HOURS INACTIVE TIME

¼ cup (60 g) turbinado sugar
1 vanilla bean
1¼ cups plus 2 tablespoons (280 g) granulated sugar
2½ cups (300 g) all-purpose flour
½ cup (60 g) corn flour
½ teaspoon baking soda
1 teaspoon kosher salt

(ingredients continue)

3. **WHISK TOGETHER THE DRY INGREDIENTS.** In a medium bowl, whisk together the all-purpose flour, corn flour, baking soda, and kosher salt; set aside.

4. **CREAM THE BUTTER AND VANILLA SUGAR.** In a stand mixer fitted with the paddle (or in a large bowl using a handheld mixer), cream the softened butter and vanilla sugar together on medium speed until fluffy and lightened in color (like frosting), 4 to 5 minutes.

5. **ADD THE EGGS AND EXTRACT.** Drop in the eggs one at a time, beating after each addition and stopping to scrape the bowl with a spatula, 1 to 2 minutes total. Add the vanilla extract and paddle to combine.

6. **ALTERNATE THE DRY AND WET INGREDIENTS.** With the mixer off, add half of the flour mixture to the mixer bowl. Turn the mixer on to the lowest speed and beat for 5 seconds (the mixture should still look very streaky and undermixed). Gently scrape the bottom of the bowl with a spatula. Add half of the buttermilk and half of the lemon juice. Turn the mixer back on to the lowest speed and beat for 3 to 4 seconds. Add the rest of the flour mixture and beat for 5 seconds. Finally, add the rest of the buttermilk and lemon juice, taking care to undermix. Turn off the mixer and finish combining the batter with a spatula by hand, using a light touch.

7. **BAKE THE LOAF.** Scrape the cake batter into the prepared loaf pan and smooth the surface evenly with the spatula. Sprinkle the remaining 2 tablespoons turbinado sugar on top. Scatter a pinch of flaky sea salt on the surface as well. Immediately transfer to the oven and bake until a cake tester inserted into the center of the loaf comes out clean, 60 to 70 minutes, rotating the pan front to back after 30 minutes. Begin to check for doneness at the 50-minute mark.

8. **SLICE AND TOAST.** Lift the cake out of the pan and remove the parchment. You can eat the cake warm and untoasted, cut into 1-inch (2.5 cm) slices. Or cool the loaf completely, 3 to 4 hours. (The unsliced cake can be wrapped tightly and stored at room temperature for up to 5 days, or in the freezer for up to 1 month.) To toast the cake slices, heat a small nonstick or cast-iron skillet over medium heat and add 1 tablespoon (15 g) salted cultured butter. Add a slice of cake and toast until fragrant and hot, about 3 minutes on each side. Repeat with as many cake slices as you are serving, adding more salted butter as necessary. Serve warm, with spoonfuls of yogurt or jam or with fresh fruit.

10 ounces (285 g) unsalted butter, cubed, at room temperature

3 eggs (150 g), at room temperature (see tip #3)

1 teaspoon vanilla extract

¾ cup plus 2 tablespoons (190 g) buttermilk, at room temperature

2 tablespoons (30 g) fresh lemon juice

Flaky sea salt

Salted cultured butter

Yogurt or jam, for serving (optional)

Fresh fruit, for serving (optional)

TIP 1 — *A coating of cooking spray on the parchment will glue any number of crunchy toppings to the sides of your cake, creating an outrageously yummy crust. Small seeds like flax and sesame and crunchy sugars like turbinado add texture and visual interest.*

TIP 2 — *Never throw away "spent" vanilla pods. You can steep them in simple syrup for poaching fruit or soaking cakes, or in vodka or bourbon to make your own vanilla extract. Vanilla beans are really expensive because they require so much time and energy to harvest and cure—so maximize their potential!*

TIP 3 — *If you've forgotten to temper your eggs, fill a deep bowl with hot water, drop the eggs (still in their shells) right into the bowl, and leave them there until they feel room temperature in your palm. And, unless you live in a superhot and humid climate, you can leave your butter, eggs, and buttermilk out overnight, which is what I do when I want to get a jump-start on baking the next morning.*

MODERN LAYER

CAKES

Though there are an infinite number of ways to construct a layer cake, I have a very particular method. My approach emphasizes the mouthfeel of the cake just as much as the outside decorative choices. The key to a delicious cake is in the thickness of the cake layers, which should be thin—no taller than ½ inch (1.25 cm). Alternate the cake layers—which should be very moist, either from the cake itself or from the application of a full-flavored soak—with juicy, creamy fillings. I stay away from butter-based cakes for my layer cakes, since they tend to dry out. (There are plenty of buttery cakes in the single-layer cake chapter, starting on page 74.)

The cake sets I've provided on these pages are meant to guide you, but the components of a layer cake can be mixed and matched to suit your preferences and whims, a little like the baker's version of the surrealist game Exquisite Corpse. Pair the components as thoughtfully as you would a plated dish, with elements of richness, acidity, and brightness. As the cake rests, the different flavors and textures mingle and combine, creating a masterpiece that is so much greater than the sum of its parts.

I use frostings strictly to bind the exterior of the cake together; they're too sweet and rich to use for inside layers. Instead, use the layers as an opportunity to add less stable but delicious fillings, like not-too-sweet custards, curds, and mousses. Time is also a very important factor in building a successful layered cake—but in the amount of time the cake has to sit, the layers can slide around unless there is something to stop them. This is why every cake in this chapter is assembled in a dish lined with plastic wrap to firmly support the layers as the cake sits in the fridge or freezer overnight.

For the final decorations, I love to play around with singular aesthetic expressions, like a playful squiggle of frosting, or a monochromatic topping of edible leaves and flowers (as in the Espresso, Chocolate, and Hazelnut Cake, page 151). I hope that you find inspiration in these pages and create ways to make these cakes your own.

HOW TO USE THIS CHAPTER

The cakes, soaks, fillings, and buttercream recipes are meant to be mixed and matched to create the layer cake of your dreams. At the end of this chapter, you'll find five tried-and-true combinations—my most victorious layer cake triumphs—and you can use those as a guideline or a place to start. Those recipe sets are also helpful to understand how I build layer cakes, and those methods can be applied to a unique layer cake of your own devising. (There's also a helpful step-by-step photo guide so you can properly see how I put one of these cakes together; see pages 136–137). I've made you a map, but which path you choose is up to you. Let's go!

CAKE + SOAK + FILLING + FROSTING = YOUR OWN UNIQUE LAYER CAKE

SOAKS

Tequila and Coconut Soak

Prosecco and Strawberry Soak

Maple and Vanilla Milk Soak

FILLINGS

Mascarpone Mousse

Green Tea Diplomat Cream

Toasted Honey and Chocolate Ganache

Yuzu and Olive Oil Curd

Fennel and White Balsamic Jam

Blueberry and Sumac Compote

Pineapple and Lime Marmalade

Sweet and Spicy Hazelnuts

Coconut Streusel

Candied Grapefruit Peel

Black Sesame and Cream
Cheese Frosting

Vanilla Bean Swiss
Buttercream

Italian Espresso
Buttercream

Vanilla Sponge Cake

Sponge cake reminds me of the fluffy, light-as-air Chinese bakery cakes I gobbled up as a child. Because the lift and tender crumb comes from aerating the eggs (no chemical leaveners needed), the flavor has a delicious eggy taste similar to that of traditional Chinese pastries. The crumb is also extremely absorbent—just like a sponge!—and neutral in flavor, making it ideal for moistening with intense, complex cake soaks.

MAKES 1 HALF-SHEET PAN CAKE,
ENOUGH FOR ONE 8-INCH (20 CM)
LAYER CAKE

20 MINUTES ACTIVE TIME
20 MINUTES INACTIVE TIME

6 eggs (300 g), well chilled
   (see tip #2)
¾ cup (150 g) sugar
1 tablespoon (15 g) vanilla extract
¾ cup plus 2 tablespoons (105 g)
   all-purpose flour
½ teaspoon kosher salt

TIP 1——*For the tallest, lightest sponge, do not grease your pans or use pans with nonstick surfaces. Because there is no chemical leavener, it has to be able to grip the sides of the pan in order to climb.*

TIP 2——*Chilled eggs make for an airy sponge (they also make it easier to separate the yolks from the whites).*

1. **PREHEAT THE OVEN AND PREP THE PAN.** Preheat the oven to 350°F (175°C). Line a half-sheet pan with parchment paper (see tip #1).

2. **WHIP THE EGG YOLKS.** Crack the eggs one by one into a small bowl, plucking out each yolk with clean fingertips as you go. Transfer the yolks to the bowl of a stand mixer fitted with the whisk (or to a large bowl if using a handheld mixer). Set the egg whites aside. Add ¼ cup plus 2 tablespoons (75 g) of the sugar to the yolks and whip on high speed until buttery yellow, at least 5 minutes. Stream in 2 teaspoons of the vanilla and whip to combine. Pour this mixture into a large wide bowl and set aside.

3. **MAKE THE MERINGUE.** Clean the mixer bowl well and pour in the egg whites. Whip on high speed until they begin to foam and turn white. With the mixer running, slowly stream in the remaining ¼ cup plus 2 tablespoons (75 g) sugar. Continue to whip on high speed until the mixture is climbing to the top of the bowl and the meringue holds a soft, floppy peak (see tip #3), about 4 minutes. To check this, detach the whisk, dunk it into the meringue, and then turn it over; the meringue crest should flop over on its side but not be drippy. Stream the remaining 1 teaspoon vanilla into the meringue, whipping to combine.

4. **ADD THE FLOUR.** As soon as the meringue is ready, work quickly to sift the flour and salt on top of the whipped yolks. The mixture will be very stiff; work it with a spatula or spoon to incorporate the flour completely. Immediately add one-third of the meringue mixture and gently stir to combine. Add the rest of the meringue, and fold to combine (see tip #4). The batter should be very loose and billowy.

More Than Cake

5. BAKE THE CAKE. Pour the batter into the sheet pan and smooth the surface with an offset spatula. Transfer to the oven and bake until the center of the cake springs back with a poke, 15 minutes. Let cool completely, then use a paring knife to loosen and remove the cake from the pan. Wrap the cake, still on its parchment, well in plastic wrap and store at room temperature for up to 3 days or in the freezer for up to 3 weeks.

TIP 3 — *Do not overbeat the meringue! If the meringue gets overly stiff, or looks curdled, it will be difficult to fold into the yolk mixture. In a pinch, I'll slip in an extra egg white and beat it again, which helps smooth out the texture. But always err on the side of underbeating a meringue—the network of air bubbles in a meringue is surprisingly strong, and the cake batter will still lift and rise in the oven.*

TIP 4 — *Fold confidently and with strength! It's better to make ten powerful, urgent folds than thirty half-hearted ones.*

Whole Wheat and Almond Chiffon Cake

Chiffon cake is richer than a classic genoise sponge, and its tender crumb makes it a reliable foundation for any layer cake. Unlike the Vanilla Sponge Cake (opposite), chiffon requires a bit of chemical leavener (here, a decent amount of baking powder) as well as whipped meringue to buoy its batter. The addition of an intense nut puree is what sets this chiffon cake apart from others. You want something smooth and rich, like tahini, creamy peanut butter, or a fancy pistachio or hazelnut spread. Avoid chunkier spreads, which might complicate the even crumb of the chiffon.

1. PREHEAT THE OVEN AND PREP THE PAN. Preheat the oven to 350°F (175°C). Line a half-sheet pan with parchment paper and lightly mist the paper with cooking spray.

2. MIX THE WET INGREDIENTS. Crack the eggs one by one into the bowl of a stand mixer fitted with the whisk, plucking out each yolk with clean fingertips as you go. Transfer the yolks to another bowl. Add the almond butter to the bowl of yolks and whisk by hand until smooth, then add ¾ cup (150 g) of the sugar, the water, oil, and vanilla and almond extracts and whisk until smooth.

→

MAKES 1 HALF-SHEET PAN CAKE, ENOUGH FOR ONE 8-INCH (20 CM) LAYER CAKE

20 MINUTES ACTIVE TIME
20 MINUTES INACTIVE TIME

3 eggs (150 g)
3 tablespoons (45 g) almond butter or almond praline paste
1 cup (200 g) sugar
¼ cup (60 g) water, at room temperature

(ingredients continue)

¼ cup (60 g) neutral oil, like
   grapeseed
1 teaspoon vanilla extract
¼ teaspoon almond extract
1 cup minus 1 tablespoon (110 g)
   whole wheat pastry flour
½ teaspoon kosher salt
2 teaspoons baking powder

3. MIX THE DRY INGREDIENTS. In another medium bowl, whisk together the whole wheat pastry flour and salt. Sift in the baking powder through a tea strainer, then whisk to combine. Pour the yolk mixture into the dry ingredients and gently stir to combine.

4. MAKE THE MERINGUE. Whip the egg whites on medium-high speed until a soft, foamy white peak forms. With the mixer running, slowly stream in the remaining ¼ cup (50 g) sugar and whip until a glossy, thick meringue has formed, 2 to 3 minutes.

5. FOLD IN THE MERINGUE. Using a large spatula, scoop up about one-third of the meringue and add to the flour and yolk mixture. Gently fold until the batter has loosened. Then add the remaining meringue and gently fold it in until incorporated. Pour the batter into the prepared sheet pan. Smooth the batter evenly with an offset spatula.

6. BAKE THE CAKE. Bake until the center springs back to the touch and the edges of the cake are beginning to pull away from the sides of the pan, 18 to 20 minutes. Let cool completely in the pan, then use a paring knife to loosen and remove the cake from the pan. Wrap the cake, still on its parchment, tightly in plastic wrap. Store at room temperature for up to 3 days or in the freezer for up to 3 weeks.

More Than Cake

Black Sesame Chiffon Cake

The addition of black sesame paste—typically found in Japanese and Korean supermarkets—gives this chiffon cake a velvety cement-colored crumb. It's so dramatic in layer cakes, especially when paired with a zippy jam.

1. **PREHEAT THE OVEN AND PREP THE PAN.** Preheat the oven to 350°F (175°C). Line a half-sheet pan with parchment paper and mist the paper with cooking spray.

2. **MIX THE WET INGREDIENTS.** Crack the eggs one by one into the bowl of a stand mixer fitted with the whisk, plucking out each yolk with clean fingertips as you go. Transfer them to another bowl. Add the black sesame paste, ¾ cup (150 g) of the sugar, the water, oil, and vanilla to the bowl of yolks and whisk by hand until smooth (see tip).

3. **MIX THE DRY INGREDIENTS.** In another medium bowl, whisk together the flour and salt. Sift in the baking powder through a tea strainer, then whisk to combine. Pour the yolk mixture into the dry ingredients and gently stir to combine.

4. **MAKE THE MERINGUE.** Whip the egg whites on medium-high speed until a soft, foamy white peak forms. With the mixer running, slowly stream in the remaining ¼ cup (50 g) sugar and whip until a glossy, thick meringue has formed, 2 to 3 minutes.

5. **FOLD IN THE MERINGUE.** Using a large spatula, scoop up about one-third of the meringue and add to the flour and yolk mixture. Gently fold until the batter has loosened. Then add the remaining meringue and gently fold it in until incorporated. Pour the batter into the prepared sheet pan and smooth the top with an offset spatula.

6. **BAKE THE CAKE.** Bake until the center springs back to the touch, 18 to 20 minutes. Let cool completely in the pan, then use a paring knife to loosen and remove the cake from the pan. Wrap the cake, still on its parchment, tightly in plastic wrap. Store at room temperature for up to 3 days or in the freezer for up to 3 weeks.

MAKES 1 HALF-SHEET PAN CAKE, ENOUGH FOR ONE 8-INCH (20 CM) LAYER CAKE

20 MINUTES ACTIVE TIME
20 MINUTES INACTIVE TIME

3 eggs (150 g)
¼ cup (60 g) black sesame paste
1 cup (200 g) sugar
¼ cup (60 g) water, at room temperature
¼ cup (60 g) neutral oil, like grapeseed
1 teaspoon vanilla extract
1 cup minus 1 tablespoon (110 g) all-purpose flour
½ teaspoon kosher salt
2 teaspoons baking powder

TIP —— *Never let raw yolks sit with sugar or extracts without agitating (both will "burn" your eggs, leaving unappealing, stringy cooked proteins in your batter).*

Hazelnut Dacquoise

Dacquoise is a fancy name for a cake based on ground nuts suspended in meringue; it is intense, sticky, and moist, like the cake version of a French macaron. You can play around with the amount of almond flour, which will change the texture of the final cake, but I love the nubby, rich mouthfeel of a dacquoise heavy with ground nuts.

MAKES 1 HALF-SHEET PAN CAKE,
ENOUGH FOR ONE 8-INCH (20 CM)
LAYER CAKE

20 MINUTES ACTIVE TIME
20 MINUTES INACTIVE TIME

1½ cups (175 g) almond or hazelnut
    flour (see tip)
¾ cup (98 g) blanched hazelnuts,
    toasted and finely ground
1 cup plus ¼ cup (150 g) powdered
    sugar
7 to 8 large egg whites (225 g)
½ teaspoon kosher salt
¼ cup plus 2 tablespoons (75 g)
    granulated sugar

TIP ——*For an even deeper, nuttier flavor, gently toast the almond or hazelnut flour in a 300°F (150°C) oven for 15 minutes. Let cool completely before using.*

1. **PREHEAT THE OVEN AND PREP THE PAN.** Preheat the oven to 350°F (175°C). Line a half-sheet pan with parchment paper. Lightly mist the paper with cooking spray.

2. **MIX THE DRY INGREDIENTS.** In a wide bowl, whisk together the almond flour and finely ground hazelnuts. Sift the powdered sugar on top and whisk together.

3. **MAKE THE MERINGUE.** In a stand mixer fitted with the whisk, whip the egg whites and salt on high speed until they begin to turn white and foamy. Gradually stream in the granulated sugar until the meringue is glossy and thickened and holds a floppy peak.

4. **MAKE THE BATTER AND FILL THE PAN.** Transfer the meringue to the almond flour/hazelnut mixture and gently fold to combine. The batter will be slightly runny. Spread the batter into the prepared sheet pan.

5. **BAKE THE CAKE.** Bake the cake until just set, about 15 minutes. Let cool completely in the pan, then run a paring knife around the edges of the pan to loosen and remove the cake. Wrap the cake, still on its parchment, tightly in plastic wrap. Store at room temperature for up to 3 days or in the freezer for up to 3 weeks (the cake will get sticky at room temperature).

More Than Cake

Olive Oil Cake

Because the cake is so olive oil forward, it doesn't need water or a milk-based syrup to hydrate the crumb. You can't go wrong with a spoonful of finishing olive oil brushed onto the cake layers, as in the Olive Oil, Mascarpone, and Fennel Layer Cake (page 145). An additional splash of something boozy—try a fortified wine like sherry—to an olive oil soak is a great way to build even more flavor.

1. **PREHEAT THE OVEN AND PREP THE PAN.** Preheat the oven to 350°F (175°C). Line a half-sheet pan with parchment paper. Lightly mist the paper with cooking spray.

2. **WHISK THE WET AND DRY INGREDIENTS SEPARATELY.** In a medium bowl, whisk together the buttermilk, sugar, eggs, olive oil, lemon juice, and vanilla. Use a small tea strainer to sift the baking soda and baking powder into a second medium bowl to remove clumps. Add the flour and salt and whisk to combine.

3. **MAKE THE BATTER AND FILL THE PAN.** Pour the wet ingredients into the dry ingredients and whisk just to combine. The batter should be runny, with some small lumps. Pour the batter into the lined pan and smooth the surface with an offset spatula. Poke out any large lumps with the tip of your finger if needed.

4. **BAKE THE CAKE.** Bake until the cake is fragrant and the center springs back with a poke, 15 to 18 minutes. Let cool completely in the pan, then run a paring knife around the edges of the pan to loosen and remove the cake. Wrap the cake, still on its parchment, tightly in plastic wrap. Store at room temperature for up to 3 days or in the freezer for up to 2 weeks.

MAKES 1 HALF-SHEET PAN CAKE, ENOUGH FOR ONE 8-INCH (20 CM) LAYER CAKE

20 MINUTES ACTIVE TIME
20 MINUTES INACTIVE TIME

1 cup (250 g) buttermilk, at room temperature
1 cup (200 g) sugar
2 eggs (100 g)
½ cup plus 2 tablespoons (150 g) olive oil
1 tablespoon (15 g) fresh lemon juice
1 teaspoon vanilla extract
¾ teaspoon baking soda
1 teaspoon baking powder
2 cups (240 g) all-purpose flour
1 teaspoon kosher salt

The trick to a mesmerizing-looking cake is to not overthink it; you
want your final masterpiece to feel effortless and lively. Below,
a minimal application of decor—such as a handful of petite
plums and a few carefully chosen flowers—creates surprising
impact and plenty of open space for the composition to breathe.
Opposite, tugging the petals off just one or two common flowers
(try daisies or marigolds) and scattering them across the surface
of a cake is an instant confetti-speckled party.

Tequila and Coconut Soak

This not-too-sweet soak adds richness and a sharp finish to simple sponges, like the Vanilla Sponge Cake (page 112). Rum would also be delicious here.

MAKES 1 CUP (240 G), ENOUGH FOR ONE 8-INCH (20 CM) LAYER CAKE

5 MINUTES ACTIVE TIME

¾ cup (180 g) unsweetened full-fat coconut milk
¼ cup (60 g) tequila

IN A SCREW-TOP JAR, combine the coconut milk and tequila and shake until smooth. Seal and store in the refrigerator for up to 1 week. Gently warm in a pot or in the microwave before applying to a cake.

Prosecco and Strawberry Soak

This vibrant strawberry syrup is so delicious it inspired "party water," a faux cocktail of fruit syrup and fizzy water I used to whip up for thirsty pastry cooks during a busy restaurant service. I have yet to find a better way to draw big flavor from out-of-season berries.

MAKES 1 CUP (240 G), ENOUGH FOR ONE 8-INCH (20 CM) LAYER CAKE

10 MINUTES ACTIVE TIME
1 HOUR INACTIVE TIME

1 pound (450 g) strawberries, hulled and roughly chopped
3 tablespoons (40 g) sugar
½ cup (120 g) sparkling wine

1. STEAM THE STRAWBERRIES. In a small pot, bring 2 inches (5 cm) of water up to a low simmer. Place the strawberries and sugar in a small heatproof bowl. Cover the bowl tightly with plastic wrap and place over the small pot; the bottom of the bowl should not touch the water. Gently steam until a thick syrup has gathered in the bottom of the bowl, 40 to 50 minutes. Remove from the heat.

2. PREPARE THE SYRUP. Gently strain the syrup through a sieve set over a bowl. Try not to press too firmly on the solids, which would cloud the liquid. Let cool completely and then keep chilled until ready to use. When ready to soak the cake, mix ¼ cup (60 g) of the syrup with the sparkling wine.

Maple and Vanilla Milk Soak

Whole milk is an easy way to add moisture and richness to cake. For an extra little kick, add a splash of maple syrup and freshly scraped vanilla seeds.

USING A SMALL SHARP KNIFE, split the vanilla bean in half lengthwise and scrape out the seeds into a small saucepan. Add the vanilla pod and maple syrup and bring to a boil over medium heat. Let simmer, uncovered, until the maple syrup looks thick and sticky, about 3 minutes. Stream in the milk and whisk well to combine. Remove from the heat and let cool completely before using. Transfer to an airtight container and store in the refrigerator for up to 1 week.

MAKES 1 CUP (240 G), ENOUGH FOR ONE 8-INCH (20 CM) LAYER CAKE

5 MINUTES ACTIVE TIME

½ vanilla bean
3 tablespoons (45 g) maple syrup
1 cup (240 g) whole milk

Mascarpone Mousse

For a fluffy yet stable filling, this is your go-to mousse for cake building. Save and freeze the leftover egg whites for the Plum Nests (page 186) or Citrusy Macaroons (page 23).

MAKES 3½ CUPS (480 G), ENOUGH FOR ONE 8-INCH (20 CM) LAYER CAKE

15 MINUTES ACTIVE TIME

3 large egg yolks (60 g)
2 tablespoons (25 g) sugar
¼ teaspoon kosher salt
1 teaspoon vanilla extract
8 ounces (225 g) mascarpone, chilled
1 cup (240 g) cold heavy cream

TIP——*If the mousse sits longer than 24 hours, re-whip for several minutes with a handheld mixer or in a stand mixer until stiff (whisking by hand won't apply enough force to bring it back to stiffness).*

1. **COOK THE YOLKS.** In a heatproof bowl set over a pot of steaming-hot (but not simmering) water, whisk the yolks, sugar, salt, and vanilla until the sugar has melted and the mixture feels warm to the touch, about 3 minutes. Remove from the heat and continue to whisk until the mixture is no longer hot to the touch and "ribbons" around the whisk and into the bowl, about 2 minutes.

2. **COMBINE THE YOLKS WITH THE MASCARPONE.** In a stand mixer fitted with the paddle (or in a large bowl using a handheld mixer), cream the mascarpone and the egg yolk/sugar mixture and paddle until smooth, about 2 minutes. Scrape this mixture into a small bowl and set aside.

3. **WHIP THE CREAM.** Pour the heavy cream into the mixer bowl (no need to clean it) and whip on medium-high speed until soft peaks are formed. Add the mascarpone mixture and continue to whip until the mixture is very stiff and thick, about 3 minutes. Stored in an airtight container in the refrigerator, the mousse will keep for up to 3 days (see tip).

VARIATION

To make the cream cheese mousse for the Black Sesame, Cream Cheese, and Pineapple Layer Cake (page 142), substitute 8 ounces (225 g) full-fat cream cheese for the mascarpone and proceed with the recipe as directed.

Green Tea Diplomat Cream

On its own, pastry cream is slightly too rich and runny for balanced layer cakes. Diplomat cream, which is lighter than pastry cream yet richer than whipped cream, is the perfect filling to spread into your layer cakes. It has the right kind of structure for building cakes and tastes silky on the palate. This version is infused with the transporting notes of green tea, a delicate counterpoint to cakes with bright citrus, berry, or stone fruit notes.

1. **BLOOM THE GELATIN.** If using sheet gelatin, fill a medium bowl with ice cubes, then cover them with water. Slip the sheet gelatin in and let sit until ready to use (it will fully soften after about 5 minutes). If using powdered gelatin, put the granules in a small dish containing 1 tablespoon of water and let sit for 5 minutes.

2. **MAKE THE PASTRY CREAM.** In a small saucepan, heat the milk and green tea over medium heat until hot and steaming. In a small bowl, whisk together the cornstarch, salt, and 1 tablespoon (12 g) of the sugar. Add a big spoonful of the hot milk to the cornstarch bowl and whisk to form a paste-like slurry. Transfer the slurry to the saucepan of milk and whisk well. Whisking constantly so the milk doesn't burn, watch until the mixture starts to noticeably thicken, then cook for no longer than 1 minute.

3. **ADD THE EGG.** Crack the egg into the bowl you just used for the cornstarch and add the remaining 1 tablespoon (12 g) sugar. Whisk to combine. While whisking the egg mixture constantly, stream half of the hot milk mixture into the bowl. Transfer the warmed egg mixture back to the saucepan and stir constantly to slightly thicken, about 2 minutes. Remove from the heat.

4. **ADD THE BUTTER AND GELATIN.** Whisk the cubed butter and vanilla into the custard. Wring out the excess water from the gelatin sheet and add the gelatin to the pan, or add the bloomed powdered gelatin mixture to the pan. Stir rapidly with a spatula to combine. Strain through a fine-mesh sieve into a clean, dry container. Let cool completely at room temperature, stirring occasionally so the cream sets up evenly; you should have about 1½ cups (275 g) pastry cream. The pastry cream can be made up to 3 days in advance and kept chilled (see tip).

→

MAKES 3½ CUPS (500 G), ENOUGH FOR ONE 8-INCH (20 CM) LAYER CAKE

20 MINUTES ACTIVE TIME
2 HOURS INACTIVE TIME

1 sheet (2.5 g) silver-strength gelatin or 1 teaspoon unflavored gelatin powder
1 cup (240 g) whole milk
1½ tablespoons (5 g) loose green tea leaves
2 tablespoons (20 g) cornstarch or tapioca starch
¼ teaspoon kosher salt
2 tablespoons (25 g) sugar
1 egg (50 g)
2 tablespoons (1 ounce/30 g) unsalted butter, cubed
1 teaspoon vanilla extract
1 cup (240 g) cold heavy cream

TIP —— *If making the diplomat cream right away, leave the pastry cream out at room temperature, so it's smooth and easy to fold into the whipped cream. (If you've made the pastry cream in advance, work the chilled pastry cream with a spatula first to loosen; it may be a bit lumpy from the gelatin but will smooth out.)*

Anything that can be infused into hot milk can be substituted for the green tea here; other teas like Earl Grey or chai are very elegant. Another great substitute is a powder that dissolves in the milk, like matcha green tea, instant coffee, cocoa powder, or ground turmeric. Or infuse with 2 tablespoons hardy, intense herbs, like rosemary, sage, lavender, or thyme (toast the leaves in the dry saucepan first, then add the milk to cover and gently warm).

5. LIGHTEN WITH WHIPPED CREAM. In a stand mixer fitted with the whisk (or in a large bowl using a handheld mixer), whip the heavy cream until very stiff, about 4 minutes. Add half of the pastry cream and use a spatula to gently combine. Fold in the remaining pastry cream. (You can make the diplomat cream up to 2 days in advance. Re-whip with a mixer on high speed for 3 to 4 minutes, until stiff again, before using.)

Toasted Honey and Chocolate Ganache

This ganache is incredibly rich, so apply it in smaller amounts, as a thin binder between cake layers and crunchy additions. I prefer to stabilize ganache with a bit of gelatin, which isn't discernible on the palate but helps with the overall structure and look of the finished layer cake. This ganache is very stiff when chilled but gradually loosens into a rich, glossy spread as it comes to room temperature.

If you have any ganache left over, it's also delicious in the Coffee-Hazelnut Linzers (page 39).

1. BLOOM THE GELATIN. If using sheet gelatin, fill a medium bowl with ice cubes, then cover them with water. Slip the gelatin sheet in and let sit until ready to use (it will fully soften after about 5 minutes). If using powdered gelatin, put the granules in a small dish containing 1 tablespoon of water and let sit for 5 minutes.

2. MAKE THE HONEY MIXTURE. In a small saucepan, bring the honey to a boil over medium-high heat. As the honey wildly foams, swirl the pan occasionally and cook until the honey has reduced by half and smells toasted, 3 to 4 minutes. Reduce the heat and stream in the heavy cream, milk, and salt. Whisk well to combine and continue to heat until the mixture is smooth. Remove the honey/milk mixture from the heat.

3. MAKE THE GANACHE. Wring out the excess water from the sheet gelatin and add the gelatin to the saucepan, or scrape in the bloomed powdered gelatin mixture. Stir rapidly with a spatula to combine. Dump in the chocolate and let sit for 1 minute. Transfer to a blender and puree on high speed until smooth (or whisk rapidly by hand). Pour through a strainer into a 1-quart (1 L) container. Chill until completely set before using, 1 to 2 hours. Store in an airtight container in the refrigerator for up to 2 weeks or in the freezer for up to 2 months.

MAKES 2 CUPS (510 G), ENOUGH FOR ONE 8-INCH (20 CM) LAYER CAKE

10 MINUTES ACTIVE TIME
2 HOURS INACTIVE TIME

1 sheet (2.5 g) silver-strength gelatin or 1 teaspoon unflavored gelatin powder
3 tablespoons (60 g) honey
¾ cup (180 g) heavy cream
½ cup (120 g) whole milk
¼ teaspoon kosher salt
5 ounces (150 g) dark chocolate (see tip), finely chopped or chips (about 1¼ cups)

TIP ——*Dark (bittersweet) chocolate usually clocks in at around the 70% cacao range, but sweeter chocolates can be used as well. Gianduja, a milk chocolate made with hazelnuts, is delicious with the burnt honey here, and even white chocolate works as long as it is paired with less-sweet layer cake elements.*

Yuzu and Olive Oil Curd

Creamy, fruit-based curds are a classic layer cake filling. Because of the high amount of sugar in the traditional recipe (which both preserves the curd and gives it its velvety mouthfeel), always choose a not-sweet fruit for your curd. Strong, abundantly tart citrus fruits like grapefruit and lemon are classic choices, and for more unexpected variations, try dusty, floral bergamot juice or passion fruit puree.

MAKES 2 CUPS (480 G), ENOUGH
FOR ONE 8-INCH (20 CM) LAYER
CAKE

20 MINUTES ACTIVE TIME

1 sheet (2.5 g) silver-strength gelatin
    or 1 teaspoon unflavored gelatin
    powder
½ cup (120 g) yuzu juice
    (see tip)
1 cup (200 g) sugar
2 teaspoons cornstarch or tapioca
    starch
½ teaspoon kosher salt
2 eggs (100 g)
2 large egg yolks (40 g)
¼ cup plus 1 tablespoon (75 g)
    extra-virgin olive oil

TIP —— *Substitute any high-acid citrus, like lemon, Meyer lemon, lime, and grapefruit for the yuzu juice. If you are using fresh whole citrus, for extra oomph, grate the zest into the sugar and juice before cooking, then strain it out at the end.*

1. **BLOOM THE GELATIN.** If using sheet gelatin, fill a medium bowl with ice cubes, then cover them with water. Slip the gelatin in and let soften until ready to use. If using powdered gelatin, put the granules in a small dish containing 1 tablespoon of water and let sit for 5 minutes.

2. **MELT THE SUGAR.** In a medium saucepan, combine the yuzu juice and ¾ cup (150 g) of the sugar. Gently bring up to the barest simmer, stirring to lift and dissolve the sugar. Don't let the mixture boil!

3. **ACTIVATE THE CORNSTARCH.** In a small bowl, whisk together 1 tablespoon (15 g) of the sugar, the cornstarch, and salt. Add a ladleful of the hot yuzu syrup and whisk to form a paste-like slurry. Pour the slurry into the saucepan and whisk well. Cook for 1 minute to thicken, no longer.

4. **MAKE THE CUSTARD.** In the bowl you just used for the cornstarch, combine the whole eggs, egg yolks, and the remaining 3 tablespoons (45 g) sugar. Whisk well to combine. While whisking the egg mixture constantly, stream in several ladlefuls of the hot yuzu syrup. Transfer the warmed egg mixture to the pan and stir constantly with a spatula over medium heat until the mixture has thickened enough to thickly coat the back of your spoon and the foam has melted away, 3 to 4 minutes, then remove from the heat. (Overcooking the curd can actually "break" the cornstarch and loosen the mixture.) Wring the excess water from the bloomed gelatin and whisk it in until it has fully melted into the custard, or scrape in the powdered gelatin mixture and stir to combine.

5. FINISH THE CURD. Whisking constantly, stream in the olive oil until well combined. Pass the curd through a fine-mesh sieve into a small bowl. Press a small piece of plastic wrap directly on the curd as it cools. Store in an airtight container in the refrigerator for up to 2 weeks or in the freezer for up to 2 months.

VARIATIONS

To make Passion Fruit and Olive Oil Curd for the Passion Fruit, Coconut, and Tequila Layer Cake (page 138) or the Passion Fruit Roll-Up Cake (page 97), replace the yuzu juice with ½ cup (120 g) passion fruit puree or ½ cup (120 g) 100% passion fruit juice. I love the consistency of Boiron fruit purees (see Resources, page 311).

Fennel and White Balsamic Jam

This bracing jam tastes just as nice with a pork chop as it does in a layer cake. Be sure to chop the fennel finely after it's cooked, so the filling isn't overly chunky in the cake.

1. PREP THE FENNEL. Slice the fennel on the thickest setting of a mandoline (or by hand) to about ⅛ inch (3 mm) thick.

2. COOK THE FENNEL. In a large skillet or Dutch oven, heat the olive oil over medium-low heat. Add the fennel and salt and gently sauté until softened but not browned, about 15 minutes. Add ¼ cup (60 g) of the vinegar and ¼ cup (50 g) of the sugar and reduce the heat to low. Press a round of parchment paper directly on the fennel, which will prevent the vinegar from evaporating too quickly. Let simmer until mostly reduced, about 20 minutes, stirring occasionally. Add the remaining ¼ cup (60 g) vinegar and ¼ cup (50 g) sugar and continue to cook for another 30 minutes. The fennel should be translucent and tender. Remove from the heat and let cool completely.

3. FINISH THE JAM. Spread the fennel mixture out on a large cutting board and chop finely. (Alternatively, you can process the jam in a food processor, but be careful to not take it too far so it becomes pasty.) Store in an airtight container in the refrigerator for up to 3 weeks.

MAKES 1½ CUPS (300 G), ENOUGH FOR ONE 8-INCH (20 CM) LAYER CAKE

15 MINUTES ACTIVE TIME
30 MINUTES INACTIVE TIME

2 bulbs fennel, stalks and fronds trimmed off (about 600 g)
1 tablespoon (15 g) olive oil
½ teaspoon kosher salt
½ cup (120 g) white balsamic vinegar
½ cup (100 g) sugar

Blueberry and Sumac Compote

A tart, vivid compote of blueberries, lemon juice, and sumac is ideal for spooning in between cake layers and creamy whips. The powdered agar-agar gives it a little extra set, but the secret ingredient is dried sumac, which adds brightness and sourness, crucial in Mediterranean and Middle Eastern dishes like hummus and grilled fish.

MAKES 1 HEAPING CUP (260 G),
ENOUGH FOR ONE 8-INCH (20 CM)
LAYER CAKE

10 MINUTES ACTIVE TIME

8 ounces (230 g) blueberries
  (about 1¼ cups), fresh or frozen
¼ cup (50 g) sugar
2 teaspoons dried sumac
1 tablespoon (15 g) fresh lemon juice
½ teaspoon agar-agar powder
Pinch of kosher salt

1. **COOK THE FRUIT.** In a deep pot, combine the berries, sugar, sumac, lemon juice, agar-agar, and salt and bring to a rolling boil over high heat. Boil for 7 to 8 minutes, stirring occasionally so the berries don't scorch. Remove from the heat and let cool slightly.

2. **PUREE THE COMPOTE.** Transfer the blueberry mixture to a food processor (or use an immersion blender) and puree slightly, so the compote has a little texture. Let cool completely. Store in an airtight container in the refrigerator for up to 2 weeks or in the freezer for up to 2 months.

Pineapple and Lime Marmalade

This marmalade is magic. It tastes so fresh and bright, an energetic foil for the richer, heavier elements in your layer cakes.

MAKES ABOUT 3 CUPS (700 G),
ENOUGH FOR ONE 10-INCH
(20 CM) LAYER CAKE

25 MINUTES ACTIVE TIME
1 DAY INACTIVE TIME

4 cups finely diced fresh pineapple
  (about 24 ounces/700 g)
1 lime, thinly sliced and finely
  chopped (about 70 g)
1 cup (200 g) sugar
½ teaspoon kosher salt
Citric acid if necessary

1. **MACERATE THE PINEAPPLE.** In a large bowl or container, combine the pineapple, lime, sugar, and salt. Refrigerate for at least 12 hours, and up to 2 days.

2. **COOK THE MARMALADE.** In a medium pot, bring the pineapple and sugar mixture to a strong simmer over medium heat. Cook, stirring occasionally, until the pineapple has turned translucent and the liquid has boiled off, 40 to 50 minutes. For the freshest taste, try not to let the fruit caramelize. Remove from the heat and let cool slightly, then pulse 4 to 5 times in a food processor (or chop by hand) until chunky, not smooth. Taste and add a pinch of citric acid if needed (the jam should taste sour and bright). Store in an airtight container in the refrigerator for up to 1 month.

More Than Cake

Sweet and Spicy Hazelnuts

My method for candying nuts is inspired by the delicious kettle-cooked nuts sold by street vendors in New York City: Sugar, water, and nuts are boiled together until the water evaporates and the sugar caramelizes evenly and deeply. These candied hazelnuts will not get sticky, will not melt, will not taste chewy. They are pure, deep, rich crunch—and perfect for pulverizing into a sandy rubble for a layer cake. Try this recipe with peanuts, pistachios, and almonds, too.

1. BOIL THE NUTS AND EVAPORATE THE WATER. In a medium saucepan, combine the hazelnuts, sugar, and water and bring to a boil. The mixture will look soupy and wet. Boil over medium-high heat until the water evaporates, 5 to 6 minutes.

2. CARAMELIZE THE SUGAR. Once the water has evaporated, the sugar and nut mixture will "seize" and begin to look sandy, chalky, and white. Immediately reduce the heat to low and continue to stir the nuts with a spatula or large spoon. They don't need to be stirred nonstop, but they will burn if left alone. After about 10 minutes, the sugar will begin to melt once again. Stir constantly so the sugar caramelizes evenly, breaking up clumps of nuts that stick together as you go.

3. SEASON THE NUTS. Keep stirring until the hazelnuts are golden, shiny, and fragrant. Add the ground chile and ground nori and stir. Line a sheet pan with parchment. Carefully transfer the nuts to the pan, spreading them out into a single layer. Let cool completely, then store tightly covered in the freezer.

4. PROCESS FOR THE CAKE FILLING. Grind the hazelnuts in a spice grinder or food processor until pebbly.

MAKES 1½ CUPS (190 G), ENOUGH FOR ONE 8-INCH (20 CM) LAYER CAKE

20 MINUTES ACTIVE TIME
20 MINUTES INACTIVE TIME

1 cup (140 g) hazelnuts
½ cup (100 g) sugar
2 tablespoons plus 1 teaspoon (35 g) water
½ teaspoon ground chile
1 tablespoon (1 g) finely ground nori powder, or one 3-by-8-inch/ 7.5 by 20 cm sheet nori, processed to a powder in the blender (see tip)

TIP —*Keep nori powder on hand for adding to tart doughs, cookies, icings, and even jams, for a subtle, sea-flavored infusion.*

Coconut Streusel

This tropical streusel brings so much flavor and texture to layer cakes. It's also vegan and gluten-free and feels moderately virtuous, so I always keep a jar in my fridge for topping scoops of sorbet and yogurt parfaits. The white rice flour is crucial to the slightly grainy, soft texture, so don't substitute all purpose flour if you can help it.

MAKES 1 CUP (157 G), ENOUGH
FOR TWO 8-INCH (20 CM)
LAYER CAKES

10 MINUTES ACTIVE TIME

½ cup (75 g) white rice flour
¼ cup (50 g) sugar
½ teaspoon kosher salt
2 tablespoons (30 g) coconut oil

1. PREHEAT THE OVEN AND PREP THE PAN. Preheat the oven to 350°F (175°C). Line a half-sheet pan with parchment paper.

2. MIX THE INGREDIENTS. In a small bowl, mix the white rice flour, sugar, and salt with your fingertips. Drizzle in half of the coconut oil and lightly combine with the tips of your fingers. Try not to compress the crumbs too tightly. Continue to add the remaining coconut oil, mixing until the mixture begins to clump together but is not soggy, like wet beach sand. Spread the crumbs out on the lined half-sheet pan.

3. BAKE THE STREUSEL. Bake until deeply fragrant and slightly tan around the edges, 10 to 11 minutes. Remove from the oven and chop the crumbs with a bench scraper. Let the streusel cool completely. Store in an airtight container in the refrigerator for up to 2 weeks or in the freezer for up to 2 months.

More Than Cake

Candied Grapefruit Peel

If you find yourself with a surplus of spent rinds after juicing oranges, lemons, grapefruits, or limes, consider saving them for candying. It's one of my favorite ways of savoring their naturally intense flavor. The method may seem painstaking, but the process of blanching and then candying is actually quite intuitive and can be applied to so many other firm-fleshed ingredients, too (see tip #1). Candied peel can be added to a number of other recipes (see tip #2), so I like to make a big batch.

1. **PREPARE THE PEELS.** Use a small, sharp knife to slice the peel away from the fruit, keeping the pith (the spongy white part) attached. Slice the peel into strips ½ inch (1.25 cm) wide. Transfer to a medium pot and add the water to cover so they float freely.

2. **BLANCH THE PEELS.** Simmer the mixture over medium-low heat until tender, about 15 minutes. (The peel is blanched when it still has some bite but a knife slides in easily.) Do not overcook the peels at this stage, as they will continue to boil in the syrup.

3. **CANDY THE PEELS IN SUGAR.** Add 2 cups (400 g) of the sugar to the pot and stir. Continue to cook over low heat until the syrup looks thick and the peel is translucent, 1 hour to 1½ hours. Stir occasionally. Remove from the heat and let the peels cool completely in the syrup.

4. **DEHYDRATE THE PEELS.** In a small bowl, combine the remaining 1 cup (200 g) sugar with the citric acid and kosher salt. Taste the mixture; it should make your mouth pucker, in a good way. In a sieve set over a bowl, drain the peels and gently pat dry with a towel. Roll each piece of peel in the citric acid/sugar mixture and transfer to a baking sheet or cooling rack. Let the peels air-dry at room temperature, uncovered, until they feel firm, dry, and chewy; flip the peels after 8 hours so the undersides can dry out, too. Store in an airtight container at room temperature for up to 1 month.

5. **TO USE THE PEEL IN LAYER CAKES.** Chop the peel to scatter on top of a mousse or curd, or slice into spears for exterior decor.

MAKES 3 CUPS (480 G), ENOUGH FOR ONE 8-INCH (20 CM) LAYER CAKE

25 MINUTES ACTIVE TIME
2 DAYS INACTIVE TIME

2 grapefruits, scrubbed clean
2 cups (480 g) water
3 cups (600 g) sugar
1 teaspoon citric acid, or more to taste (see tip #3)
½ teaspoon kosher salt

TIP 1 —*Try it with sliced ginger, pineapple (a personal favorite), quince, and even pumpkin.*

TIP 2 —*Candied peel is so much more than a garnish. Fold it into the Millet, Parsnip, and Chocolate Chunk Muffins (page 282); add it to the Malted Cocoa Fudge (page 59); chop it into the Fennel, Chocolate, and Hazelnut Spears (page 27).*

TIP 3 —*Though the peel (and its inner pith) is naturally quite bitter, it isn't very acidic. That's where citric acid—a weak acid found naturally in all citrus fruits—comes in. (Just thinking about it makes my mouth pucker!) You can skip the final sugar rolling (in step 4) and use the candied peel straight from the syrup, too.*

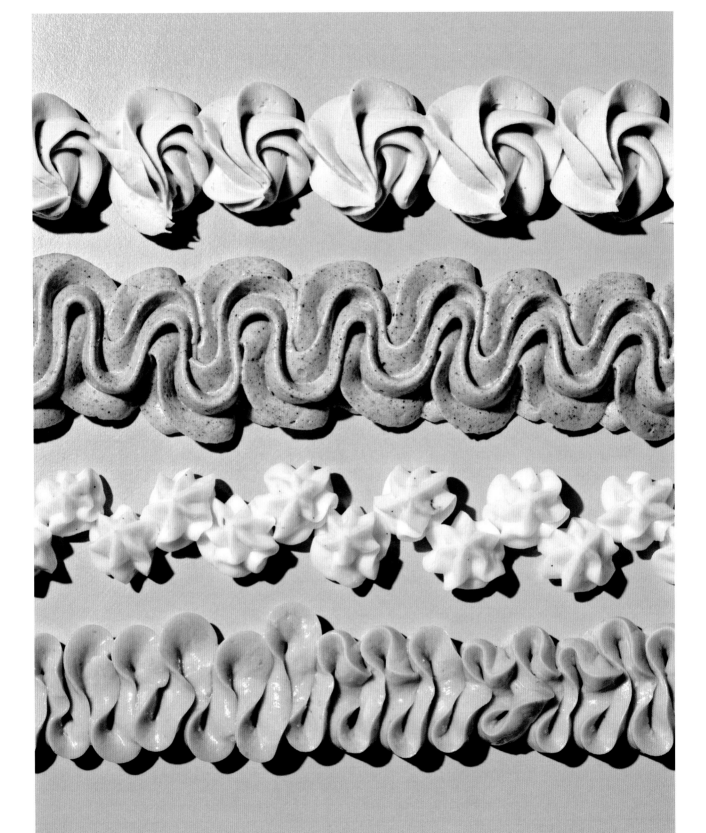

Black Sesame and Cream Cheese Frosting

Two of the most important tenets of baking successfully—temperature and time—are also crucial when it comes to making fluffy frostings for layer cakes. Butter and cream cheese need to be at room temperature (I leave butter out overnight, but 3 to 4 hours in a moderate climate is sufficient) before they can be whipped into oblivion, which takes time—your stand mixer is best here, unless you want to build up wrist muscles with a handheld mixer.

IN A STAND MIXER fitted with the paddle, beat the butter on medium speed until creamy and aerated, about 3 minutes. Add the cream cheese and beat to combine, about 2 minutes. Scrape the bowl well with a spatula after each ingredient addition. Add 1 cup (120 g) of the powdered sugar and beat on medium speed until combined, about 2 minutes. Add the rest of the powdered sugar and continue to beat until fluffy, 8 to 10 more minutes. Add the black sesame paste, vanilla, and salt and paddle to combine. Taste and add more salt if necessary. Refrigerate until ready to use; re-paddle the frosting to aerate before using.

MAKES 4 CUPS (800 G), ENOUGH FOR ONE 10-INCH (20 CM) SHEET CAKE

15 MINUTES ACTIVE TIME

10 tablespoons (5 ounces/145 g) unsalted butter, at room temperature
10½ ounces (300 g) cream cheese, at room temperature
2⅓ cups (300 g) powdered sugar
¼ cup (60 g) black sesame paste
1 teaspoon vanilla extract
½ teaspoon kosher salt, or to taste

VARIATION

If you'd prefer to make a more classic cream cheese frosting, omit the black sesame and replace it with something glossy and tangy, like sour cream or yogurt.

Vanilla Bean Swiss Buttercream

My go-to layer cake is not too sweet, sumptuous but not greasy, and easy to customize with extracts and spices. The meringue base of the buttercream comes together in a double boiler before being whipped into a thick cloud. Once it is cool, nearly a pound (!) of butter is introduced into the meringue, which gives the frosting outlandish richness.

MAKES 3 CUPS (615 G), ENOUGH FOR TWO 8-INCH (20 CM) LAYER CAKES

15 MINUTES ACTIVE TIME

4 large egg whites (120 g)
1 cup (200 g) granulated sugar
⅓ cup plus 1 tablespoon (48 g) powdered sugar
1 vanilla bean
10½ ounces (300 g) unsalted butter, cubed, at room temperature
1 teaspoon kosher salt

VARIATION

To make Silky Pistachio Buttercream for the Olive Oil, Mascarpone, and Fennel Layer Cake (page 145), add ½ cup (140 g) pistachio paste after adding the cubed butter. Many Italian specialty markets (see Resources, page 311) carry pistachio paste; I love Marco Colzani products, imported by the online retailer Gustiamo.

1. **COOK THE EGG WHITES.** In a heatproof medium bowl, combine the egg whites and granulated sugar and whisk well. Set the bowl over a pot of steaming-hot (but not simmering) water, and whisk until the mixture is hot and the temperature is 115°F (45°C), 4 to 5 minutes.

2. **BEAT THE MERINGUE.** Transfer the mixture to the bowl of a stand mixer fitted with the whisk (or to a large bowl if using a handheld mixer) and whip on high speed until slightly cooled, about 2 minutes. Turn the mixer off and add the powdered sugar. Whip on medium-high speed; the meringue should look glossy and stiff.

3. **HARVEST THE VANILLA SEEDS.** Use a small sharp knife to halve the vanilla bean lengthwise, pry open the halves, and use the knife to scrape the vanilla seeds out into the meringue. Whip to combine, about 1 minute.

4. **ADD THE BUTTER.** With the mixer running on medium-high speed, add the cubed butter, piece by piece, over 3 to 4 minutes. The buttercream may look like it will break, but keep beating; it will come back together. Add the salt and beat the buttercream for another 5 minutes. Use immediately or refrigerate in an airtight container for up to 2 weeks.

5. **TO ICE A CAKE.** When ready to ice a layer cake, let the buttercream come to room temperature for at least 2 hours (or overnight) and then re-whip for 5 minutes so it is fluffy and light.

More Than Cake

Italian Espresso Buttercream

This is an elegant buttercream with a unique satin finish, due to the egg yolks, which give it a luxurious richness. Unlike a Swiss buttercream, in which the egg whites are cooked in a double boiler, Italian buttercream cooks the eggs with a hot sugar syrup, so a digital thermometer is essential.

1. MAKE THE SUGAR SYRUP. In a small pot, combine the sugar, water, and vanilla. Bring to a boil over high heat and cook until the syrup registers 255°F (125°C), 6 to 7 minutes.

2. WHIP THE EGGS AND HOT SYRUP. In a stand mixer fitted with the whisk (or in a large bowl using a handheld mixer), whip the whole egg and egg yolk together on medium-high speed. With the mixer running, very slowly stream in the hot syrup. Add the salt. Continue to whip on high speed until the bowl no longer feels superhot to the touch, about 5 minutes.

3. ADD THE ESPRESSO AND BUTTER. Stream in the espresso and continue to whip for another 2 minutes. Add the butter one piece at a time, beating until the buttercream appears emulsified, glossy, and fluffy. Taste and add more salt, if desired. Use immediately or refrigerate in an airtight container for up to 2 weeks.

4. TO ICE A CAKE. When ready to ice a layer cake, let the buttercream come to room temperature for at least 2 hours (or overnight) and then re-whip for 5 minutes, until buoyant and silky.

MAKES 2½ CUPS (350 G), ENOUGH FOR AN 8-INCH (20 CM) LAYER CAKE

20 MINUTES ACTIVE TIME

1 cup (200 g) sugar
3 tablespoons (45 g) water
1 teaspoon vanilla extract
1 egg (50 g)
1 large egg yolk (20 g)
½ teaspoon kosher salt, or more to taste
2 tablespoons (30 g) brewed strong espresso, at room temperature
14 tablespoons (7 ounces/208 g) unsalted butter, cubed, at room temperature

HOW TO BUILD A LAYER CAKE

Using thin, large sheets of cake, punched to specific circular shapes, allows you to have any size cake you desire. A cake pan, lined in plastic wrap, provides a safe environment to build a soaring masterpiece layered with sticky and creamy fillings, as well as a convenient vessel to store in the fridge for chilling. The process is meditative; no teetering cakes here.

PASSION FRUIT, COCONUT, AND TEQUILA LAYER CAKE

This cake is always a hit, as popular with couples who want a boozy wedding finale as with friends looking for a really good time. I like to call this cake the Sammy Hagar, in honor of his iconic tequila Cabo Wabo.

MAKES ONE 8-INCH (20 CM) LAYER
CAKE
SERVES 8 TO 10

45 MINUTES ACTIVE TIME
1 DAY INACTIVE TIME

1 cup (240 g) cold heavy cream
Vanilla Sponge Cake (page 112)
¾ cup (180 g) Tequila and Coconut
   Soak (page 120)
2 cups (480 g) Passion Fruit and
   Olive Oil Curd (see page 127),
   at room temperature
½ cup (60 g) Coconut Streusel
   (page 130)
2½ cups (535 g) Vanilla Bean Swiss
   Buttercream (page 134), at room
   temperature
A large handful flowers or leaves,
   like tulips, roses, or pansies

TIP ——*I prefer to age layer cakes at least 2 or even 3 days, so all the harmonious flavors can mingle and marry.*

1. **PREP THE CAKE MOLD.** Line a deep 8-inch (20 cm) round cake pan (at least 3 inches/7.5 cm deep), a springform pan, or a saucepan with straight sides with plastic wrap, being sure that the wrap has plenty of overhang.

2. **CUT OUT THE CAKE LAYERS.** Using a small serrated knife and the bottom of the cake mold as a guide, trace an 8-inch (20 cm) circle on the upper left-hand corner of the sheet. Trace another 8-inch (20 cm) circle on the lower right-hand corner of the sponge sheet. Carefully cut out the rounds with the knife and set aside. Use the bottom of the cake mold to trace a half-moon shape on the upper right-hand corner of the sheet, and then another one on the lower left-hand corner of the sheet, and cut these out. Finally, cut out a rectangle 8 inches (20 cm) long and 1 inch (2.5 cm) wide from the center of the sheet. You'll piece these 3 scraps together to form a circle for the center layer of the cake. (See illustration on page 141.)

3. **WHIP THE CREAM.** In a stand mixer fitted with the whisk (or in a large bowl using a handheld mixer), whip the heavy cream until stiff, about 3 minutes. Keep chilled until ready to build the cake.

4. **BUILD THE CAKE.** Place one round cake layer in the bottom of the plastic wrap–lined pan. Dab ¼ cup (60 g) of the tequila and coconut soak onto the cake. Add ⅔ cup (160 g) of the passion fruit curd and spread it evenly. (If the curd feels overly stiff in the container, work it a bit with a small offset spatula or spoon to make it easier to spread.) Sprinkle ¼ cup (30 g) of the coconut streusel on top. Spoon half of the whipped cream on top and gently smooth and press it out to the edges. (To avoid lifting up any of the coconut crumbs, dab the cream in spoonfuls all over the surface

More Than Cake

and gently press down to smooth.) Arrange the two half-moons and the rectangular piece on top to form a round, then add ¼ cup (60 g) soak. Layer ⅔ cup (160 g) curd, the remaining ¼ cup (30 g) coconut streusel, and the other half of the whipped cream on top. Finally, place the second round on top to seal the cake shut, and brush the remaining ¼ cup (60 g) soak on top. (You will have about ⅔ cup/160 g passion fruit curd left over, which you need for the buttercream.) Securely wrap the entire cake form in plastic wrap and transfer to the refrigerator to rest for at least 8 hours (or longer; see tip) or to the freezer for at least 5 hours, or up to 3 days, so the flavors can meld.

5. MIX THE PASSION FRUIT BUTTERCREAM. After the cake has rested, it will be stable enough to be iced. In a stand mixer fitted with the whisk, whip the buttercream until smooth, about 2 minutes. Add the remaining passion fruit curd and whip until smooth, glossy, and thick, another 3 minutes.

6. FROST THE CAKE. Invert the chilled cake onto a platter or a 10-inch (25 cm) cardboard cake round. (If you have a cake turntable, place the cake, resting on a cardboard round, on the center of the turntable.) Remove the cake form, then peel off the plastic wrap. Use an offset spatula to dollop half of the whipped buttercream all over the surface of the cake. Spread the buttercream all the way to the edges of the cake. Dab the remaining buttercream along the sides of the cake, smoothing each dab to touch the one before, until none of the cake is visible. Once the sides of the cake are roughly covered in buttercream, run the offset spatula along the surface again to smooth. Then run the offset spatula along the sides of the cake, where the excess buttercream will have gathered, to wipe away excess frosting.

7. DECORATE THE CAKE. Scatter the flower petals or leaves over the surface of the cake, letting them fall in a natural way. The cake can sit out in a cool environment for 5 to 6 hours, but on a hot day, beware of greasy-looking icing. And the cake tastes best if the slices are still slightly chilled. If the cake was fully frozen before icing, allow at least 4 hours to thaw before serving.

Trace an 8-inch (20 cm) circle on the upper left-hand corner (1) and lower right-hand corner (5) of the sponge sheet. Cut out the rounds and set aside. Trace a half-moon shape on the upper right-hand corner (2) and lower left-hand corner (4) of the sheet, and cut those out. Finally, cut out a rectangle 8 inches (20 cm) long and 1 inch (2.5 cm) wide from the center of the sheet (3).

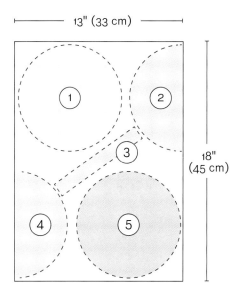

YIELD: Three 8-inch (20 cm) circular cakes

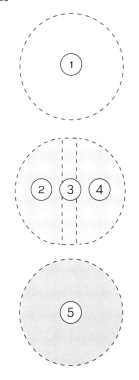

BLACK SESAME, CREAM CHEESE, AND PINEAPPLE LAYER CAKE

My preferred sheet cakes are built for travel: from long, bumpy car rides to multiple transfers on the subway, I always feel more relaxed when I'm carrying a precious layer cake to its final destination if it is shaped like a low, long rectangle. Plus, you get more surface area for decorating—a sheet cake is the perfect canvas to practice your piping skills.

MAKES ONE 10-INCH (25 CM)
LAYER CAKE
SERVES 10 TO 12

45 MINUTES ACTIVE TIME
1 DAY INACTIVE TIME

Black Sesame Chiffon Cake
(page 115)
¼ cup plus 2 tablespoons (90 g)
Maple and Vanilla Milk Soak
(page 121)
1⅓ cups (350 g) Pineapple and
Lime Marmalade (page 128)
3 cups (410 g) Cream Cheese
Mousse (see page 122),
re-whipped
3 cups (600 g) Black Sesame
and Cream Cheese Frosting
(page 133)
A handful of petite decorations,
such as the flowers from a sprig of
fresh lilac

1. PREP THE CAKE MOLD. Line a deep 9-by-13-inch (23 by 33 cm) baking dish with plastic wrap, being sure that the wrap has plenty of overhang.

2. CUT THE CAKE. Trim the edges of the chiffon cake so that the sheet measures 12 by 16 inches (30 by 40 cm). Cut the cake into 3 equal rectangles: To do so, orient the cake with a short side facing you. Cut the cake widthwise 6 inches (15 cm) from the top, then trim 2 inches (5 cm) off the long side to yield a rectangle 6 inches (15 cm) wide and 10 inches (25 cm) long. Cut the remaining rectangle in half lengthwise to yield two rectangles that are 6 inches (15 cm) wide and 10 inches (25 cm) long. (See illustration on page 144.)

3. BUILD THE CAKE. Place one rectangle of cake on the bottom of the plastic wrap–lined baking dish. Dab on 2 tablespoons of the maple milk soak. Add ⅔ cup (155 g) pineapple and lime marmalade and spread it evenly. Spoon 1½ cups (205 g) of the cream cheese mousse on top and gently smooth and press it out to the edges. Place a second cake rectangle on top and add 2 tablespoons soak, then follow with the remaining ⅔ cup marmalade and then the remaining 1½ cups cream cheese mousse. Add the final cake layer and finish with the remaining 2 tablespoons soak. Securely wrap the entire cake in plastic wrap and transfer to the refrigerator to rest for at least 8 hours (or overnight) or to the freezer for at least 5 hours, or up to 3 days, so the flavors can meld.

4. RE-WHIP THE FROSTING. After the cake has rested, it will be stable enough to be iced. In a stand mixer fitted

More Than Cake

Orient the cake with the short side facing you. Cut the cake widthwise 6 inches (15 cm) from the top, then trim 2 inches off the long side to yield a rectangle 6 inches (15 cm) wide and 10 inches (25 cm) long (1). Cut the remaining rectangle in half lengthwise to yield two rectangles that are 6 inches (15 cm) wide and 10 inches (25 cm) long (2 and 3).

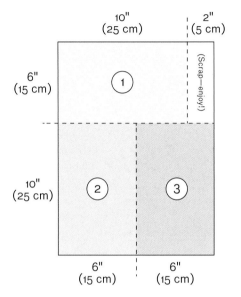

with the paddle (or in a large bowl using a handheld mixer), whip the black sesame and cream cheese frosting for about 3 minutes. Transfer ⅔ cup (130 g) of the frosting to a piping bag fitted with a large star tip.

5. FROST THE CAKE. Invert the chilled cake onto a platter, board, or cake stand and remove the plastic wrapping. Use a serrated knife to trim the uneven edges of the cake. Frost the sides of the cake with the remaining 2⅓ cups icing, then pipe 3-inch (7.5 cm) squiggles across the cake.

6. DECORATE THE CAKE. Arrange the cake decorations over the surface and all sides of the cake. If the cake was fully frozen before icing, allow at least 4 hours to thaw and temper before serving. To portion, use a serrated knife to cut the cake into squares.

OLIVE OIL, MASCARPONE, AND FENNEL LAYER CAKE

Forget roses and peonies—I prefer the lush, romantic folds and flecks of Little Gem lettuces, Castelfranco chicories, and Treviso radicchio for decorating my cakes.

1. **PREP THE CAKE MOLD.** Line a deep 8-inch (20 cm) round cake pan (at least 3 inches/7.5 cm deep), a springform pan, or a saucepan with straight sides with plastic wrap, being sure that the wrap has plenty of overhang.

2. **CUT OUT THE CAKE LAYERS.** Using a small serrated knife and the bottom of the cake mold as a guide, trace an 8-inch (20 cm) circle on the upper left-hand corner of the cake sheet. Trace another 8-inch (20 cm) circle on the lower right-hand corner of the sheet. Carefully cut out the rounds with the knife and set aside. Use the bottom of the cake mold to trace a half-moon shape on the upper right-hand corner of the sheet, and then the lower left-hand corner, and cut these out. Finally, cut out a rectangle 8 inches (20 cm) long and 1 inch (2.5 cm) wide from the center of the sheet. You'll piece these 3 scraps together to form a circle for the center layer of the cake. (See illustration on page 141).

3. **BUILD THE CAKE.** Place one cake round in the bottom of the plastic wrap–lined pan. Brush the cake with 1 tablespoon (15 g) of the olive oil. Add ¾ cup (145 g) of the fennel jam. Spoon 1½ cups (210 g) of the mascarpone mousse on top and gently press it out to the edges. Arrange the two half-moons and the rectangular pieces on top to form a second layer and brush with 1 tablespoon (15 g) olive oil. Add the remaining ¾ cup fennel jam, then the remaining 1½ cups mascarpone mousse. Add the final cake round and soak with the last tablespoon of olive oil. Securely wrap the cake in plastic wrap and transfer to the refrigerator for at least 8 hours (or overnight) or to the freezer for at least 5 hours, or up to 3 days.

4. **RE-WHIP THE BUTTERCREAM.** After the cake has rested, it will be stable enough to be iced. In a stand mixer fitted with the whisk (or in a large bowl using a handheld mixer), whip the pistachio buttercream until silky, 3 to 4 minutes.

5. **FROST THE CAKE.** Invert the chilled cake onto a platter or 10-inch (25 cm) cardboard cake round. (If you have a cake turntable, place the cake, resting on a cardboard round, on the center of the turntable.) Remove the cake form, then peel off the

→

MAKES ONE 8-INCH (20 CM) LAYER CAKE
SERVES 10

45 MINUTES ACTIVE TIME
1 DAY INACTIVE TIME

Olive Oil Cake (page 117)
3 cups (420 g) Mascarpone Mousse (page 127), re-whipped
3 tablespoons (45 g) olive oil
1½ cups Fennel and White Balsamic Jam (page 127)
3 cups (640 g) Silky Pistachio Buttercream (page 134), at room temperature (see tip)
A big handful of assorted chicories, lettuces, and other greens

TIP —— *Because of its high butter content, buttercream can crack if temperatures fluctuate. If transporting a cake from your kitchen to another venue, always travel with a jar of extra buttercream for spackling and filling in the little cracks. Don't worry about the stability of your cake—the gelatin in the creamy fillings ensures that they won't get drippy or soft, and the thin layers of cake mean that they won't slide around at all.*

plastic wrap. Use an offset spatula to dollop half of the whipped buttercream all over the surface of the cake. Spread the buttercream all the way to the edges of the cake. Dab the remaining buttercream along the sides of the cake, smoothing each dab to touch the one before, until none of the cake insides are visible. Once the sides of the cake are roughly covered in buttercream, run the offset spatula along the surface again to smooth. Then run the offset spatula along the sides of the cake, where the excess buttercream will have gathered, to wipe away excess frosting.

6. DECORATE THE CAKE. Arrange the leaves all over the surface of the cake, creating undulating, natural patterns. The cake can sit out in a cool environment for 5 to 6 hours, but on a hot day, beware of greasy-looking icing. And the cake tastes best if the slices are still slightly chilled. If the cake was fully frozen before icing, allow at least 4 hours to thaw and temper before serving.

ALMOND, GREEN TEA, AND BLUEBERRY BOMBE

Bombe-shaped layer cakes provide an adorable spherical surface for draping flowers, gobbing on buttercream swirls, or festooning with candles. Plus, their sturdy architectural design makes them the easiest to transport, by far—this is one cake that will never fall over.

MAKES ONE 8-INCH (20 CM)
BOMBE
SERVES 10

45 MINUTES ACTIVE TIME
1 DAY INACTIVE TIME

2½ cups (400 g) Green Tea
   Diplomat Cream (page 123)
Whole Wheat and Almond Chiffon
   Cake (page 113)
¼ cup plus 1 tablespoon (75 g)
   Prosecco and Strawberry Soak
   (page 120)
¼ cup (80 g) Blueberry and Sumac
   Compote (page 128)
2 cups (430 g) Vanilla Bean Swiss
   Buttercream (page 134), at room
   temperature
3 to 4 edible flowers, like tulips,
   dahlias, or zinnias, with stem
   attached

1. **PREP THE CAKE MOLD.** Line a bowl 8 inches (20 cm) wide and about 3 inches (7.5 cm) deep with plastic wrap, being sure that the wrap has plenty of overhang.

2. **RE-WHIP THE CREAM.** In a stand mixer fitted with the whisk (or in a large bowl using a handheld mixer), whip the green tea diplomat cream until stiff, about 3 minutes. Keep chilled until ready to build the bombe.

3. **BUILD THE BOMBE.** Use a small knife to cut out 4 rounds from the sheet cake layers: one 3-inch (7.5 cm), one 5-inch (12.5 cm), one 6-inch (15 cm), and one 7-inch (18 cm). Place the smallest round of the cake in the bottom of the plastic wrap–lined pan. Dab 1 tablespoon of the prosecco soak onto the cake layer. Add 1 tablespoon (20 g) of the blueberry compote and spread it out. Spoon ½ cup (80 g) of the diplomat cream on top and gently smooth and press it out to the edges. Place the second-smallest cake round on top and brush with 1 tablespoon soak. Add 1 tablespoon blueberry compote and 1 cup (160 g) diplomat cream. Add the third-smallest cake round and brush on 1 tablespoon soak. Follow with the remaining 2 tablespoons compote, then the remaining 1 cup (160 g) diplomat cream. Top with the 7-inch (18 cm) cake round and brush on the remaining 2 tablespoons soak. Securely wrap the bowl in plastic wrap and transfer to the refrigerator to rest for at least 8 hours (or overnight) or in the freezer for at least 5 hours, or up to 3 days, so the flavors can meld and the cake can settle and firm up.

4. **RE-WHIP THE BUTTERCREAM.** After the cake has rested, it will be stable enough to be iced. In a stand mixer fitted with the whisk (or in a large bowl using a handheld mixer), whip the buttercream for 3 to 4 minutes. Transfer ¼ cup (55 g) of

the buttercream to a small pastry bag fitted with a small plain pastry tip (or skip the piping tip and snip a ¼-inch/0.5 cm opening in the tip of the bag). Set the piping bag aside.

5. FROST THE BOMBE. Invert the chilled bombe onto a platter or cake stand. (If you have a cake turntable, invert the cake onto a cardboard cake round and then place it in the center of the turntable.) Remove the bowl, then peel off the plastic wrap and discard. Use an offset spatula to dollop the remaining 1¾ cups (175 g) whipped buttercream all over the surface of the bombe, then smooth it evenly over the entire exterior. Using the reserved piping bag of buttercream, pipe small pearls of buttercream all over the surface.

6. DECORATE THE CAKE. Arrange 3 or 4 full flowers, with stems still attached, all over the surface of the cake. The cake can sit out in a cool environment for 5 to 6 hours, but on a hot day, beware of greasy-looking icing. And the cake tastes best if the slices are still slightly chilled. If the cake was fully frozen before icing, allow at least 4 hours to thaw and temper before serving. Slice the cake with a serrated knife for the cleanest look.

More Than Cake

ESPRESSO, CHOCOLATE, AND HAZELNUT CAKE

Café Sabarsky, nestled into one of my favorite New York City museums, the Neue Galerie, is inspired by the great Viennese cafés of the early twentieth century. Best of all are the elegant rows of desserts that line the dining room, filled with all manner of traditional Austro-German tortes, strudel, and more. Inspired by those rich, sticky, nutty sweets, I modeled this tempting gluten-free cake after their most popular dessert, a hazelnut and chocolate ganache torte named after the famed artist Gustav Klimt.

1. **PREP THE CAKE MOLD.** Line a deep 8-inch (20 cm) cake pan (at least 2 inches/5 cm deep), a springform pan, or a saucepan with straight sides with plastic wrap, being sure that the wrap has plenty of overhang.

2. **CUT OUT THE CAKE LAYERS.** Using a small serrated knife and the bottom of the cake mold as a guide, trace an 8-inch (20 cm) circle on the upper left-hand corner of the cake. Trace another 8-inch (20 cm) circle on the lower right-hand corner of the cake. Carefully cut out the rounds with the knife and set aside. Use the bottom of the cake mold to trace a half-moon shape on the upper right-hand corner of the cake, and then the lower left-hand corner of the cake, and remove them. Finally, cut out a rectangle 8 inches (20 cm) long and 1 inch (2.5 cm) wide from the center of the cake. You'll piece these 3 scraps together to form a circle for the center layer of the cake. (See illustration on page 141.)

3. **BUILD THE CAKE.** Place one round of the cake in the bottom of the plastic wrap–lined pan (see tip). Add 1 cup (255 g) of chocolate ganache and spread it evenly. Sprinkle ½ cup (65 g) of the finely ground candied hazelnuts on top. Dust 1 teaspoon of the cocoa powder all over with a small tea strainer. Arrange the two half-moons and the rectangular piece on top to form the second layer, then add the remaining 1 cup (255 g) ganache, the remaining ½ cup (65 g) candied hazelnuts, and the remaining 1 teaspoon cocoa powder. Place the final round of cake on top. Securely wrap the entire cake form in plastic wrap and transfer to the refrigerator to

MAKES ONE 8-INCH (20 CM) LAYER CAKE
SERVES 10 TO 12

45 MINUTES ACTIVE TIME
1 DAY INACTIVE TIME

Hazelnut Dacquoise (page 116)
2 cups (510 g) Toasted Honey and Chocolate Ganache (page 125), chilled
1 cup (160 g) finely ground Sweet and Spicy Hazelnuts (page 129)
2 teaspoons unsweetened cocoa powder
2½ cups (350 g) Italian Espresso Buttercream (page 135), at room temperature
A handful dried flowers and leaves (like dried thistles, twigs, seed pods, and grasses)

rest for at least 8 hours (or overnight) or to the freezer for at least 5 hours, or up to 3 days, so the flavors can meld.

4. RE-WHIP THE BUTTERCREAM. In a stand mixer fitted with the whisk (or in a large bowl using a handheld mixer), whip the buttercream until glossy and super fluffy, 3 to 4 minutes.

5. FROST THE CAKE. Invert the chilled cake onto a platter or 10-inch (25 cm) cardboard cake round. (If you have a cake turntable, place the cake, resting on a cardboard round, in the center of the turntable.) Remove the cake form, then peel off the plastic wrap and discard. Use an offset spatula to dollop half of the whipped buttercream all over the surface of the cake. Spread the buttercream all the way to the edges of the cake. Dab the remaining buttercream along the sides of the cake, smoothing each added dab to touch the one before, so that none of the cake insides are visible. Once the sides of the cake are roughly covered in buttercream, run the offset spatula along the surface again to smooth.

6. DECORATE THE CAKE. Arrange the dried flowers and leaves on the surface of the cake. This cake tastes best if the slices are still slightly chilled. If the cake was fully frozen before icing, allow at least 4 hours to thaw and temper before serving. Slice the cake with a large, dry hot knife for the cleanest look.

TIP —— *Sticky dacquoise can easily tear in the process of being transferred from the sheet pan to the cake form. But because the cake will rest, chilled, for a long period of time, even torn pieces of cake will come back together seamlessly. Think of it as putting together a puzzle in the cake mold and fit them together as best you can. The creamy ganache will take care of the rest.*

NOTES ON CAKE DECORATING

Nothing makes a first impression quite like a decorated layer cake, a showstopping dessert that combines baking technique with artistic flair. The feasting begins with your eyes, well before the first slice is cut, so I believe that cakes should look as delicious and inviting as they taste. There are as many ways to decorate a layer cake as there are to bake one, but my general approach is one of effortlessness, like a vase of flowers tipping over onto your buttercream.

For years I stayed away from layer cakes, because I felt intimidated by both their complex construction and the intricate decor that characterizes multitiered wedding cakes. The most popular celebration cakes, I felt, were either a model of irreproachable formality

and exacting engineering—think icy, razor-sharp sugar roses or meticulous piped edges—or intentionally childlike, rolled in primary-color sprinkles or wrapped in thick, smooth sheets of fondant.

I wanted to decorate cakes that reminded me more of natural things, like the frilly rosettes of lettuces and swaying lilac branches in my garden. I wanted to make cakes that felt romantic, lush, and joyful but also deconstructed and abstract. I didn't

want to drench my cakes in blooming roses; I wanted to pull those roses apart and scatter the petals all over the cake, creating a dappled, bobbing surface. I worked to develop my own aesthetic, instinctively tapping into what I knew about composition, color, movement, and texture from years spent drawing and painting.

I think layer cakes—a niche of pastry that is perhaps most held back by conventional norms—are a spectacular opportunity to explore new ways of seeing and making. The cakes on these pages have a natural movement and fullness to them and can be decorated with whatever you have available, from the bundle of parsley in your refrigerator to a spindly branch found on a long walk. The final look shouldn't feel too studied or fussy; it should feel loose and fun and easy. Cake decor has another sneaky purpose, too, and that is as camouflage for a layer cake's small imperfections. Petals, fruits, and leaves can cover up cracks in buttercream or mask a slightly slanted surface.

Look for inspiration outside of food. Your favorite sculptor, florist, farmers' market stand, or pebble-lined beach can give you hints on how you can honor nature on your cake. It is easy to go overboard on decor when there are so many dramatic options before you, but the most elegant and arresting cakes actually make the most of very little. A monochromatic palette or a single type of flower applied with a sparing hand can make a big difference in the final look. I also love cakes that remind me of a place and time—a chocolate layer cake coated in glittering jingle shells, from a summer spent in Long Island, or a wedding cake for an old childhood friend, decorated with eucalyptus branches from my parents' backyard in San Diego.

I don't spend too long arranging and readjusting decor once it's on the cake—I try to just go with it. It helps to "test-drive" the look of the cake by using an overturned cake pan as a mock cake surface, to play around with different textures, colors, and scale. Like piling your hair into a messy bun, it does take a little practice to get just the right look.

FRUIT

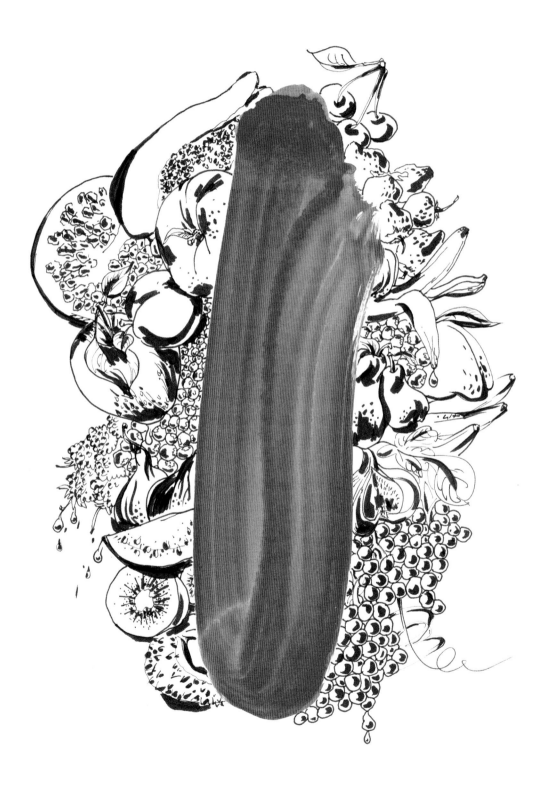

EXPRESSIONS

I fantasize and daydream about fruit the way other chefs dream about caviar and truffles. I think about how many months it is until raspberries will appear in the market. I fly home to California in the winter to raid our neighbor's passion fruit vine. I plan whole dinner party menus around a bunch of grapes. I sketch pears from memory and mail the drawings to my parents.

I vastly prefer making fruit-forward desserts to all others. The act of baking with fruit is a transformative experience for you *and* the fruit. Witness the way cherries twinkle in the sun but then bubble up and bleed their juices in the oven. Breathe in as apricots swell into a soft pudding state, their fleecy skins pooling around them like a wrinkled sweater. Poke the glittering geode cavern of a fig as it surrenders its juices into crisping pastry. There is no kind of baking that pulls me more deeply into bliss.

For me, baking with fruit means doing all you can to elevate its form and flavor. Of course, some fruits are so ephemeral and expressive that too much sugar or heat can mute, distract from, or even ruin their nuances. In general, I don't love fresh fruit swallowed up by clouds of cake batter or cornstarch, or paired with other strong flavors like chocolate or coffee.

My favorite way to create fruit desserts is by constantly riffing on what a former co-worker dubbed my "fruit pizzas." Unlike a deep-dish style American pie, I prefer a thin French-style tart, or a galette, which has an elegant, free-form quality that, for me, best emphasizes the explosive, delirious sensation of in-season, ripe fruit.

I'm extremely particular about how fruit is treated before it's baked, to the point of pedantic, almost prim, detail. First, observe the fruit, feeling its weight and taking in its scent, so you have a better understanding of how to best cook with it. Pears should be poached before baking, because they can get dry and mealy in oven heat. Peel apples before roasting them, as the skins can get chewy and tough. Rhubarb should be sliced lengthwise, to slowly draw out the water as it bakes. And, of course, no part of precious fruit should go to waste. Apple peels can tint a sticky glaze for brushing on fruit. Boiling water extracts flavor from plum pits. There is a use for everything.

The act of sharing a fruit-forward dessert is the best thrill of all. These desserts taste nourishing and vivid. They're scaffolded with butter, sugar, or nuts, or gilded with surprising additions like candied herbs, sticky jam, and miso paste. Try packing up one of the thin fruit tarts, frozen and unbaked, from this chapter (like the pineapple, apple, or rhubarb variations) in an empty pizza box lined with parchment—a gift to someone of future pleasure.

PINEAPPLE TILE GALETTE

Galette, tarta, crostata, pie, torte: so many words from so many cultures to describe fresh or preserved fruit enrobed in a tender crust. Beyond the American classics of peaches, apples, and pears, consider the highly delicious fruits from tropical climates—like pineapple, bananas, papayas, guava, lychee, and mango—when you assemble dramatic fruit-forward desserts. My soul responds to the tropical variations in the cold winter months, when the sunny, aromatic fruits effortlessly lift the spirits and senses.

Freshly sliced pineapple is the best and easiest place to start. (Avoid the canned slices, which are often packed in cloying corn syrup.) Here, the pineapple flesh is sliced into slender polygonal tiles, like the shimmering scales of a fish, darting across a buttery crust. Don't toss the tough skin and core as you chop your way through the fruit—they'll simmer in water and sugar to yield a tart syrup for a final lacquer.

1. **PREHEAT THE OVEN.** Preheat the oven to 425°F (220°C).

2. **ROLL THE PÂTE BRISÉE.** Let the chilled dough sit at room temperature until slightly softened but still cool to the touch, 10 to 15 minutes. Sprinkle a large sheet of parchment paper with flour and place the dough on top. Using firm, even pressure, roll the dough out from the middle of the round in a radius pattern, rotating the parchment like a turntable, until you have a large round about 14 inches (35 cm) wide. Use a small knife to trim the dough into a neat round. Slide the dough and parchment onto a half-sheet pan and return to the fridge to chill.

3. **PREP THE FILLING.** Grate the zest from the lime into a small bowl. Add the flour and 1 tablespoon of the sugar and pinch together with the zest. Use a sharp knife to cut the pineapple in half crosswise. Place each half on the cutting board and slice off the skin, top crown, and bottom, saving all the scraps. Cut each piece in half lengthwise (through the core) and then in half lengthwise

MAKES ONE 12-INCH (30 CM) GALETTE
SERVES 6 TO 8

30 MINUTES ACTIVE TIME
1 HOUR INACTIVE TIME

Pâte Brisée (recipe follows)
1 tablespoon (8 g) all-purpose flour, plus more for rolling the dough
1 lime
¾ cup (150 g) plus 2½ tablespoons (30 g) sugar
1 small to medium pineapple (choose one that yields slightly with a good squeeze)
2 tablespoons (30 g) coconut oil, melted
2 cups (480 g) water

(ingredients continue)

½ teaspoon citric acid
Flaky sea salt
8 Shiso Chips (recipe follows)

again, to yield a total of 8 spear-shaped pieces. Set each one on its side and slice out the core at an angle, setting the cores aside with the rest of the scraps. Then slice each piece crosswise into slices ¼ inch (0.5 cm) thick. You should have 4 to 5 cups (about 750 g) of sliced fruit. (You may not need it all. You can use any leftover pineapple to make Pineapple and Lime Marmalade, page 128.)

4. SHAPE THE GALETTE BASE. Remove the sheet pan from the refrigerator and sprinkle the lime/sugar/flour mixture all over the dough. Use the tip of your fingers to bring 1 inch (2.5 cm) of the dough up and over itself all around, making a braid-shaped crimp about ¾ inch (2 cm) high.

5. ADD THE PINEAPPLE. Starting at the top of the galette, arrange rows of pineapple, overlapping the pieces so no dough underneath peeks through. As you move down the galette, adding new rows, make sure to overlap each new row over the row before it. (The fruit will shrink in the oven, so pack it in tightly.) Brush the galette edges and the pineapple with the coconut oil and sprinkle 1½ tablespoons of the sugar all over.

6. BAKE THE GALETTE. Transfer the pan to the oven and bake until the pineapple is slightly blackened on the edges and the crust is deeply golden, about 40 minutes.

7. MEANWHILE, MAKE THE GLAZE. Transfer all the pineapple scraps (minus the spiky crown) to a pot and add the remaining ¾ cup (150 g) sugar and the water. Simmer over medium heat until the peels and core are softened, about 20 minutes. Lift out the solids with tongs and continue to reduce the liquid until it is thickened and syrupy, about 10 minutes longer. Pass through a fine-mesh sieve into a small jar and sprinkle in the citric acid. Set aside to cool.

8. FINISH THE GALETTE. Remove the galette from the oven and let cool slightly, about 10 minutes. Brush on the pineapple glaze and sprinkle with flaky sea salt. Scatter the shiso chips on top, then slice into 8 wedges to serve.

Shiso Chips

Candying preserves ephemeral plants like herbs and petals by coating them in a veil of sugar. Other tender, fruity herbs, like basil, mint, lemon verbena, or anise hyssop, candy just as well. Once candied, the herbs last almost indefinitely in the refrigerator, satisfying unexpected cravings for something sweet-and-sour. Try them tossed into popcorn, granola, trail mix, and pretzels. They can also be used for decorating layer cakes or cookies, for scattering on fruit plates or scoops of ice cream, even for garnishing a cocktail.

This is an easy, soothing project for any skill level, especially little kids, whose tiny fingers are ideal for dabbing on the egg-white wash.

1. COAT THE LEAVES. In a small bowl, whisk together the sugar and citric acid. Taste the mixture with the tip of your finger and add more citric acid until it is the balance of sweet and tart that you like. In another small bowl, gently whisk the egg white. Use a small pastry brush or your fingertips to paint a very thin layer of egg white on both sides of one shiso leaf, making sure every surface is covered (any exposed areas will oxidize and wilt). Remove any excess egg white with the side of a clean finger or a pastry brush. Transfer the leaf to the bowl with the sugar and citric acid mixture, turning to coat. Lay the leaf on a flat dry surface (like a sheet pan or cooling rack). Repeat until all the leaves are coated.

2. DRY THE LEAVES. Let the leaves dry at room temperature for 12 hours, then flip each leaf carefully and dry out the other side, another 8 to 10 hours. The leaves are fully candied when they are crunchy like potato chips and have no sticky bits. Transfer to an airtight container and store at room temperature, where the leaves will last for up to 3 weeks.

$\rightarrow$

MAKES 12 CHIPS

10 MINUTES ACTIVE TIME
24 HOURS INACTIVE TIME

¼ cup (50 g) sugar
½ teaspoon citric or malic acid,
   or more to taste
2 large egg whites (60 g)
12 shiso leaves, rinsed and dried

Pâte Brisée

I picked up this indispensable technique for making pâte brisée from Ashley Whitmore, who ran the pastry department for Marlow & Sons and Diner, both in Brooklyn, from 2010 to 2014. We used a giant food processor to make huge batches of dough, which came in handy once the Thanksgiving pie orders started rolling in. This pastry is tender and has enough structure to support heavy fruit and more.

MAKES 1 POUND (455 G), ENOUGH FOR A 12-INCH (30 CM) GALETTE

10 MINUTES ACTIVE TIME
2 HOURS INACTIVE TIME

2 cups (240 g) all-purpose flour
½ teaspoon kosher salt
9 tablespoons (4½ ounces/135 g) unsalted butter, cut into ½-inch (1.25 cm) cubes, cold
6 to 8 tablespoons (90 to 120 g) ice-cold water

TIP — *Clear plastic wrap offers a window into how the dough will eventually roll out. A distinctly pebbled pattern should be visible through the plastic, with only a few larger circles of butter; any gray smears indicate gummy, overworked dough. If the dough looks frayed and white on the edges (meaning the flour was not adequately hydrated by the water), the crumbs were not packed tight enough in the plastic wrap. Direct your rolling pin energy to the edges of the plastic to compact the crumbs properly.*

1. **COMBINE THE DRY INGREDIENTS AND BUTTER.** In a food processor, combine the flour and salt and pulse twice to blend. Add the cold cubed butter all at once and pulse 8 to 10 times to combine. The butter should mostly be the size of a pea or lentil, with just a few chickpea-size pieces.

2. **STREAM IN THE WATER.** Jogging the pulse button of the food processor as quickly as you can, stream in 6 tablespoons (90 g) water, so that it hits the blade and is sprayed in every direction, thus coating the flour mixture indirectly. Once the dough begins to climb up the sides of the bowl, stop adding water. The mixture should look like damp bread crumbs, with some larger pieces of butter. If it feels powdery, add up to 2 more tablespoons (30 g) ice water, flicking it across the crumbs with the tips of your fingers, like drips from a watering can.

3. **DOUBLE-CHECK THE TEXTURE.** Pick up a handful of the damp crumbs and firmly grip them in your palm to press them into a mass. Open your hand. Poke the mass with a finger—it should fall back into crumbs. If it feels stretchy and gummy (meaning the gluten was overworked), it is overhydrated and will bake into a tougher crust. If it doesn't stay together, clenched in your fist, it's too dry and needs more water.

4. **PACK INTO PLASTIC WRAP.** Dump the crumbs onto a large sheet of plastic wrap, pull the edges of the plastic up, and gather the edges into the center, pressing down to seal. Press out the extra air with a rolling pin until the pack is airtight, forming a disc about ½ inch (1.25 cm) thick and 6 inches (15 cm) across. Roll the surface all over with the pin to seal (see tip). Refrigerate for at least 2 hours. The dough pack can be stored in the refrigerator for up to 5 days or in the freezer for up to 3 weeks.

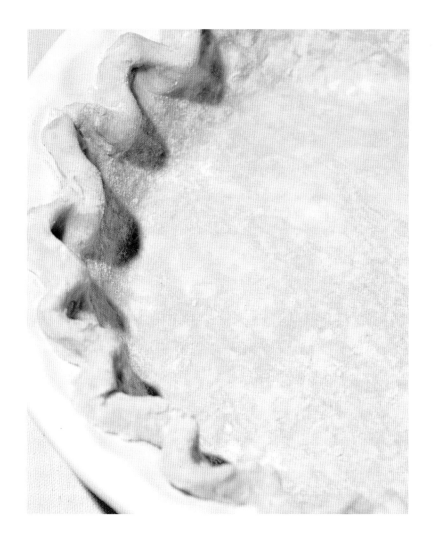

Dried nori sheets, typically used for Japanese sushi and onigiri, are a great swap for salt because they are packed with nutrients and oceanic flavor. Process the sheets on high speed in a blender or spice grinder until fine, iridescent flakes form. For the Miso Soup Danish (page 197), substitute 2 tablespoons (2 g) finely ground nori for the kosher salt.

You'll need a little less dough to make the Adzuki Bean and Brown Butter Pie (page 249). Before pressing the dough into a disc, measure out ¼ cup (55 g) of the crumbs and set those aside. (They can be wrapped in plastic wrap and saved to make the Flaky Poppy Seed Crackers, page 66).

For a flakier pie dough, the butter needs to be "sheeted," or shingled into the flour. Freeze the butter completely, then shred on the large holes of a box grater. Toss the butter into your flour mixture, like you'd fluff up a green salad. Then add the water 1 tablespoon at a time until it is hydrated sufficiently. Pack into plastic wrap as described here before chilling.

TRIPLE APPLE TART

Though familiar to the point of ubiquity, the truth is that a great apple is the most appealing and flat-out delicious of all the myriad fruits to add to baked goods, particularly tarts and pies. Over the years, I've riffed on the apple tart over and over again, looking at this timeless pastry from all different angles. I've paired Pink Lady apples with nutty, almond frangipane (classic and buttery); Granny Smith apples with sugared shiso (sour and refreshing); and poached Red Dragon apples with vinegar, ice cream, and whipped cream (drippy and fussy but still great).

    With so many ideas bobbing around, the recipes that will live in your repertoire will be the ones that are the most direct and impactful. Here, the apple stands alone, exuding nuance and versatility. No American-style warming spices like cinnamon or nutmeg, no rich additions like frangipane or cheese, no secondary fruit like cranberries or strawberries. To further emphasize the tart's resolute apple-ness, there's a swipe of electrifying apple butter on the bottom and a tangy, sticky apple glaze shot through with apple cider vinegar.

1. PREHEAT THE OVEN. Preheat the oven to 425°F (220°C); see tip #1.

2. ROLL OUT THE BRISÉE. Let the chilled dough sit at room temperature until slightly softened but still cool to the touch, 10 to 15 minutes. Sprinkle a sheet of parchment paper with the flour and place the disc of dough on top. Using firm, even pressure, roll the dough out from the middle of the round in a radius pattern, rotating the parchment like a turntable, until you have a large circular shape about 14 inches (35 cm) in diameter and ¼ inch (6 mm) thick. Use a small knife to trim the dough into a neat round. Slide the dough and parchment onto a half-sheet pan and transfer to the refrigerator to chill.

3. PREP THE APPLES. Peel the apples, reserving the peels for the glaze. Cut the apples in half through the core and then in half lengthwise again. Place each quarter apple cut side down and

MAKES ONE 10-INCH (25 CM) TART
SERVES 6 TO 8

25 MINUTES ACTIVE TIME
40 MINUTES INACTIVE TIME

Pâte Brisée (page 164)
All-purpose flour, for rolling the
   dough
3 large Honeycrisp apples
¼ cup (80 g) Apple Butter (recipe
   follows)
1 large egg white (30 g), lightly
   whisked
½ cup (100 g) sugar
¾ cup (180 g) water
2 teaspoons (10g) apple cider vinegar
Flaky sea salt

TIP **1** ——*The hot oven prevents the butter from melting out of the dough and scorches the edges of the apples, resulting in an intense, concentrated apple flavor. So don't be afraid to crank your oven way, way up. (Imagine you're baking a pizza—you want it in and out as quickly as possible in order to promote deep color and caramelized toppings!)*

TIP **2** ——*If you can't get the slices of fruit to lie flat or look perfect before baking, don't fret! You can always adjust the placement of the fruit after the tart is pulled from the oven, when the fruit is hot and malleable.*

carefully slice out the core at an angle, saving the cores for the glaze. Cut each quarter lengthwise into 4 equal wedges. If the apples are huge, cut into slices about ¼ inch/6 mm thick.

4. SHAPE THE TART BASE. Remove the dough from the refrigerator. Spread the apple butter on the surface of the dough, all the way to the edges. Use the tips of your fingers to bring 1 inch (2.5 cm) of the dough up and over itself all around, creating a braid-shaped crimp about ¾ inch (2 cm) high. (If the dough cracks, let it warm up on the counter for 5 minutes and then try again.)

5. ARRANGE THE APPLES. Begin laying down apple slices, starting at the outside perimeter, overlapping each slice by one-third (see tip #2). When the outside ring of apples is complete, start the next ring, this time with the apple slices facing in the other direction, making sure to overlap each ring of apples by ½ inch (1.25 cm). Continue until you have reached the center of the tart. Brush the braided crust with the egg white and sprinkle ¼ cup (50 g) of the sugar all over, particularly on the crust.

6. BAKE THE TART. Transfer the pan to the oven and bake until the crust is golden, 35 to 40 minutes.

7. MEANWHILE, MAKE THE TART GLAZE. Transfer the reserved apple peels and cores to a small pot and add the remaining ¼ cup (50 g) sugar. Add the water and simmer over medium heat until the color is drained from the peels, about 15 minutes. Strain the mixture into a small jars. Taste the glaze—it should be viscous and slightly tart. Add the apple cider vinegar. If the glaze still appears watery, place the syrup back on the heat and reduce for an additional 5 minutes.

8. GLAZE THE TART AND SERVE. Remove the tart from the oven and let cool for 15 minutes before applying the glaze with a brush. Sprinkle the surface with flaky sea salt. Slice into 6 to 8 wedges and serve.

VARIATION

Just as a savory chef might finish a dish with artful drizzles of vinegar and oil, I prefer to dress many of my desserts à la minute. A splash of cold-pressed sunflower seed oil on a slice of apple tart adds nutty, intense flavor at the last moment.

Apple Butter

1. PREHEAT THE OVEN. Preheat the oven to 300°F (150°C).

2. PREPARE THE APPLES. Cut the apples into quarters and cut out the cores. Place the apples and water in a 9-by-13-inch (12 by 33 cm) baking dish and drizzle the honey on top.

3. BAKE THE APPLES. Cover the pan with foil and bake until the apples are very soft and falling apart, about 2 hours. Remove the foil and bake, stirring occasionally, until the mixture looks reduced and dried out, about 2 hours longer. The darker the puree, the more intense the final apple butter will taste. Remove from the oven and let cool briefly.

4. MAKE THE APPLE BUTTER. Transfer the apples to a blender or food processor and puree on high for several minutes, until velvety. Refrigerate in an airtight container until ready to use. This can be refrigerated for up to 2 weeks; frozen, the apple butter keeps for up to 2 months.

MAKES 2 CUPS (500 G)

10 MINUTES ACTIVE TIME
3 TO 4 HOURS INACTIVE TIME

6 apples (aim for a mix of sweet and tart varieties, like Honeycrisp and Granny Smith)
2 tablespoons (30 g) water
1 tablespoon (20 g) honey

CHECKERED RHUBARB TART

Rhubarb can be a bit high maintenance, so easily slumping into stringy gray mush, and often approached by home cooks from a mildly panicky, troubleshooting perspective: How to make it sweeter? Or give it more structure? Lightly scoring the surface of the rhubarb, parallel to its fibrous grain, helps maintain its shape. The sugar, which acts as a protective blanket, settles into the slits, allowing the water to evaporate evenly and gradually. Because of its significant water content, rhubarb shrinks quite a bit as it bakes, so it's crucial to nestle the rhubarb batons tightly together so the final look is bountiful.

1. **PREHEAT THE OVEN AND PREP THE PAN.** Preheat the oven to 425°F (220°C). Line a half-sheet pan with parchment paper and mist the paper with cooking spray.

2. **ROLL OUT THE DOUGH.** Let the chilled dough sit at room temperature until slightly softened but still cool to the touch, 10 to 15 minutes. Sprinkle a sheet of parchment paper with flour and place the disc of dough on top. Using firm, even pressure, roll the dough out from the middle in a radius pattern, rotating the parchment like a turntable, until you have a circular shape about 14 inches (35 cm) wide. Use a small knife to trim the dough into a neat 13-inch (33 cm) circle. Slide the dough onto the prepared sheet pan and transfer to the refrigerator to chill.

3. **SCORE THE RHUBARB.** Using a sharp knife, score a series of 3 or 4 long cuts halfway through each rhubarb piece, running parallel with the grain; do not cut all the way through.

4. **SHAPE THE TART BASE.** Remove the chilled dough from the refrigerator. Spread the rhubarb jam over the surface of the dough, all the way to the edges. Fold over the dough edges to create a crust edge 1 inch (2.5 cm) wide.

$\rightarrow$

MAKES ONE 12-INCH (30 CM) TART
SERVES 8

30 MINUTES ACTIVE TIME
40 MINUTES INACTIVE TIME

Pâte Brisée (page 164)
All-purpose flour, for rolling the
  dough
4 to 6 stalks rhubarb, cut into 2-inch
  (5 cm) lengths (about 5 cups/
  600 g total; save all the scraps)
¼ cup (90 g) Quick Rhubarb Jam
  (recipe follows)
1 large egg white (30 g)
½ cup (100 g) sugar
¼ cup (60 g) water
Flaky sea salt
Whipped cream, for serving

5. **ARRANGE THE RHUBARB.** Starting in the top left-hand corner, working from left to right, place 3 of the rhubarb pieces vertically in a row, like matchsticks. Place 3 more pieces directly next to them but running perpendicular to them, creating a checkerboard pattern, and then continue to fill the whole tart this way. Be sure that the rhubarb is fitted very snugly together, as it will shrink during baking. Brush the tart edges with the egg white and sprinkle ⅓ cup (65 g) of the sugar all over the crust and fruit.

6. **BAKE THE TART.** Transfer the pan to the oven and bake until the rhubarb is singed and slightly blackened in parts and the crust is deeply golden, about 40 minutes.

7. **MEANWHILE, MAKE THE TART GLAZE.** Transfer all the rhubarb scraps to a small pot and add the rest of the sugar. Add the water, bring to a boil over high heat, and cook until the color is leached from the rhubarb, about 10 minutes. Strain. The glaze should be viscous and slightly tart.

8. **GLAZE THE TART.** Remove the baked tart from the oven and let cool for 15 minutes. If the juices have run over the edge, gluing it to the parchment, run an offset spatula along the edges to loosen; do this immediately, before the sugar sets in place. Brush the rhubarb with the glaze and sprinkle with flaky sea salt. Transfer the tart to a platter (see tip), slice into 8 pieces, and serve with plenty of whipped cream.

Quick Rhubarb Jam

I love the clean, sour flavor of just rhubarb and sugar, but it can be easily dressed up with a splash of Campari and orange juice.

MAKES 1 CUP (240 G)

15 MINUTES ACTIVE TIME
30 MINUTES INACTIVE TIME

2 cups (240 g) chopped rhubarb
½ cup (100 g) sugar
Pinch of kosher salt

IN A MEDIUM SAUCEPOT, combine the rhubarb, sugar, and salt and let sit for 10 minutes to macerate. Set the pot over medium heat and bring the mixture up to a boil, stirring occasionally. Let simmer until the rhubarb has broken down and most of the water has evaporated, about 15 minutes. The mixture will foam heavily and the bubbles will shrink in size as the rhubarb cooks down. Remove from the heat and transfer to a small bowl. Let cool completely and store in an airtight container in the fridge for up to 1 week.

SOUR CHERRY AND SUNFLOWER SEED TART

Fresh sour cherries have a brief, elusive season, often appearing at farmers' markets for just a few weeks before slipping away for the year, making way for sweet cherries, stone fruits, and melon. Fortunately, frozen sour cherries (sometimes labeled "pie cherries") are widely available year-round, their vivid, racy flesh preserved for our pleasure.

While sturdier fruits like apples, peaches, rhubarb, and figs will happily caramelize and roast in an open-faced galette, delicate fruits like sour cherries, berries, or very small, ripe plums tend to lose their structure as they bake, the precious juices streaming out of the tart and burning on the sheet pan. (That's why sour cherries work so well in American-style deep-dish or double-crust pies, where they're protected by a sturdy dough fortress.)

Instead, fragile fruits like currants, cherries, blueberries, and raspberries can be lightly macerated first, then spooned onto a rich, nutty bed of frangipane. As the frangipane puffs and swells, it protects the fruits from the heat of the oven.

A generous spoonful of plain yogurt or crème fraîche lifts this dessert with cooling tang.

1. **PREP THE FILLING.** In a small bowl, combine the sour cherries, kirsch, and lemon juice, toss lightly, and set aside.

2. **MIX THE WET INGREDIENTS FOR THE DOUGH.** In a stand mixer fitted with the paddle, combine the sugar and butter and paddle on medium-high speed for 1 to 2 minutes. Scrape the bowl with a spatula so it is mixed evenly, then paddle again for 10 seconds. Add the whole egg, egg yolk, and vanilla and paddle to combine, another 1 to 2 minutes.

3. **BLEND IN THE DRY INGREDIENTS.** In a small bowl, whisk together the flour, ground sunflower seeds, baking powder, and kosher salt. Tip the mixture into the mixer bowl and paddle on the lowest speed until just combined, 10 to 15 seconds.

→

MAKES ONE 10-INCH (25 CM) TART
SERVES 8

30 MINUTES ACTIVE TIME
1 HOUR INACTIVE TIME

1 pound (455 g) sour cherries, pitted
1 tablespoon (15 g) kirsch, Armagnac, or your favorite brandy
1 tablespoon (15 g) fresh lemon juice
½ cup (100 g) sugar

(ingredients continue)

6 tablespoons (3 ounces/90 g) unsalted butter, at room temperature

1 egg (50 g)

1 large egg yolk (20 g)

1 teaspoon vanilla extract

1 cup (120 g) all-purpose flour

½ cup (60 g) sunflower seeds, toasted and finely ground

1½ teaspoons baking powder

½ teaspoon kosher salt

Sunflower Seed Frangipane (recipe follows), at room temperature (see tip), re-whipped

Flaky sea salt

2 cups (255 g) whole-milk yogurt or crème fraîche, for serving (optional)

TIP —— *Because of its high butter content, frangipane will chill into a firm block, so let the spread sit at room temperature for at least 1 hour before using. Paddle right before using so it becomes fluffy and spreadable.*

4. ROLL AND CHILL THE DOUGH. Cut two pieces of parchment 12 inches (30 cm) wide and 16 inches (40 cm) long. Place the dough in the middle of a piece of parchment and gently shape it into a square. Place the second piece of parchment on top of the dough square. Use a rolling pin to firmly press the dough down, sandwiching it between the sheets of parchment. (Don't peel off the parchment!) Using strong, forceful motions radiating from the center, roll the dough out to a round 15 inches (38 cm) in diameter. Transfer the parchment pack to a half-sheet pan and freeze for 20 to 30 minutes to chill thoroughly.

5. PREHEAT THE OVEN. Preheat the oven to 350°F (175°C).

6. SHAPE THE TART SHELL. Lightly mist a fluted 10-inch (25 cm) tart pan with cooking spray. (A tart pan with a removable bottom will make slicing later easier, but it's not essential.) Peel off the top piece of parchment from the chilled dough and flip to invert it into the tart mold. Peel off the other piece of parchment. Gently press the dough into the corners of the tart pan and up the sides, and pinch off any extra dough with your fingers. If the dough cracks, just press it back together with your fingers. Prick the bottom all over with a fork. Freeze again for 15 minutes to chill.

7. BLIND-BAKE THE TART SHELL. Press the reserved sheet of parchment back onto the shaped tart shell and fill to the top with pie weights, like dried beans or rice. Bake until the edges are golden and the bottom is cooked through but still pale, 25 to 30 minutes. Let cool slightly, then gently tug the top piece of parchment out and dump the hot pie weights into a bowl to cool. Leave the oven on.

8. ADD THE FILLINGS AND BAKE. Spread the frangipane over the bottom of the cooled shell. Spoon the macerated cherries on top of the frangipane. Crimp foil around the edges of the tart so the dough does not continue to darken in the oven. Return to the oven and bake until the frangipane is puffed up and feels set (it will have a cakey crumb; a toothpick or knife slid in should come out clean) and the cherries are juicy and bubbling, about 30 minutes.

9. COOL AND SERVE. Let the tart cool for at least 30 minutes before portioning with a sharp knife. Sprinkle the surface with flaky sea salt and serve with a cold scoop of yogurt or crème fraîche, if desired.

Sunflower Seed Frangipane

This recipe for frangipane is modeled on a very easy-to-remember ratio of ingredients: nearly equal weights of sugar, butter, eggs, and seeds. The easiest and most intuitive substitutions are with the type of flours, seeds, and nuts that give frangipane its characteristic richness; almonds, pistachios, hazelnuts, walnuts, pecans, and even peanuts, when finely ground, make delicious spreads for fruit tarts.

IN A STAND MIXER fitted with the paddle (or in a large bowl using a handheld mixer), cream the sugar and butter on medium speed until the mixture looks fluffy and pale, 5 to 6 minutes. Add the eggs, beating well and scraping the bowl with a spatula. Add the vanilla and almond extracts and paddle to combine. The mixture may look split; this is okay. Add the salt and ground sunflower seeds and paddle on low speed until combined, about 30 seconds. Transfer to a small container and set aside at room temperature if using immediately. If making ahead, store in an airtight container in the refrigerator for up to 2 weeks or in the freezer for up to 2 months.

MAKES 2 CUPS (440 G)

15 MINUTES ACTIVE TIME

½ cup (100 g) sugar
8 tablespoons (4 ounces/115 g) unsalted butter, at room temperature
2 eggs (100 g), at room temperature
1 teaspoon vanilla extract
½ teaspoon almond extract
½ teaspoon kosher salt
1 cup (120 g) sunflower seeds, toasted and finely ground

NECTARINE AND MISO TARTE TATIN

Tarte Tatin is a truly iconic dessert, embodying both old-school technique and chic simplicity. And yet, simple desserts are the trickiest to execute, because it's much harder to hide mistakes. A caramel too dark or too light, fruit cooked too long or not long enough, or soggy puff pastry are all ways this timeless dessert can go sideways in a matter of seconds.

My solution is to partially deconstruct this technically thorny dessert, baking the fruit and pastry separately, so it can be easily assembled at the moment of eating for maximum texture and freshness. If you love the unique, slippery mouthfeel of potato gratin, you will go crazy for this method of slow-cooking the fruit into translucent, even layers. Look for slightly underripe fruit, which is so much easier to slice into thin slivers. In the fall, swap out the nectarines for apples, pears, or quinces, or a cocktail of all three.

MAKES ONE 9-INCH (23 CM)
TARTE TATIN
SERVES 6 TO 8

40 MINUTES ACTIVE TIME
4 HOURS INACTIVE TIME

½ cup (100 g) sugar
4 tablespoons (2 ounces/60 g)
    unsalted butter
2 tablespoons (30 g) white miso
    paste
6 to 8 slightly underripe nectarines
One 12-inch (30 cm/225 g) sheet
    Rough Puff Pastry (recipe
    follows), chilled
1 large egg white (30 g), lightly
    whisked
Flaky sea salt
1 cup (225 g) cold crème fraîche,
    for serving

1. **PREHEAT THE OVEN.** Preheat the oven to 300°F (150°C).

2. **COOK THE CARAMEL.** Line a 9-inch (23 cm) round cake pan with parchment paper and set aside. In a small pot, melt the sugar and butter over medium-high heat. Continue to cook until the sugar is deeply golden, like the color of an amber lager, using a whisk throughout to emulsify the butter and sugar into a smooth sauce. Remove from the heat and stir in the miso paste. Pour the caramel into the parchment-lined cake pan and slowly tilt the pan so it covers the entire bottom. Set aside to cool completely.

3. **PREP THE NECTARINES.** Use a sharp knife to slice off the 2 fattest lobes of the nectarines, just away from the pit, and then the other two sides, for 4 pieces. Set a mandoline to an ⅛-inch (3 mm) thickness (test a few pieces of fruit to calibrate) and slice all the fruit thinly. (In the absence of a mandoline, a small sharp knife is adequate, but the layers of the tart won't be as precise or even.)

4. **MAKE THE NECTARINE CONFIT.** Arrange the nectarine slices in neat circular rings in the cake pan, stacking

TIP 1 ——*Lightly weighting down the puff pastry with a half-sheet pan controls the rise of the pastry by applying even weight, resulting in a tidy, crisp bar of pastry, and prevents it from shrinking drastically, always a disappointing sight.*

TIP 2 ——*If an excess of caramel is still stuck to the pan after inverting, place the pan in a warm but turned-off oven, to melt and loosen the caramel. Drizzle the extra on top.*

more on top of the layers as you go. Press a piece of foil or parchment paper on top of the nectarines to cover. Place a smaller cake pan or pot on top and weight it down with something heavy, like pie weights. Transfer to the oven and bake for 1 hour. Remove from the oven and remove the weights and foil covering. Return to the oven and bake, uncovered, for 1 hour longer. Remove and set aside. Increase the oven temperature to 425°F (220°C).

5. PREPARE THE PANS. Line a sheet pan with parchment paper and have a second sheet pan at the ready.

6. PREPARE THE PUFF PASTRY. Use an overturned bowl, a cake pan, or a 10-inch (25 cm) parchment round as a guide to cut the puff into a round 10 inches (25 cm) in diameter. Transfer the pastry to the lined sheet pan and freeze for 10 minutes.

7. BAKE THE PASTRY. Remove the sheet pan from the freezer and cut six slashes ⅜ inch (1 cm) long in the puff pastry round. Brush the surface with the egg white. Lightly mist another piece of parchment with cooking spray and set over the pastry sprayed side down. Set the second sheet pan on top to weight the pastry down (see tip #1). Transfer to the oven and bake for 25 minutes. Reduce the oven temperature to 375°F (190°C). Remove the upper sheet pan and peel off the parchment. Place the uncovered puff back in the oven and bake until deeply golden, glossy, and crisp, 7 to 10 minutes (keep an eye on it so it doesn't burn). Remove from the oven and transfer to a cooling rack.

8. ASSEMBLE THE TART. Place the puff pastry disc on top of the cake pan containing the confit. Carefully place an inverted serving platter on top. Gently lift the cake pan, holding the top steady, and flip it all over. Slowly remove the cake pan and peel off the parchment paper (see tip #2). Nudge any wayward fruit back into place. Use a serrated knife to slice the tarte Tatin into wedges. Sprinkle with flaky sea salt and serve with the crème fraîche.

Rough Puff Pastry

Classically made puff pastry involves a complicated set of time-and-temperature-sensitive folds and rolls that encase thin sheets of butter in a lean dough. Rough puff pastry, on the other hand, incorporates small cold cubes of butter right into the dough, just like Pâte Brisée (page 164). The result is still flaky and delicate, but the process is dramatically easier and faster.

1. **MIX THE DOUGH.** In a stand mixer fitted with the paddle, combine the flour, sugar, salt, and butter and mix on low speed until the butter pieces are the size of chickpeas and lentils, about 2 minutes. With the mixer running on low speed, stream in the ice water and vinegar for no more than 10 seconds.

2. **BEGIN THE FOLDS.** Turn the mixture out onto a large piece of parchment paper. Pat the dough into a rectangle about 6 by 12 inches (15 by 30 cm) and 2 inches (5 cm) thick. It will look damp and shaggy with patches of wet spots; this is okay.

3. **MAKE THE FIRST SET OF FOLDS.** Using a rolling pin, press down the length of this rectangle, flattening it until it is no thicker than ¾ inch (2 cm). With a long side facing you, and using the parchment paper to support and cradle the dough, lift the right third of the dough up and over to fall on top of the middle third. Repeat the same motion with the left third of the dough, bringing it up and over to fall on top of the middle section, pressing any loose, shaggy pieces back into place. This is called a letter fold.

   Repeat the letter fold two more times, using the rolling pin to firmly press and flatten the dough into a rectangle. Transfer the parchment packet to the refrigerator and let rest for 30 minutes.

4. **MAKE TWO MORE SETS OF FOLDS.** Remove the parchment packet from the refrigerator and repeat the process of making three letter folds. Refrigerate the dough and let rest for 30 minutes. Then make a final set of three letter folds. As the dough becomes increasingly smoother and more elastic, shift your rolling pin movements from a pressing-down motion to a more standard rolling-out motion, aiming for a rectangle about 12 by 20 inches (30 by 50 cm). If the dough is excessively sticking to the rolling pin or parchment, sprinkle on a minimal amount of all-purpose flour.

5. **WRAP AND STORE.** After the final set of letter folds, wrap the dough package tightly in plastic wrap and transfer to the refrigerator for at least 30 minutes. If you will be using the dough for tart recipes (see pages 176 and 180), cut the chilled puff pastry into thirds. Wrap each chunk separately and refrigerate for up to 1 week. If planning on using later, roll out each third into a 12-inch (30 cm) square, then freeze; the thinner pastry will thaw more evenly. If using the dough for other recipes, wrap well and refrigerate or freeze.

MAKES 1½ POUNDS (675 G) PUFF PASTRY

20 MINUTES ACTIVE TIME
2 HOURS INACTIVE TIME

2 cups (240 g) all-purpose flour, plus more for rolling the dough

1 tablespoon (15 g) sugar

1 teaspoon kosher salt

12 ounces (340 g) unsalted butter, cut into ½-inch (1.25 cm) cubes, very cold

¼ cup plus 1 tablespoon (75 g) ice-cold water

1 teaspoon distilled white vinegar

STILL LIFE TART

This tart is a still life painting sprung to actual life, a love letter to the farmers'
market rows of baskets brimming with sparkling fruits. It starts with a sheaf of puff
pastry, cut to create ruffly, scalloped edges, like a flower or a doily, and baked into a
bronzed disc. The pastry is your canvas, ready for your vision. Whichever fruits you
choose, aim for visual abundance, a variety of ready-to-eat tart and sweet fruits, and
plenty of refreshing, tender herbs like mint or shiso.

MAKES ONE 11-INCH (28 CM) TART
SERVES 6

20 MINUTES ACTIVE TIME
30 MINUTES INACTIVE TIME

One 12-inch (30 cm/225 g) sheet
    Rough Puff Pastry (page 178),
    chilled
1 large egg white (30 g), lightly
    whisked
¾ cup plus 1 tablespoon (100 g)
    powdered sugar
Grated zest and juice of 1 lemon
3 cups (about 450 g) mixed fresh
    fruit, nothing larger than a fig
12 leaves mixed fresh herbs, like
    mint, basil, tarragon, shiso, and
    sorrel

1. PREHEAT THE OVEN AND PREP THE PAN. Preheat
the oven to 425°F (220°C). Line a sheet pan with parchment
paper and have a second sheet pan at the ready.

2. SHAPE THE PUFF. Use a sharp paring knife to trim the
chilled puff pastry into a scalloped round about 12 inches
(30 cm) in diameter, like the shape of a cartoon flower. (You can cut
the pastry free-form, or draw a daisy shape on a piece of paper, cut it
out, and use that as a guide.) Prick the pastry all over with a fork.

3. BAKE THE PASTRY. Transfer to the lined sheet pan and
brush the surface with the egg white. Top with another piece
of parchment paper lightly misted with cooking spray, followed by
the second half-sheet pan to weight it down. Transfer to the oven
and bake until the pastry is golden and puffed, about 20 minutes.
Carefully remove the parchment covering and the top sheet pan and
continue to bake, uncovered, until the pastry is deeply golden, 5 to
6 minutes longer. Let cool completely on a cooling rack.

4. MAKE AND APPLY THE ICING. In a small bowl,
combine the powdered sugar and lemon zest. Stream in the
lemon juice until the icing is the consistency of buttermilk. Spoon
the icing over the cooled puff pastry round.

5. DECORATE WITH THE FRUITS. Arrange the fresh
fruit in a cluster, tucking in the herbs throughout. Serve
immediately (see tip).

TIP —— *If assembling the tart later—
at a friend's dinner party, or a picnic—
wrap the iced puff pastry round
in plastic wrap, store the fruit in
protective containers, and finish
the tart on-site.*

SUNCHOKE AND APRICOT TART

Perched somewhere between American peach pie, Italian Montebianco, and French Basque cake is this irresistible double-crust sunchoke and apricot tart. The burnished, crumbly crust gives way to a silky duet of tart apricot preserves and nutty sunchoke cream. Each bite is a soft, gentle journey.

1. **ROLL AND CHILL THE DOUGH.** Cut four pieces of parchment 12 by 16 inches (30 by 40 cm). Divide the tart dough in half. Place one dough portion in the middle of a piece of parchment and gently shape it into a square. Place another piece of parchment on top of the dough square. Use a rolling pin to firmly press the dough down, sandwiching it between the sheets of parchment. (Don't peel off the parchment!) Using strong, forceful motions radiating from the center, roll the dough out to a 13-inch (33 cm) round. Repeat with the second dough portion. Transfer both dough rounds encased in their parchment sheets to a half-sheet pan and freeze for at least 20 minutes.

2. **ASSEMBLE THE PIE.** Mist an 8-inch (20 cm) fluted tart pan with cooking spray. Peel off the top piece of parchment on one round of chilled almond dough and flip to invert it into the tart pan. Peel off the other piece of parchment. Gently press the dough into the corners and up the sides of the tart pan and trim the excess dough with your fingertips so the shaped tart shell is 1 inch (2.5 cm) high. (If the dough cracks or tears, you can press softened extra bits of dough to patch.) Freeze again for 15 minutes.

3. **PREHEAT THE OVEN.** While the tart shell is freezing, preheat the oven to 350°F (175°C).

4. **ADD THE FILLINGS.** Spread the apricot jam evenly over the bottom of the tart. Dollop the custard on top and gently smooth flat (try not to mix the two spreads together too much).

5. **PRESS ON THE LID.** Remove the second round of almond dough from the refrigerator and peel off one piece of parchment. Invert the round on top of the tart and peel off the

MAKES ONE 8-INCH (20 CM) TART
SERVES 8

25 MINUTES ACTIVE TIME
2 HOURS INACTIVE TIME

Almond Tart Dough (recipe follows)
1 cup (about 320 g) apricot jam
1 cup (300 g) Sunchoke Custard (recipe follows), chilled
1 large egg white (30 g), lightly whisked
Flaky sea salt

second piece of parchment. Use the palm of your hand to press down, attaching it to the exposed filling and pressing out any air inside. Use a small knife to trim the excess dough around the perimeter, sealing the top lid to the walls of the tart.

6. BAKE THE PIE. Brush the egg white all over the top crust. Cut three small vents in the surface. Transfer to the oven and bake until deeply golden and bronzed, 40 to 45 minutes. Let cool for at least 1 hour before cutting. Sprinkle with flaky sea salt to serve and slice into 8 wedges.

Almond Tart Dough

MAKES ABOUT 1 POUND (475 G)

15 MINUTES ACTIVE TIME
1 HOUR INACTIVE TIME

½ cup (100 g) sugar
6 tablespoons (3 ounces/90 g)
    unsalted butter, at room
    temperature
1 egg (50 g)
1 large egg yolk (20 g)
1 teaspoon vanilla extract
1 cup (120 g) all-purpose flour
½ cup (60 g) almond flour
1½ teaspoons baking powder
½ teaspoon kosher salt

1. MAKE THE TART DOUGH. In a stand mixer fitted with the paddle (or in a large bowl using a handheld mixer), combine the sugar and butter and paddle on medium-high speed for 1 to 2 minutes. Add the whole egg, egg yolk, and vanilla and paddle to combine, another 1 to 2 minutes.

2. ADD THE DRY INGREDIENTS. In a small bowl, whisk together the all-purpose flour, almond flour, baking powder, and salt. Tip the mixture into the stand mixer and paddle on the lowest speed until the ingredients are combined, 8 to 10 seconds. Wrap tightly in plastic wrap and refrigerate until ready to use. The dough will keep in the fridge for up to 1 week or in the freezer for up to 1 month.

Sunchoke Custard

Sunchokes, sometimes called Jerusalem artichokes, are an earthy, nutty foil for bright, acidic stone fruits like apricots. Treat sunchokes like potatoes or squash, and you'll be rewarded with a satiny puree that will add unique richness to a simple pastry cream. (A bit of the puree would also be excellent folded into the Chocolate and Earl Grey Mousse, page 244.)

1. **MAKE THE SUNCHOKE PUREE.** Cut the sunchokes into coins ½ inch (1.25 cm) thick. Add to a small pot and cover with ½ cup (120 g) of the milk. Bring to a low simmer, cover, and cook until the sunchokes are very tender and almost falling apart, 20 to 25 minutes. Transfer the entire mixture to a blender (remove the steam vent from the blender cap) and puree while still hot; the mixture should be thick and creamy. Set aside to cool.

2. **MAKE THE CUSTARD.** Use a small knife to halve the vanilla bean lengthwise and scrape the vanilla seeds out into a small pot. Add the spent vanilla pod to the pot and pour in the remaining 1 cup (240 g) milk. While the milk is heating, in a small bowl, whisk together the cornstarch, salt, and 1 tablespoon (15 g) of the sugar. When you see the first few bubbles in the pot, add a spoonful of hot milk to the cornstarch bowl and whisk to form a paste-like slurry. Add the slurry to the pot and bring back up to a simmer. Simmer for 1 minute, whisking throughout so the milk doesn't burn.

3. **ADD THE EGG.** Crack the egg into the bowl you just used for the cornstarch and add the remaining 2 tablespoons (30 g) sugar. Whisk to combine. While whisking the egg mixture constantly, stream in a ladle of the hot milk. Pour the warmed egg mixture into the pot and stir until thickened, about 2 minutes.

4. **ADD THE SUNCHOKE PUREE.** Remove the custard from the heat and whisk in the butter and sunchoke puree. Pass the custard through a fine-mesh sieve into a medium bowl and set aside to cool, about 1 hour. Transfer to an airtight container and refrigerate until ready to use. It will keep in the fridge for up to 4 days.

MAKES 2 CUPS (500 G)

25 MINUTES ACTIVE TIME
1 HOUR INACTIVE TIME

5 ounces (140 g) sunchokes (2 to 3 large sunchokes), scrubbed clean and peeled
1½ cups (360 g) whole milk
½ vanilla bean
2 tablespoons (15 g) cornstarch or tapioca starch
½ teaspoon kosher salt
3 tablespoons (45 g) sugar
1 egg (50 g)
2 tablespoons (1 ounce/30 g) unsalted butter

PLUM NESTS

If you love making egg yolk–rich custards or curds, pastry cream, or ice cream, chances are good that you are in constant excess of egg whites. Meringues extend a second life to leftover egg whites, and these crisp, sweet nests offer a neutral-tasting, gluten-free alternative to the flour-based doughs featured in this chapter. A balance of sweet, rich, and sour components is important in assembling this dessert because meringues run quite sweet. Segments of raw plums, not yet ripe and still with a bit of crunch, are macerated in vinegar and honey. Ricotta and mascarpone are whipped together. And a final drizzle of emerald olive oil captures the vibrant essence of fresh herbs.

MAKES 10 TO 12 NESTS

30 MINUTES ACTIVE TIME
2 HOURS INACTIVE TIME

3 large egg whites (90 g)
½ teaspoon cream of tartar
½ teaspoon kosher salt
¾ cup (150 g) sugar
1 teaspoon vanilla extract
½ teaspoon almond extract
½ cup (125 g) ricotta cheese,
    preferably whole-milk
½ cup (125 g) mascarpone
5 or 6 slightly underripe plums
1 teaspoon honey
1 teaspoon (8 g) white wine vinegar
½ cup (160 g) stone fruit jam
3 tablespoons (45 g) Herb Oil
    (recipe follows)
Flaky sea salt

1. PREHEAT THE OVEN AND PREP THE PANS. Preheat the oven to 250°F (120°C). To bake in batches, line two half-sheet pans with parchment paper.

2. MIX THE MERINGUE. In a stand mixer fitted with the whisk (or in a large bowl using a handheld mixer), combine the egg whites, cream of tartar, and kosher salt. Begin whipping on high speed until the mixture foams up and begins to turn white, 2 to 3 minutes. Slowly stream in the sugar and continue whipping on high speed until the mixture has quadrupled in size and is glossy and stiff with a little flop, another 5 minutes or so. Add the vanilla and almond extracts. Transfer the meringue to a piping bag (see tip #1) fitted with a star tip.

3. FORM THE NESTS AND BAKE. To form a nest, pipe a circle 2 to 2½ inches (5 to 6.5 cm) wide and ¾ to 1 inch (2 to 2.5 cm) high onto a lined sheet pan, then pipe another circle directly resting on top. The cavity in the center of the nest should be at least 1 inch (2.5 cm) across. Continue piping nests, spacing them 4 inches apart, until the sheet pans are full. Bake until dry to the touch, about 1 hour. Turn off the oven, crack open the door, and let the meringues sit for 20 minutes. The meringues should be crisp all the way through. (If not using right away, store in the freezer; see tip #2.)

→

TIP 1 —*In the absence of pastry bags, the mixture can be portioned with an ice cream scoop or spoon. Scoop ¼-cup (15 g) mounds of meringue onto the sheet pan, flicking it off the spoon with your finger. Use the back of the spoon to create a crater in the center.*

TIP 2 —*Humidity is the enemy of meringues, causing their fragile shells to weep. To combat molar-clogging stickiness, store your meringues in an airtight container in the freezer, where it is cold and dry. They'll stay crunchy for up to 3 weeks.*

4. **MEANWHILE, MIX THE FILLING.** In a stand mixer fitted with the paddle (or in a large bowl using a handheld mixer), beat the ricotta and mascarpone on medium-low speed until smooth and fluffy, about 5 minutes. Scrape the mixture out into a bowl and keep chilled until ready to use.

5. **MACERATE THE FRUIT.** Halve the plums lengthwise and pull out the pits. Slice the plums into thin crescents and toss with the honey and vinegar in a small bowl.

6. **ASSEMBLE THE NESTS.** Fill the center of each meringue nest with 1 tablespoon of the whipped ricotta. Add a tablespoon of jam. Cover with a generous spoonful of macerated plums. Finish with a drizzle of herb oil and a pinch of flaky sea salt. Serve immediately.

VARIATION

Who doesn't love an edible vessel? Use these cute nests for everything! Make mini sundaes with ice cream, whipped cream, Sweet and Spicy Hazelnuts (page 129), and Cocoa Gloss (page 82). Or pipe in the Chocolate and Earl Grey Mousse (page 244) and dust with cocoa powder. Or fill with store-bought sorbet and Passion Fruit Jellies (page 54).

Herb Oil

FILL A SMALL BOWL with ice and cover with water. Bring a small pot of water to a boil. Add the herbs and blanch to set the color, 5 to 10 seconds. Remove with tongs and drop into the ice bath. Then remove, wring out the excess water with your hands, and add the herbs and olive oil to a blender. Process on high until the herbs and oil have made a fine puree. Line a sieve with a coffee filter and set over a bowl. Slowly pour the mixture into the sieve and let stand overnight to drip. The oil should be crystal clear, neon green, and extremely fragrant. Store in an airtight container in the refrigerator for up to 3 months.

MAKES 1 CUP (240 G)

10 MINUTES ACTIVE TIME
12 HOURS INACTIVE TIME

4 cups packed fresh herb leaves,
   like anise hyssop, basil, mint,
   lovage, parsley, or lemon verbena
1½ cups (360 g) olive oil

B
A
K
I
N
G

W
I
T
H

V
E
G
E
T
A
B
L
E
S

<blockquote>
Good cooking is the result of balance struck between frugality and liberality. . . . Once we lose touch with the spendthrift aspect of nature's provisions epitomized in the raising of a crop, we are in danger of losing touch with life itself. When Providence supplies the means, the preparation and sharing of food takes on a sacred aspect.
</blockquote>

—PATIENCE GRAY

Some people, when they see a fat tomato, a swaying bunch of herbs, or a basket brimming with mushrooms, immediately think about what salad or vegetable dish they'd like to make. But my baking-addled brain starts spinning a long list of ways I'd like to shingle that tomato into a flaky galette, stir the herbs into a peppery biscuit, or chop those mushrooms into a whole-grain scone. I'm all about balance, and savory pastries have both a nourishing *and* a decadent side.

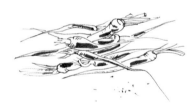

Incorporating vegetables into pastries is an excellent way to develop your imagination in the kitchen as well as increase your understanding of these plants. Thinking about vegetables in this way can lead you to become the most resourceful, thrifty, and creative baker you have ever been in your life—truly! In fancy restaurant kitchens, the pastry department is often the recipient of the savory side's "refuse." Many pastry chefs love the challenge of incorporating a line cook's waste into a new dish. Onion scraps are caramelized and stirred into dense kale fillings for pies. Meyer lemon peels get sliced thinly and pressed into focaccia before baking. Yesterday's potatoes are crumbled and folded up in thinly stretched strudel dough.

Baking thoughtfully with vegetables is like putting on glasses after a lifetime of blurry vision—you feel incredibly grateful to take in the details and quirks around these ingredients, because suddenly you're closer to them than you ever have been before. You'll start to discover uses for ingredients that you've never thought of before, like how long stalks of herbs can be woven into a flaky dough, or how seaweed can add unexpected crunch to pie filling.

Conversely, showcasing vegetables in pastry allows you to get more grandiose, over-the-top, and architectural than a salad or bowl of soup. A graphic Kabocha Galette (page 199) can stop you in your tracks, just like a meticulously decorated layer cake or a sleek, plated dessert.

The best thing about these savory treats is that unlike elaborate multi-dish dinners, they are entire, compact meals in and of themselves, and need little more than a napkin to cradle them. These pastries emerge from the oven baked in their edible containers, which makes them both terrific gifts and sturdy and efficient travelers.

More Than Cake

HALF-MOON PIE

Archestratus Books + Food, run by the indefatigable first-generation Sicilian Paige Lipari, is my favorite bookstore in New York City, not least because the kitchen turns out some of the most delicious sandwiches I've ever had. The crunchy, gooey Darren Vito sandwich layers mortadella, sliced caciocavallo, roasted red peppers, and a thick bread crumb spread into a slab of crunchy focaccia as big as a paperback novel.

I was inspired to pay homage to Paige's epic sandwiches with a flaky, buttery pastry. You'll need a deli-style meat (like ham or smoked turkey); a melty, stretchy Italian cheese (like fontina or mozzarella); a spicy fermented element (like crushed Calabrian chiles or hot sauce); and a few bright and green things (like parsley, broccoli, bell peppers, or spinach) for balance.

The pie is even better the next day, served at room temperature, with a simple escarole salad.

MAKES ONE 14-INCH (35 CM) PIE
SERVES 8

30 MINUTES ACTIVE TIME
40 MINUTES INACTIVE TIME

Pâte Brisée (page 164), chilled
All-purpose flour, for rolling the
  dough
3 cups (300 g) broccoli or
  cauliflower florets
1 egg (50 g), separated
2 teaspoons crushed Calabrian
  chiles in oil (see Resources,
  page 311)
2 tablespoons (30 g) olive oil
¼ cup (60 g) chopped roasted
  red peppers
4 ounces (115 g) sliced ham or
  mortadella
¾ cup (75 g) grated fontina cheese
Dijon mustard, for serving

1. PREHEAT THE OVEN. Preheat the oven to 375°F (190°C).

2. ROLL OUT THE DOUGH. Let the chilled dough sit at room temperature until slightly softened but still cool to the touch, 10 to 15 minutes. Sprinkle a large sheet of parchment paper with flour and place the disc of dough on top. Using firm, even pressure, roll the dough out into a large round about 15 inches (38 cm) in diameter. Use a small knife to trim the dough to a 14-inch (35 cm) round. Slide the dough on its parchment onto a sheet pan and refrigerate.

3. PREP THE FILLING. Finely chop the broccoli. In a medium bowl, combine the chopped broccoli, egg yolk, Calabrian chiles, olive oil, and roasted peppers. Use a spoon to mix evenly.

4. SHAPE THE PIE. Remove the rolled-out dough from the refrigerator. Shingle the ham on the right half of the pastry round. Spoon the broccoli filling on top of the ham, stopping 1 inch (2.5 cm) from the edges of the pastry. Sprinkle the fontina cheese on top. Fold the empty left half of the dough over. Starting at the

top, fold over the edges into a pleat, crimping downward to form a decorative pattern.

5. BAKE THE PIE. Cut several tiny vents in the pastry to allow steam to escape in the oven. Brush the lightly whisked egg white all over the pastry. Transfer to the oven and bake until deeply golden and sizzling, about 40 minutes. Remove from the oven and let cool slightly before slicing into 8 wedges. Serve with Dijon mustard on the side.

VARIATION

There are plenty of ways to jazz up the basic Pâte Brisée (page 164). Add 2 tablespoons (4 g) chopped sturdy herbs (like fresh rosemary or oregano) for a fragrant, speckled finish. You can replace up to ¼ cup (30 g) of the all-purpose flour with a nut flour or add up to 2 tablespoons (15 g) whole seeds (like poppy, sesame, or flax) for extra texture and crunch. Up to one-quarter of the butter can be replaced with a grated firm, salty cheese (like Parmesan or Pecorino Romano).

MISO SOUP DANISH

At Marlow & Sons, where I held my very first pastry job in New York City, I clocked in every morning at 6:30 to prepare for the 8:00 a.m. rush. I made the sunrise commute on foot, starting from my apartment in Greenpoint and crossing underneath the Williamsburg Bridge. The walk was brutal in the winter, when the icy winds would blow off the East River and sting my cheeks. To warm up, I began to simmer large batches of dashi at night, which I'd pour into a thermos every morning, shaking it up with miso paste and chopped herbs before heading out the door.

    This cozy Danish, stuffed with seaweed, chopped vegetables, and cubed tofu, reminds me of those quiet, dark mornings. As an extra touch, I weave in shoots of scallion, which dart in and out of the pastry like silky ribbons peering through a girl's braid.

1. **PREPARE THE SEAWEED FILLING.** Trim and halve the scallions, separating the green tops from the white bottoms. Finely dice the scallion whites. Place the dark green scallion tops and dried wakame in a bowl and soak in hot water until softened, about 10 minutes. Remove the softened scallion tops and set aside. Drain the wakame, pat dry, and finely chop. In a large bowl, combine the sliced scallion whites, chopped seaweed, chopped dark greens, and shredded carrot. Add the miso paste and olive oil and massage with your hands. Add the diced tofu and stir to combine.

2. **PREHEAT THE OVEN.** Preheat the oven to 375°F (190°C).

3. **ROLL OUT THE DOUGH.** Remove the dough from the refrigerator and let sit at room temperature until slightly softened but still cool to the touch, 10 to 15 minutes. Dust a large sheet of parchment paper with some flour and place the disc of dough on top (see tip). Using firm, even pressure, roll the dough out into a rough rectangle about 13 by 17 inches (33 by 43 cm)—just a bit larger than a standard 12-by-16 inch (30 by 40 cm) sheet of parchment paper. Slide this sheet of dough onto a sheet pan.

$\rightarrow$

MAKES ONE 12-INCH (30 CM)
DANISH
SERVES 8

30 MINUTES ACTIVE TIME
1 HOUR INACTIVE TIME

1 bunch scallions (about 100 g)
1 cup (10 g) broken pieces of dried
    seaweed, such as wakame
1 cup (75 g) packed chopped bitter
    or dark greens, such as kale,
    collard greens, or escarole
1 carrot, shredded (125 g)
2 tablespoons (35 g) white miso
    paste
2 tablespoons (30 g) olive oil
5 ounces (150 g) extra-firm tofu,
    cut into ½-inch (1.25 cm) dice
    (about 1 cup)
Pâte Brisée (page 164), made
    with nori (see Variation)

(ingredients continue)

All-purpose flour, for rolling the
  dough
1 large egg white (30 g), lightly
  whisked

VARIATION

If you like to visit your local
farmers' market or have a garden
of your own, you could enhance
the woven fronds of scallion with
even more decor. Flowers aren't
just for decorating sweet treats.
Many plants—like broccoli, kale,
cilantro, and peas—produce
delicious blossoms that add
beauty to savory dishes.

4. ADD THE FILLING. With a short side facing you, use a
   knife to make two small cuts at the top of the dough rectangle
spaced 4 inches (10 cm) apart, thus marking the dough into three
vertical columns. Spread the tofu and vegetable filling down the
middle third of the dough. Make a cut in the top of the left third of
the dough at a 45-degree angle to the vertical, stopping when you
get to the filling. Continue to cut the dough into strips 3 inches
(7.5 cm) wide down the length of the dough. Repeat with the right side,
cutting the dough into strips 3 inches (8 cm) wide at a 45-degree
angle downward. There should be 3 or 4 strips on each side.

5. BRAID THE STRIPS. Starting from the top left, fold the
   first strip diagonally across the tofu filling. Fold the top right
strip over that, creating an X. Tuck some of the reserved softened
green scallion tops into the pastry. Continue to create the X shape
with the remaining strips, weaving in the remaining scallions. Pinch
the top and bottom ends closed. Brush the surface of the Danish all
over with the egg white.

6. BAKE THE DANISH. Transfer to the oven and bake until
   the pastry is golden brown, 45 to 50 minutes. Remove from the
oven and cool for at least 15 minutes, then slice into 8 pieces.

KABOCHA GALETTE

"Kabocha," like "apple" or "tomato," is an umbrella term for many varieties of Japanese pumpkin and winter squash. Kabocha squash are exceptional in open-faced, free-form galettes because of their sweet, succulent flesh and edible skin (no peeling required), which caramelize and sizzle in a hot oven.

For baking, slice the kabocha into thin irregularly shaped tiles, which are shingled tightly together into asymmetrical psychedelic patterns, like a jigsaw puzzle. Here, the sweetness of the squash is offset by aromatic sautéed leeks and a barley tea–infused lacquer.

1. PREHEAT THE OVEN. Preheat the oven to 400°F (200°C).

2. COOK THE LEEKS. Preheat a skillet over medium heat and add the leeks, 1 tablespoon of the olive oil, and a big pinch of kosher salt. Cook until tender, 10 to 12 minutes. Transfer the leeks to a cutting board and roughly chop, then transfer to a small bowl and stir in the vinegar.

3. ROLL OUT THE DOUGH. Let the chilled dough sit at room temperature until slightly softened but still cool to the touch, 10 to 15 minutes. Sprinkle a large sheet of parchment paper with flour and place the disc of dough on top. Using firm, even pressure, roll the dough out into a rough round shape about 14 inches (35 cm) in diameter. Use a small knife to trim the dough into a neat round about 13 inches (33 cm) wide. Transfer the dough and parchment to a sheet pan and refrigerate.

4. SLICE THE KABOCHA. Cut the kabocha into pieces ¼ inch (6 mm) thick and no more than 2 inches (5 cm) long. Sprinkle with ½ teaspoon kosher salt, the remaining 2 tablespoons olive oil, and the black pepper and toss to coat.

5. SHAPE AND BAKE THE TART. Remove the pan of dough from the fridge. Spread the cooled cooked leeks evenly over

MAKES ONE 12-INCH (30 CM) TART
SERVES 6

30 MINUTES ACTIVE TIME
60 MINUTES INACTIVE TIME

2 cups (400 g) sliced leek coins,
    ³⁄₈ inch (1 cm) thick (from about
    3 medium leeks), well rinsed
3 tablespoons (45 g) olive oil
Kosher salt
1 tablespoon (15 g) rice vinegar
Pâte Brisée (page 164), chilled
All-purpose flour, for rolling the
    dough
1 pound (455 g) kabocha squash
    (about ½ medium squash;
    see tip #1), halved and seeded
¼ teaspoon freshly ground black
    pepper
1 large egg white (30 g), lightly
    whisked
¼ cup (35 g) hulled pumpkin seeds
Barley Tea Lacquer (recipe follows)
Flaky sea salt

the surface of the dough, right up to the edges (see tip #2). Use your fingers to crimp the edges of the tart, forming a border 1 inch (2.5 cm) wide. Arrange the kabocha slices on top, fanning them tightly together so they overlap. (At this point, if you'd like, you can freeze the tart and bake it later; see tip #3.) Brush the edges of the crust with the egg white and press the pumpkin seeds onto the crust. Transfer to the oven and bake until the kabocha is sizzling and the crust is golden and fragrant, about 40 minutes.

6. GLAZE THE SQUASH. Remove from the oven and let the tart cool for 20 minutes. Use a pastry brush to paint the lacquer onto the squash. Sprinkle flaky sea salt all over. Cut into wedges and serve.

TIP 1 —*If you can't find kabocha at your grocery store or farmers' market, try pumpkin, butternut squash, acorn squash, or sweet potato, and cut into shapes of similar size. (Peel the pumpkin and butternut squash first!)*

TIP 2 —*When you fold or twist up the edges of the dough to make a border, the dough will seal in the spread (think stuffed-crust pizza).*

TIP 3 —*After adding the squash, slide the tart onto a cardboard cake round and tightly wrap the parcel in plastic wrap. Bake the tart right from frozen, transferring it to a parchment-lined half-sheet pan and applying the egg-white wash and pumpkin seeds right before baking.*

Barley Tea Lacquer

IN A SMALL SAUCEPAN, bring the barley tea, vinegar, honey, coconut aminos, and fish sauce to a boil over medium heat. Continue to boil until slightly thickened and reduced, 5 to 7 minutes. Strain the lacquer into a small jar or dish. The lacquer can be made up to 1 week in advance and stored in a jar in the fridge.

MAKES ⅓ CUP (80 G)

5 MINUTES ACTIVE TIME

2 teaspoons (1 or 2 tea bags) roasted barley tea, like mugicha
⅓ cup (80 g) rice vinegar
¼ cup (80 g) honey
1 tablespoon (15 g) coconut aminos or soy sauce
1 teaspoon fish sauce

MUSHROOM, CHEDDAR, AND APPLE TART

Sometimes a dish is so delicious, I can't help but reverse-engineer it into a handheld pastry. (I tend to think that most food can be improved with the addition of buttery dough.) Several years ago at a wine bar in Greenpoint, Brooklyn, called Achilles Heel, I ate a warm mushroom salad, scattered over brothy grains and topped with crunchy slices of apple. The salad was unpretentious and direct, but still surprising—the kind of effortless food their former chef Desiree Tuttle is known for.

Here, the mixture of temperatures—sizzling mushrooms, warm cheddar custard, and crisp, cool apple slices—heightens the pleasure. Using only cremini mushrooms feels a bit boring given the vast array of both cultivated and wild mushrooms available. Frilly, meaty maitake and oyster mushrooms, and the miniature, cute-as-a-button shimeji varieties, all of which are sold in many grocery stores, especially Asian grocers (where the prices are often better, too), are wonderful here. Aim for visual abundance. If you're traveling or gifting the tart, package the apples in a separate container, then garnish it with them right when you're ready to eat.

MAKES ONE 10-INCH (25 CM)
FLUTED TART
SERVES 6 TO 8

45 MINUTES ACTIVE TIME
1 HOUR INACTIVE TIME

Seeded Rye Dough (recipe follows)
1 large egg white, lightly whisked
1 tablespoon (15 g) olive oil
1 pound (455 g) mixed mushrooms,
    thickly sliced or broken down into
    2-inch (5 cm) pieces
2 shallots, sliced lengthwise into
    thin spears
½ teaspoon kosher salt

(ingredients continue)

1. **PREHEAT THE OVEN AND PREP THE PAN.** Preheat the oven to 375°F (190°C). Lightly mist a 10-inch (25 cm) fluted tart pan with a removable bottom with cooking spray.

2. **SHAPE THE TART SHELL.** Make the dough as directed, and while it is still warm, transfer to the center of the tart pan. Using your hands and working quickly, smoosh the hot dough over the bottom and up the sides of the tart pan. Pinch off the excess dough with your fingertips so the edges look neat and even. (Save the extra in case you need to patch the tart shell later.) Transfer the tart pan to the fridge to cool until the crust feels stiff, at least 5 to 10 minutes.

3. **BAKE THE TART SHELL.** Brush the egg white all over the tart shell. Prick the bottom all over with a fork. Bake until the edges are lightly golden and the center of the bottom is baked through but still slightly pale (the dough will look opaque and not

2 tablespoons (1 ounce/30 g)
  unsalted butter
¼ teaspoon ground black pepper
Cheddar Cream (recipe follows),
  at room temperature
½ crisp sweet-tart apple, such as
  Honeycrisp
1 teaspoon apple cider vinegar

TIP ——*In a rush to cool down your piping-hot mushrooms? In restaurants, line cooks have all kinds of clever ways to bring the heat of anything down as quickly as possible. Speed up the cooling process for caramelized onions, sautéed veggies, purees, beans, pasta, you name it, by spreading the food into a thin layer on a sheet pan or any wide flat surface. The steam will escape in a fraction of the time, which also reduces the chance of any harmful bacteria growth.*

sheer or greasy), 15 to 18 minutes. Remove from the oven and let cool completely. If there are any holes or cracks in the tart shell, patch with small pieces of raw tart scrap (no need to bake again here).

4. PARCOOK THE MUSHROOMS AND SHALLOTS. In your largest skillet, heat the olive oil over medium heat until shimmering. Add the mushrooms and shallots and stir to coat. Sprinkle in the salt and continue to cook, stirring infrequently, until the mushrooms have released most of their water, about 6 minutes. Do not overcook, as they will continue to roast in the oven. Remove from the heat and stir in the butter and pepper. Set aside to cool slightly (see tip).

5. ASSEMBLE AND BAKE THE TART. Spread the cheddar cream over the bottom of the tart shell. Pile the parcooked mushrooms and shallots on top. Slide the tart back into the oven and bake until the mushrooms are sizzling and the crust edges are deeply golden, about 15 minutes.

6. MEANWHILE, MARINATE THE APPLE. Slice the apple into slices that are slender but not floppy, just shy of ⅛ inch (2.5 mm). Transfer the slices to a small bowl and toss with the vinegar.

7. TOP THE TART. When the tart comes out of the oven, scatter the apple slices on top. Slice into 6 wedges and serve warm. Leftovers are good for 1 day and best at room temperature.

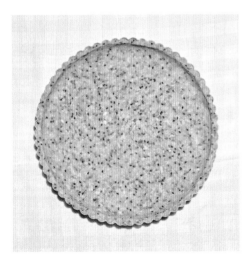

More Than Cake

Seeded Rye Dough

IN A SMALL POT, combine the butter, water, sugar, oil, and salt. Bring to a simmer over medium heat, add the seeds and all-purpose and rye flours, and remove from the heat. Stir vigorously with a spoon until a smooth ball forms, about 15 seconds. Remove from the pot and let cool briefly, about 5 minutes, before using. If making the dough in advance, let it cool completely, then tightly wrap in plastic wrap and refrigerate for up to 4 days. Allow the dough to sit at room temperature until pliable and soft before shaping in the pan.

MAKES ABOUT 12 OUNCES (350 G) DOUGH, ENOUGH FOR ONE 10-INCH (25 CM) TART

15 MINUTES ACTIVE TIME
5 MINUTES INACTIVE TIME

6 tablespoons (3 ounces/90 g) unsalted butter
3 tablespoons (45 g) water
1 tablespoon (15 g) sugar
1 tablespoon (15 g) vegetable oil
½ teaspoon kosher salt
3 tablespoons (about 30 g) mixed seeds, like sunflower, sesame, pumpkin and/or flax seeds
1 cup plus 2 tablespoons (135 g) all-purpose flour
3 tablespoons (25 g) rye flour

Cheddar Cream

The gooey, super-rich cheddar cream can be piped into the Sweet Onion and Sesame Gougères (page 300) or spread thinly in the Kabocha Galette (page 199) or the Lemony Squash Pizzettes (page 211), but it's also a delicious dip on its own, great for dunking batons of Apricot and Olive Focaccia (page 209).

SET THE YOLKS in a small heatproof bowl. In a small pot, bring the heavy cream and whole milk up to a simmer. Carefully stream the hot liquid over the yolks, whisking rapidly throughout. Pour the yolk mixture into the pot and stir over low heat until slightly thickened, about 5 minutes. Add the cheddar and stir until smooth. Press a piece of plastic wrap on top to prevent a skin from forming as it cools. The cream can be made up to 3 days in advance; store in an airtight container in the refrigerator.

MAKES 1¼ CUPS (275 G)

5 MINUTES ACTIVE TIME
30 MINUTES INACTIVE TIME

2 large egg yolks (40 g), at room temperature
¼ cup (60 g) heavy cream
¼ cup (60 g) whole milk
1 cup (115 g) grated cheddar cheese

OO-33?

As soon as my plane touches down in San Diego, I race up the 5 to Chino Farm in Rancho Santa Fe. Though it's rightfully famous for its dainty Mara Des Bois strawberries and bulging Valencia oranges, I always end up with surprising extra treats— passion fruits on the vine, a four-foot-tall cardoon frond, burgundy Brussels sprouts the size of a chickpea, speckled chicories, and so much more.

APRICOT AND OLIVE FOCACCIA

This focaccia couldn't be easier to make, and you'll go crazy for its crisp, well-oiled crust and tender, chewy insides. The key is a nice long stretch of time: make the pre-ferment at least 8 hours before baking, or age it in the fridge for 1 to 4 full days for a more low-and-slow flavor. Additionally, resting the dough overnight in your refrigerator allows it to work in a little more flavor before baking, while giving you control over the timing of the final bake.

A sheet pan of fully proofed, dimpled focaccia is an invitation to get creative. I love a bounty of dried fruits and olives in my bread, but they can get desiccated in a hot oven. Here, dried apricots and black olives soak overnight in verjus, the green juice of unripe grapes. The result is a full-flavored, sweet-and-sour topping that can withstand the hottest temperature of your oven.

1. MAKE THE PRE-FERMENT. In a large bowl, sprinkle the yeast over the warm water and let sit for 2 minutes. Add the whole wheat flour and mix with a spoon. Cover with plastic wrap and leave at room temperature for at least 8 hours, and up to 12 hours. Transfer to the refrigerator until ready to use; it can be held refrigerated for up to 4 days.

2. MAKE THE FOCACCIA DOUGH. In a large bowl, combine the pre-ferment, warm water, honey, and yeast and let sit for 4 minutes, or until the yeast looks puffy. Add the all-purpose flour and 2 tablespoons (30 g) of the olive oil. Mix well with a wooden spoon until no dry flour is visible, about 2 minutes. The mixture will be shaggy and sticky. Cover with a towel and let sit for 15 minutes. Add the kosher salt and mix again with a spoon or your hands until incorporated, another 2 minutes. Cover again with a towel and let rest for 30 minutes.

3. STRETCH AND FOLD THE DOUGH to build strength. Dip your fingertips in a little water and gently lift one edge of the dough to stretch and pull it upward, then fold it over into the center. Rotate the bowl and continue to lift and stretch the edges of the focaccia, rotating the bowl as needed, until the dough feels

MAKES ONE 12-INCH (30 CM)
FOCACCIA
SERVES 6 TO 8

PRE-FERMENT:
5 MINUTES ACTIVE TIME
8 HOURS INACTIVE TIME

DOUGH:
30 MINUTES ACTIVE TIME
12 HOURS INACTIVE TIME

FOR THE PRE-FERMENT

¼ teaspoon active dry yeast
⅓ cup (80 g) warm water
½ cup (60 g) whole wheat flour

FOR THE FOCACCIA

1 cup plus 3 tablespoons (280 g)
   warm water
1 tablespoon (20 g) honey
1 teaspoon active dry yeast

(ingredients continue)

2¾ cups (340 g) all-purpose flour
¼ cup (60 g) olive oil
1½ teaspoons kosher salt
Verjus-Soaked Apricots and Olives
   (recipe follows)
Flaky sea salt and cracked black
   pepper

bouncy and won't stretch any further. Cover and let rest for 30 more minutes.

4. DO TWO MORE SETS OF STRETCHES AND FOLDS. Repeat the stretch-and-fold process two more times, pausing for 30 minutes after the first set and letting the dough rest for 30 minutes after the second one, for an additional 1 hour of rest time. Cover the bowl tightly with plastic wrap, or transfer to an airtight container, and refrigerate for at least 8 hours, or up to 48 hours.

5. PREHEAT THE OVEN AND PREPARE THE PAN. When ready to bake, position a rack in the center of the oven and preheat the oven to 450°F (230°C). Coat a sheet pan with the remaining 2 tablespoons olive oil plus a generous misting of cooking spray.

6. BAKE THE FOCACCIA. Remove the dough from the fridge and transfer to the oiled sheet pan. Flip the dough over so it is evenly coated in the oil. Use greased fingertips to poke, press, and stretch the dough to about 12 inches (30 cm) wide and 14 inches (35 cm) long.

7. ADD THE TOPPINGS. Just before baking, drain the apricots and olives, pressing them into the surface of the focaccia. Transfer to the oven and bake until golden and fragrant, about 25 minutes. Remove from the oven and immediately slide the focaccia out onto a cooling rack. Sprinkle generously with flaky salt and cracked black pepper.

Verjus-Soaked Apricots and Olives

If you can't find verjus, substitute 1 cup (240 g) unsweetened apple or grape juice, plus ⅓ cup (85 g) apple cider vinegar.

MAKES 2 CUPS (575 G)

5 MINUTES ACTIVE TIME
8 HOURS INACTIVE TIME

½ bottle (325 ml) verjus
12 dried apricots
1 cup (180 g) oil-cured black olives
   or brine-cured green olives, pitted

IN A POT, gently warm the verjus over low heat. Add the apricots and olives and remove from the heat. Let cool completely, cover, and let sit for at least 8 hours, or overnight.

LEMONY SQUASH PIZZETTES

These individually sized pizzettes bake more quickly than a whole sheet pan of focaccia (see page 209) and have crispy edges and tender insides. Top the pizzettes with a blanket of marinated raw zucchini, which hides a core of roasted lemon slices, crushed hazelnuts, and torn shiso.

The pizzettes taste clean and summery, nice with coffee and a fried egg in the morning, or, in the afternoon, sliced into mini wedges and dunked into a brothy soup. Because of the generous amount of olive oil in the recipe, these little snacks won't dry out overnight. To reheat, slide into a toaster oven or under the broiler and heat until the zucchini is sizzling again.

1. **MAKE THE PRE-FERMENT.** In a large bowl, mix the yeast and warm water and let sit for 2 minutes. Stir in the flour with a spoon. Cover with plastic wrap and leave at room temperature for at least 8 hours, and up to 12 hours. Transfer to the refrigerator until ready to use; it can be held refrigerated for up to 4 days.

2. **SLICE THE SQUASH AND LEMON.** Use a mandoline or a sharp knife to slice the squash crosswise into slices about the thickness of a stack of three quarters, or a scant ¼ inch (5 mm). Slice the lemon crosswise very thin, about half as thick as the squash, and pick out the seeds. Set aside.

3. **MAKE THE DOUGH.** In a large bowl, combine the warm water, pre-ferment, honey, and yeast and let sit for 4 minutes, or until the yeast looks puffy. Add the all-purpose flour and 2 tablespoons (30 g) of the olive oil. Mix well with your hands or a wooden spoon until no dry flour is visible, about 2 minutes. The mixture will be shaggy and sticky. Cover with a towel and let sit for 15 minutes. Add the kosher salt and mix again with the spoon or your hands until incorporated, another 2 minutes. Cover again with a towel and let the dough rest for 30 minutes.

4. **STRETCH AND FOLD THE DOUGH** to build strength. Dip your fingertips in a little water and gently lift one edge of the dough to stretch and pull it upward and then fold it over into the

MAKES TWELVE 4-INCH (10 CM) PIZZETTES

PRE-FERMENT:
5 MINUTES ACTIVE TIME
8 HOURS INACTIVE TIME

DOUGH:
30 MINUTES ACTIVE TIME
2 HOURS INACTIVE TIME

FOR THE PRE-FERMENT

¼ teaspoon active dry yeast
⅓ cup (80 g) warm water
½ cup (60 g) all-purpose flour

FOR THE PIZZETTES

4 to 5 small summer squash or zucchini (or a mix)
1 lemon or Meyer lemon
1¼ cups (280 g) water, at room temperature
1 tablespoon (20 g) honey
1 teaspoon active dry yeast

(ingredients continue)

3 cups (360 g) all-purpose flour

¼ cup (60 g) olive oil

1 teaspoon kosher salt

Flaky sea salt

3 tablespoons (25 g) hazelnuts, lightly toasted, then chopped

4 large shiso leaves, sliced into thin ribbons

Freshly cracked black pepper

TIP ——*Rather than adding more flour to the dough mixture, I like to shape this sticky dough by wetting my hands first with water. Creating and sustaining tension is everything in getting a nice, even shape to the bread (which results in a crisp, smooth crust after it bakes). Too much water sprinkled on the work surface makes it impossible to shape the dough into balls; too little water will cause the dough to leave gluey trails on the counter. Experiment with what works best on your kitchen surface while you get the hang of the motion.*

center. Rotate the bowl and continue to lift and stretch the edges of the dough, rotating the bowl as needed, until the dough feels bouncy and won't stretch any further. Cover and let rest for 30 more minutes.

5. DO TWO MORE SETS OF STRETCHES AND FOLDS. Repeat the stretch-and-fold process two more times, pausing for 30 minutes after the first set and letting the dough rest 30 minutes after the second one, for an additional 1 hour of rest time.

6. PREHEAT THE OVEN AND PREP THE PANS. When the dough has just 30 more minutes rest time, preheat the oven to 450°F (230°C). To bake in batches, mist two half-sheet pans generously with cooking spray.

7. SALT THE SQUASH. Divide the squash in half and set half of it aside for garnishing. Pat the other half dry with a towel and sprinkle with flaky sea salt.

8. SHAPE THE PIZZETTES. Turn out the dough to a clean tabletop sprinkled with water (see tip). Divide the dough into 12 portions using a bench scraper or knife. Gently shape the dough by tucking the corners of each piece under itself and rotating the palm of your hand to shape it into a taut ball. Transfer 6 balls to each half-sheet pan. Let rest for 10 minutes, then use greased fingertips to gently poke and press each piece into a disc 3 to 4 inches (8 to 10 cm) wide. If the dough starts bouncing back, let it rest for 5 minutes before trying to stretch it further.

9. TOP THE PIZZETTES. Depress the centers of each pizzette with your fingertips to form a nest. Arrange the salted sliced squash and the lemon slices, dividing them evenly, in a tightly fanned arrangement, like a hand of playing cards, in the center of each. Drizzle the remaining 2 tablespoons olive oil on top of the squash/lemon fans.

10. BAKE THE PIZZETTES. Transfer to the oven and bake until the squash is sizzling, about 15 minutes. Remove from the oven and immediately transfer to a cooling rack. Sprinkle the squash with the crushed hazelnuts, shiso ribbons, more flaky sea salt, and pepper. Cover the pizzette centers with the reserved raw squash. Serve immediately.

BATHED PIE

Pan bagnat—a well-loved sandwich eaten across Provence—is a messy, dripping, divine thing. A large loaf of crusty bread, split and drenched in olive oil, vinegar, and the juices of other succulent ingredients, like ripe tomatoes, is weighted down, then sliced and devoured, usually standing up.

This deep-dish pie, carefully layered with Provençal-inspired ingredients like olives, tomatoes, garlic, and olive oil, is a sturdier version of this "bathed" sandwich of coastal France. Here, chopped vegetables, sliced tomatoes, and whole eggs are swaddled in a tissue-thin strudel pastry that's surprisingly resilient. It's the kind of snack you could drop into a tote stuffed with fizzy water and towels and take to the beach, no plates or utensils needed.

Though this dish should be made year-round, in the early summer, scour the markets for new potatoes, fresh eggs, frilly greens, young garlic, and ripe tomatoes.

1. **MIX THE DOUGH.** In a stand mixer fitted with the dough hook, mix the bread flour, water, olive oil, salt, and baking powder on medium-low speed until combined, 3 to 4 minutes. (If mixing by hand, knead all the ingredients until a smooth ball forms, 7 to 8 minutes.) Shape roughly into a ball, wrap in plastic wrap, and refrigerate for at least 30 minutes, or up to 2 days, to rest.

2. **PREP THE TOMATO.** Thinly slice the tomato into ¼-inch (6 mm) slices. Set the slices on a pan lined with paper towels. Sprinkle with ¼ teaspoon kosher salt and set aside.

3. **COOK THE POTATOES AND KALE.** Bring a small pot of water to a boil. Add 2 teaspoons kosher salt and the potatoes. Boil until the potatoes are very tender and the skins are splitting, about 10 minutes. Remove the potatoes with a slotted spoon or tongs and bring the water back up to a boil. Add the kale all at once and blanch (see tip #1) until just tender, about 2 minutes. Drain and let cool, then wring out excess moisture with your hands. Transfer to a cutting board and finely chop.

→

MAKES ONE 10-INCH (25 CM) TART
SERVES 8

DOUGH:
10 MINUTES ACTIVE TIME
30 MINUTES INACTIVE TIME

PIE:
45 MINUTES ACTIVE TIME
1½ HOURS INACTIVE TIME

FOR THE DOUGH

2 cups (240 g) bread flour
½ cup (120 g) water, at room
　temperature
¼ cup (60 g) olive oil
1 teaspoon kosher salt
¼ teaspoon baking powder

(ingredients continue)

1 large tomato

Kosher salt

2 small waxy potatoes, like Yukon
Gold or German Butterball

1 large bunch kale (such as lacinato),
midribs removed and leaves
roughly chopped

¼ cup (45 g) oil-cured black olives,
pitted and finely chopped

1 cup (90 g) finely grated hard salty
cheese, such as Parmesan or
pecorino

2 tablespoons (30 g) olive oil, plus
more for drizzling

¼ teaspoon freshly ground black
pepper

7 eggs (350 g)

1 head garlic, unpeeled

1 tablespoon (15 g) sugar

12 oil-packed anchovy fillets

Flaky sea salt

TIP 1 ——*Mix and match what you
have on hand, noting different cooking
times. Swiss chard, spinach, and
arugula need a brief 10- to 15-second
blanch. Tougher greens like kale,
cabbage, and dandelion greens
need 1 or 2 minutes longer in the
boiling water. The frizzy tops of root
vegetables like turnips, radishes, and
beets are delicious—just give them a
brief sauté in olive oil to soften before
adding.*

TIP 2 ——*For the best reheating
experience, gently toast pie slices in
a dry skillet over low heat until the
bottom is firm and the filling slightly
warm to the touch, about 8 minutes.*

4. **SEASON THE FILLING LAYERS.** Use your thumbs to break apart the cooled potatoes into small dice–size chunks and set aside. In a medium bowl, combine the chopped kale, chopped olives, ½ cup (45 g) of the grated cheese, the olive oil, pepper, one of the eggs, and ½ teaspoon kosher salt. Taste and add more kosher salt if necessary.

5. **PREHEAT THE OVEN AND PREP THE PAN.** When ready to assemble and bake the pie, preheat the oven to 400°F (200° C). Coat a half-sheet pan with cooking spray.

6. **STRETCH AND SHAPE THE DOUGH.** Remove the dough from the refrigerator. Lightly grease a clean countertop with cooking spray. Using your fingertips, firmly push the dough outward, flattening and stretching it as you go. If it starts to bounce back, let it rest for several minutes, then resume stretching. Don't stress if small tears form; just keep stretching, tugging, and pressing the dough until it is thin but not transparent, like a thick linen curtain. Aim for a square of pastry about 24 inches (61 cm) across.

7. **FILL THE PIE.** Carefully pick up the stretched pastry and drape it into the prepared sheet pan. Spread the greens filling into a 10-inch (25 cm) round centered on top of the pastry. Use the back of a spoon to create 6 egg-shaped divots in the filling. Arrange the crumbled potatoes around the rims of the divots, creating a barrier from one divot to the next. Crack an egg into a small dish and pour it into a divot, holding back on adding all the egg white in case there is overflow (save the excess egg white for an egg wash). Repeat until all 6 eggs are nested into the tart. Sprinkle the remaining ½ cup (45 g) cheese on top of the eggs. Pat the tomatoes dry and shingle them on top to completely cover the surface.

8. **CLOSE THE PIE.** Set the unpeeled head of garlic in the middle of the pie. Pick up the edges of the pastry and drape them around the garlic, like a blanket; artfully arrange and fold the layers to create a ruffly, dramatic exterior, leaving the garlic exposed. Brush the exterior of the pastry with the lightly whisked reserved extra egg whites and sprinkle the sugar on top.

9. **BAKE THE PIE.** Bake for 40 minutes. Remove from the oven and carefully press the anchovies on top of the pastry to adhere. Return the pie to the oven and bake until deeply golden and crisp, another 10 minutes. Remove from the oven and drizzle the head of garlic with olive oil. Let the pie cool, then cut into 8 slices. The pie will hold for 2 days, wrapped well and chilled (see tip #2).

A rainbow's worth of vivid ingredients—tomato, greens, potato, egg, cheese, and more—are carefully layered into a tissue-thin sheet of pastry, which is surprisingly resilient. The pastry cradles its insides like a softly draping blanket, while baking up to satisfying crispness.

Baking with Vegetables

ELEGANT

223 Panna Cotta with Grated Melon

225 Caramel Chocolate Chip Bombe
227 Salted Caramel Sauce
228 Chocolate Shards

229 Cheesecake and Plum Syrup
230 Plum Syrup

233 Star Anise and Vanilla Bean Crème Brûlée

235 Rose Water and Mezcal Flan
238 Condensed Milk

239 Chamomile Puff Crown
242 Chamomile Cream
243 Vanilla Craquelin

244 Chocolate and Earl Grey Mousse
246 Chocolate and Earl Grey Ganache
248 Feuilletine

249 Adzuki Bean and Brown Butter Pie

DESSERTS

Sometimes people ask me why I became a pastry chef rather than a "chef." Though I don't care much for titles—and I truly love cooking as much as baking—there is an emotional reason why I gravitated toward pastry exclusively in my professional life.

If people dismiss the dessert menu, or skip over the baking section of a bookstore, the implication is that sweets are not essential to their eating habits. I like this challenge of having to prove why my work is necessary. To me, dessert indicates a shift beyond simple calories and nutrition; dessert underlines the quest for pure pleasure, sharing, and coming together. Desserts mark family traditions and spread delight in a way that no other kind of dish can. This is something I think people really need—it's not optional.

Consider the exhilaration of an unveiled flan, caramel reflecting the dancing light; spoons clinking over a bowl of chocolate mousse; the easy glamour of sparkling crème brûlée or a tall cheesecake. Even if we don't remember the exact dish years later, we remember what counts: how we felt, how we made others feel, flashes of energy dancing through a room.

We tend to leave the showstopping desserts to the work of professionals, which is fair (and keeps pastry chefs employed!). But even the most complex-seeming desserts can be surprisingly straightforward and peaceful to mix and assemble, as long as you take your time and approach each component with thought. So next time you have something to celebrate, don't leave fancy desserts to the realm of restaurant dining rooms. Dole out the joy and the excess and the splendor right in your home.

PANNA COTTA WITH GRATED MELON

Panna cotta, so sexy in its simplicity of form, with its brevity of ingredients and slippery mouthfeel, is one of the more profound ways to enjoy extraordinary cream. If you compare the amount of time invested in any new pastry project to the showstopping power of the recipe's results, panna cotta has to be the most rewarding, yet lowest lift, of all recipes.

The key to panna cotta—Italian for "cooked cream"—is sourcing rich, sweet, fat-cap-topped heavy cream. For that, you'll want to seek out local dairy farms, instead of reaching into the supermarket dairy shelf. If you can find delicious cream, then the handful of other ingredients and, really, the recipe itself are almost an afterthought.

Most of the work happens just out of frame, while gelatin silently thickens barely sweetened cream into a wobbly form. You want to aim for that liminal place between solid and liquid—so you won't be able to unmold these panna cottas onto a plate. So I prefer to set the panna cotta in a striking dish or set of glasses, where the surface can be showered with any number of toppings. Any ripe fruit can share a spoon with panna cotta, but grated raw honeydew melon adds drenched, shaggy texture and honeyed sweetness, and a final lashing of vinegar perks the whole dish right up.

1. **BLOOM THE GELATIN.** If using sheet gelatin, fill a medium bowl with ice cubes, then cover with water. Slip the gelatin sheets in and let sit until fully softened, about 5 minutes. If using powdered gelatin, put in a small dish containing 1½ tablespoons of water and let sit for 5 minutes.

2. **MEANWHILE, MAKE THE VANILLA SUGAR.** Use a small sharp knife to halve the vanilla bean lengthwise, pry open the halves, and use the knife to scrape the vanilla seeds out into a small saucepan. Add the sugar and kosher salt and massage the seeds into the sugar/salt with the tips of your fingers. Add the spent vanilla pod to the pan.

$\rightarrow$

MAKES ONE 6-INCH (15 CM)
FAMILY-STYLE PANNA COTTA

20 MINUTES ACTIVE TIME
3 HOURS INACTIVE TIME

1½ sheets (3.75 g) silver-strength
  gelatin or 1½ teaspoons
  unflavored gelatin powder
1 vanilla bean
¼ cup (50 g) sugar
½ teaspoon kosher salt, plus more
  to taste
2 cups (480 g) heavy cream

(ingredients continue)

½ honeydew melon
1½ tablespoons (20 g) fruity vinegar
Flaky sea salt
10 to 12 fresh herb leaves, like lemon
    verbena, mint, or Thai basil

TIP 1 ——*For a silky-smooth, restaurant-quality panna cotta, try to minimize the use of a whisk, which will foam up the cream and create tiny air bubbles. If you still see some bubbles on the surface of your panna cotta, those can be easily squashed by either pressing the underside of a wet spoon on the surface or lightly rapping the container on a counter.*

TIP 2 ——*To prevent the vanilla bean flecks from sinking to the bottom of your panna cotta, wait until the gelatin is partially activated and the cream looks thickened before pouring the base into the bowl or pie plate. This will suspend the vanilla bean particles prior to refrigeration.*

3. **DISSOLVE THE SUGAR.** Add just enough cream to cover the vanilla sugar (about ½ cup/120 g), keeping the rest of the cream cold. Set the saucepan over medium-low heat and stir with a spatula until the mixture is hot and steaming. Do not bring up to a simmer or scald.

4. **ADD THE GELATIN.** Remove the cream from the heat. Wring out the excess water from the gelatin sheets (but keep the ice bath available; or prepare an ice bath now if you used powdered gelatin) and add it to the pot. If using gelatin powder, scrape the whole mixture into the pot. Whisk rapidly to dissolve. Add the remaining cold heavy cream and use a spatula to stir and combine (see tip #1). Strain through a fine-mesh sieve into a clean 1-quart (1 L) container. Nestle this container into the reserved ice bath.

5. **PARTIALLY SET THE GELATIN.** Gently stir the panna cotta base, being sure to get into the corners of your container where the gelatin may set up more quickly. Taste the mixture again and add more kosher salt if needed. Once the mixture looks viscous and thickened (see tip #2) but not set all the way, after about 30 minutes, pour it into a shallow bowl or pie plate 6 inches (15 cm) wide. Refrigerate uncovered for at least 2 to 3 hours before serving; the dish can be stored, wrapped tightly, for up to 3 days.

6. **PREPARE THE MELON.** Remove the seeds and cut the honeydew melon into large wedges. Use the largest hole on a box grater to grate the melon into a medium bowl. Stir in the vinegar.

7. **SERVE AND GARNISH.** Spoon the melon mixture onto the surface of the chilled panna cotta. Add a pinch of flaky sea salt and the torn herbs and serve immediately.

CARAMEL CHOCOLATE CHIP BOMBE

In my tiny apartment kitchen, I rarely invest in single-use appliances, like an ice cream machine—even though I love making ice cream! Fortunately, semifreddos and frozen parfaits are an elegant compromise, and as amenable to flavor variation as ice cream itself—no bulky equipment required.

I love any cross section that reveals lots of visual secrets—like the crisp shards of paper-thin chocolate, inspired by one of my favorite ice cream flavors, stracciatella.

1. **PREP THE MOLD.** Drape a large piece of plastic wrap over a deep ramen bowl (or similar; see tip) and press it in tightly to fit. There should be plenty of plastic overhang. Set aside in the freezer.

2. **MAKE THE WHIPPED CREAM.** In a large wide bowl, whisk the heavy cream until it holds a very stiff peak, 4 to 5 minutes. (You can also do this with a handheld mixer or in a stand mixer.) Keep chilled.

3. **MAKE THE CREAM CHEESE MIXTURE.** Place the cream cheese in a medium bowl and set aside. In a small heatproof bowl set over a pot containing 1 inch (2.5 cm) of barely simmering water, whisk together the egg yolks, sugar, rum, vanilla, and kosher salt. Then continue to whisk constantly until the mixture feels warm to the touch and the crystals of sugar and salt have melted, 3 to 4 minutes. Remove the bowl from the heat and continue to whisk until the mixture is at room temperature, about 2 minutes. Pour this mixture over the cream cheese and work it with a spatula until smooth. (This can also be done with the paddle attachment in a stand mixer.)

4. **MAKE THE SEMIFREDDO.** Pull the whipped cream out of the refrigerator and pour the cream cheese mixture over it. Using a large spatula and spare, sweeping motions, fold the mixture completely into the whipped cream. Drizzle ½ cup (125 g) of the chilled caramel sauce on top and fold 4 or 5 times, then crunch the

MAKES ONE BOMBE 5 INCHES
(12.5 CM) DEEP AND 8 INCHES
(20 CM) WIDE
SERVES 8

25 MINUTES ACTIVE TIME
4 HOURS INACTIVE TIME

1½ cups (360 g) cold heavy cream
4 ounces (110 g) cream cheese,
    cubed, at room temperature
60 g egg yolks (from 3 eggs)
1 tablespoon (15 g) sugar
1 tablespoon (15 g) rum or bourbon
1 teaspoon vanilla extract
½ teaspoon kosher salt
Salted Caramel Sauce (recipe
    follows), chilled
Chocolate Shards (recipe follows),
    frozen
1 tablespoon (5 g) cocoa powder
Flaky sea salt

large shards of chocolate in your fist into smaller, cornflake-size chips, letting them fall into the bowl. Gently fold 3 more times to incorporate.

5. **FREEZE THE MIXTURE.** Remove the lined bowl from the freezer. Pour the mixture into the bowl. Pull the wings of excess plastic wrap over the top to cover and freeze until the bombe feels very firm, 3 to 4 hours.

6. **SLICE AND SERVE.** Tug the plastic wrap out of the bowl (you may have to run the underside of the bowl under hot water to loosen the plastic) and invert onto a cutting board. Peel off the plastic wrap and discard. Dust the bombe with the cocoa powder sifted through a tea strainer. Use a hot clean knife to portion 8 wedges of the bombe into pre-frozen bowls. Add a drizzle of the reserved caramel sauce on top of each slice. Sprinkle the surface with flaky sea salt. Serve immediately.

TIP —— *Look for a deep, not-too-wide bowl to mold your bombe, like the kind you eat ramen out of. Shallower bowls won't give you the same height or drama, though they will work. Your baking workhorses—like cake and Bundt pans—are great options, too.*

VARIATIONS

To make an ice cream cake, press an 8-inch (20 cm) round of Olive Oil Cake (page 117) or squishy Vanilla Sponge Cake (page 112) onto the top of the bombe before chilling.

For even more pronounced marbling, drizzle ½ cup (125 g) Cocoa Gloss (page 82) after you fold in the caramel sauce.

Salted Caramel Sauce

IN A SMALL POT, bring the honey, butter, and dark brown sugar to a boil and simmer until slightly reduced, about 2 minutes. Stream in the heavy cream and whisk vigorously until emulsified. Bring back to a simmer and cook for 3 to 4 more minutes, swirling the pot occasionally. Remove from the heat and stir in the kosher salt. Let cool completely, about 30 minutes. The caramel can be refrigerated in an airtight container for up to 3 weeks.

$\rightarrow$

MAKES 1 CUP (250 G)

10 MINUTES ACTIVE TIME
30 MINUTES INACTIVE TIME

¼ cup (80 g) honey
4 tablespoons (2 ounces/60 g) unsalted butter
3 tablespoons (45 g) dark brown sugar
¼ cup plus 2 tablespoons (90 g) heavy cream
½ teaspoon kosher salt

Chocolate Shards

MAKES 105 GRAMS

10 MINUTES ACTIVE TIME
20 MINUTES ACTIVE TIME

½ cup (90 g) dark chocolate chips
1 tablespoon (15 g) coconut oil

1. MELT THE CHOCOLATE. Bring 1 inch (2.5 cm) of water up to a bare simmer in a small pot. Combine the chocolate chips and coconut oil in a small heatproof bowl and set over the pot. Stir occasionally until the chocolate is melted and glossy, about 3 minutes.

2. MAKE THE SHARDS. Pour the mixture out onto a 12-by-16-inch (30 by 40 cm) piece of parchment or a silicone baking mat and spread very thin using an offset spatula. Refrigerate until brittle, about 20 minutes. Peel the parchment off the chocolate sheet. Break the chocolate into large shards. Keep frozen until ready to use.

CHEESECAKE AND PLUM SYRUP

The components of an elegant plated dessert should have unexpected contrasts in texture, temperature, and acidity in order to create balance and harmony in the perfect final bite. A dessert's aesthetic appeal should play around with gravity, proportion, and movement while offering beguiling simplicity.

Keep these tenets in mind, like a memo tacked onto the bulletin board of your brain, especially with seemingly basic desserts like cheesecake. This cheesecake looks sleek and confident on the plate and tastes so elegant, with just a lashing of fruit syrup and balsamic vinegar—no crust needed.

The sunset-hued fruit syrup can shift depending on the season: ballet-slipper-pink rhubarb syrup in the spring; amber peach or nectarine syrups in the summer; lollipop hues of plum, fig, and cranberry into the fall.

1. PREHEAT THE OVEN. Preheat the oven to 300°F (150°C). Drape a saddle of parchment paper into an 8-inch (20 cm) loaf pan (see tip #1) and lightly mist with cooking spray.

2. MIX THE CHEESECAKE BASE. In a food processor, combine the cubed cream cheese and sugar and pulse until the mixture is combined. (The base can also be made in a stand mixer with the paddle attachment, scraping the bowl with a spatula after each addition.) Add the sour cream, eggs, kosher salt, vanilla extract, and almond extract and blend until smooth and glossy, about 2 minutes. Taste and add more kosher salt if needed.

3. PREP THE STEAMING PAN. In a kettle or saucepan, heat 1 quart (1 L) water until steaming hot. Transfer the loaf pan to a deep baking dish or roasting pan with at least 2 to 3 inches (5 to 7.5 cm) of space on all sides. Pour the cheesecake base into the loaf pan. Cover the entire setup with a large piece of foil, crimping it along the sides to seal, then peel the foil back a few inches (about 7.5 cm) at one of the narrow ends of the steaming pan so you can add the hot water.

4. STEAM THE CHEESECAKE. Pull out an oven rack and set the baking dish on the rack. Slowly pour the steaming-hot

MAKES ONE 8-INCH (20 CM) CHEESECAKE
SERVES 10

30 MINUTES ACTIVE TIME
4 HOURS INACTIVE TIME

Three 8-ounce (225 g) bricks cream cheese (see tip #2), at room temperature, cubed
¾ cup (150 g) sugar
1 cup (240 g) sour cream, at room temperature
3 eggs (150 g), at room temperature
1½ teaspoons kosher salt, or more to taste
1 teaspoon vanilla extract
½ teaspoon almond extract
Plum Syrup (recipe follows)
2 tablespoons (30 g) balsamic vinegar
Flaky sea salt

water into the pan through the opening in the foil, to a depth of 1 inch (2.5 cm). Roll the foil back into place and pinch to seal completely. Slide the oven rack back in place and steam, untouched, for 90 minutes. Peel off the foil and give the pan a gentle shake; the surface should look puffed, and the custard should jiggle uniformly.

5. COOL AND CHILL. Once out of the oven, remove the foil covering the steaming pan and let the cheesecake cool completely in the water bath. Remove the loaf pan, wrap tightly in plastic wrap, and refrigerate for at least 1 to 2 hours to chill before serving.

6. SLICE AND PLATE. To portion, invert the loaf pan onto a cutting board and peel off the parchment paper. Slice the chilled cheesecake (see tip #3) into slabs 1 inch (2.5 cm) thick and transfer with an offset spatula to individual plates. Drizzle each slice liberally with plum syrup and balsamic vinegar; really go for it. Add a pinch of flaky sea salt to each and serve.

Plum Syrup

This fruit syrup recipe works extremely well with stone fruit: the boiling method extracts flavor from the pits, not just the flesh.

MAKES ½ CUP (125 G)

15 MINUTES ACTIVE TIME
30 MINUTES INACTIVE TIME

8 ounces (225 g) plums (3 or 4)
½ cup (100 g) sugar
1 tablespoon (15 g) fresh lemon juice

COARSELY CHOP THE PLUMS and transfer to a small pot (including the pits). Add just enough water to cover (about 1 cup/240 g) and the sugar. Simmer over medium heat until the water has reduced into a thick syrup and the color has been zapped from the fruit, about 30 minutes. The plums should look spent and the syrup neon pink. Remove from the heat and add the lemon juice. Strain through a fine-mesh sieve into a jar with a lid (don't press too hard on the fruit so you end up with a clear, non-cloudy syrup). Let cool completely, then seal and refrigerate until ready to use.

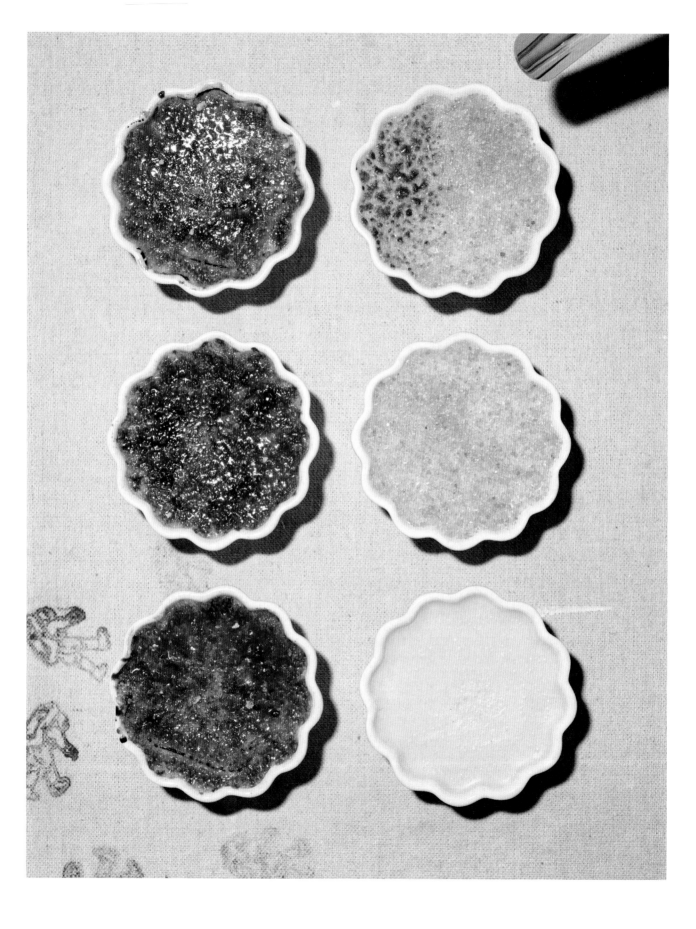

STAR ANISE AND VANILLA BEAN CRÈME BRÛLÉE

Crème brûlée is so much fun to eat. There's that cathartic tap-tap-tap of a spoon against the wide mirror of caramelized sugar, a private ice rink stretched over the unseen custard. Then the sugary shatter, and the spoon plunging into set cream. There's nothing quite like it.

Pure vanilla bean is the gold standard for crème brûlée, but a handful of toasted star anise pods adds the subtle warmth of black licorice. Once you master this recipe, the infusion possibilities are endless. Stalks of sturdy herbs like rosemary or lavender, a splash of extract or liqueur, a stick of cinnamon, or a few orange peels all add flavor without compromising the texture of the custard.

1. INFUSE THE CREAM. In a small pot, gently toast the star anise over medium-low heat until fragrant, about 4 minutes. Pour in the heavy cream and remove from the heat. Use a small sharp knife to halve the vanilla bean lengthwise, pry open the halves, and use the knife to scrape the vanilla seeds out into the cream. Add the spent pod to the pot. Let the cream steep for 20 to 30 minutes. (This can also be done the night before and kept chilled for a long, cool steep.)

2. PREHEAT THE OVEN. Preheat the oven to 275°F (135°C).

3. COOK THE CUSTARD. Remove the star anise and vanilla pod from the pot with a slotted spoon. Reheat the cream over medium-low heat until very hot but not simmering, 4 to 5 minutes. In a medium bowl, whisk together the yolks, granulated sugar, and kosher salt (see tip #1). While whisking the yolks constantly, stream in 1 cup (240 g) of the hot cream. Whisking constantly, slowly stream the warmed egg yolk mixture into the pot. (Tempering eggs into dairy: not unlike patting your head and rubbing your stomach at the same time, a solid motor skill to have!) Stir the custard constantly, just enough to melt the sugar and slightly reduce the bubbles on the surface, about 1 minute. (The custard will continue to thicken in the oven as it steams, so it will look thin and runny here.) Immediately

MAKES SIX 4-INCH-WIDE (10 CM) CRÈME BRÛLÉES

20 MINUTES ACTIVE TIME
3 TO 4 HOURS INACTIVE TIME

6 whole star anise
2 cups (480 g) heavy cream
½ vanilla bean
9 large egg yolks (180 g)
¼ cup (50 g) granulated sugar
½ teaspoon kosher salt
2 tablespoons (30 g) turbinado sugar
Flaky sea salt
Citric or malic acid (see tip #2)

TIP 1 —*Ever had a bowl jump away from you while trying to whisk its contents? Rest any mixing bowl on a kitchen towel for a grippy, no-slip surface.*

VARIATION

For a molten core, dab a teaspoon of chilled Chocolate and Earl Grey Ganache (page 246) in the bottom of each empty ramekin, then freeze for 20 minutes to set. Pour the custard on top and steam as directed.

pass the custard through a fine-mesh sieve into a large spouted measuring cup or 1-quart (1 L) pitcher.

4. SET UP THE WATER BATH. In a kettle or saucepan, heat 1 quart (1 L) water until steaming hot. Place 6 shallow ramekins (see tip #3) about 4 inches (10 cm) wide and 1½ inches (4 cm) deep in a 15-by-10-inch (38 by 25 cm) baking dish at least 3 inches (7.5 cm) deep. Portion ½ cup (about 100 g each) of custard into each ramekin. Crimp a large piece of foil on top of the baking dish, then pull back the foil at one corner of the pan to make an opening for pouring in the hot water. Place the baking dish on an oven rack and pour ½ inch (1.25 cm) of the hot water into the dish through the opening in the foil. Crimp the foil back on to seal.

5. STEAM THE CUSTARDS. Bake until the edges of the custards look set but the centers have a slight wobble, 23 to 27 minutes (the range is due to variations in vessel use, as well as the initial temperature of the custard before steaming). As it is better to err on the side of undercooking the custards, you can check the custards at 20 minutes by peeling back the foil slightly, peering inside, and giving one of the ramekins a light jab; press the foil back and continue to steam for another 5 minutes before checking again. (Alternatively, use an instant-read thermometer to check that the internal temperature is at 170°F/75°C.)

6. COOL AND CHILL. Remove from the oven and let the custards cool in the water bath before removing and patting dry; they should look firm but not curdled across the surface. Wrap the custards tightly and refrigerate for 2 to 3 hours, or up to 4 days.

7. TORCH THE SUGARY SURFACE. When ready to serve, preheat the broiler to high. Unwrap the custards and sprinkle 1 teaspoon of turbinado sugar directly on the surface of each. Rock the ramekin around with your hands, so the sugar sticks across every bit of the surface. Gently tap the ramekin on its side to remove any excess sugar (see tip #4). Place the ramekins on a small sheet pan and run under the broiler for 2 to 3 minutes—keep a close eye on them. (Alternatively, if you own a kitchen torch, hold it 4 inches/ 10 cm from the surface of each crème brûlée, moving the flame quickly, until deeply golden, about 30 seconds.) Sprinkle with flaky sea salt and just a few granules of citric acid. Serve immediately.

ROSE WATER AND MEZCAL FLAN

Oranges and mezcal envelop this traditional Mexican dessert in acid and smoke, while a few dashes of rose water extract add floral intrigue. My flan is very rich and dense, so proportion and balance become extra important in controlling the sweetness. Most flan caramels look far too anemic for my taste. I take my flan caramel far, to the point of smoking, for that essential bitterness that cuts through the custard. If you truly burn it (the bubbles will look like an iridescent oil slick), it's just a bit of sugar lost. Just clean the pan (see tip #1) and start over!

1. **COOK THE CARAMEL.** Have a clean dry 8-inch (20 cm) cake pan at the ready near the stove. In a small saucepan, combine the sugar, water, and syrup and bring to a boil over high heat. Swirl gently to combine. Continue to boil the mixture until the water has evaporated and the sugar begins to turn golden. Periodically swirl. When it reaches the color of honey, turn the heat down to medium-low. At the moment when the syrup just begins to smoke and is the color of root beer—after 5 to 6 minutes—remove from the heat.

2. **COAT THE FLAN PAN WITH CARAMEL.** Immediately pour the caramel into the cake pan. Carefully tilt and swirl the pan so the caramel coats the bottom and halfway up the sides of the mold. Set aside to cool completely; after about 20 minutes it should feel hard, like glass.

3. **PREHEAT THE OVEN.** Preheat the oven to 275°F (135°C).

4. **PREPARE THE CUSTARD.** In a large bowl, whisk together the condensed milk, egg yolks, whole egg, kosher salt, rose water, and orange zest (peel the zested orange and slice into wedges for the garnish). Set aside to let the custard steep with the orange zest for at least 15 minutes, then strain the custard through a fine-mesh sieve into the caramel-lined cake pan.

5. **SET UP THE WATER BATH.** In a kettle or pot, heat 1 quart (1 L) water until steaming hot. Set the cake pan in a

MAKES ONE 8-INCH (20 CM) FLAN
SERVES 8

30 MINUTES ACTIVE TIME
7 TO 8 HOURS INACTIVE TIME

FOR THE CARAMEL

¾ cup (150 g) sugar
¼ cup (60 g) water
3 tablespoons (60 g) glucose,
    light corn syrup, or rice syrup

FOR THE CUSTARD

2 cups (600 g) Condensed Milk
    (recipe follows)
4 large egg yolks (80 g)
1 egg (50 g)
½ teaspoon kosher salt
½ teaspoon rose water
    (see Resources, page 311)
Grated zest of 1 orange
2 tablespoons (30 g) mezcal, plus
    more (optional) for serving
Flaky sea salt

TIP 1 —— *Cooking sugar is a messy business; no amount of scrubbing will get rid of the caked-on sugar on the edges and bottom of your saucepan. Fill the pan with water—almost all the way to the top—and boil the water for 5 to 10 minutes. The sugar will loosen and dissolve in the water, leaving you with a practically spotless pot, and none of the frustrating cleanup.*

TIP 2 —— *Sometimes you'll find a thick layer of caramel still stuck to your pan, even after inverting it. Reheat on the stove or in the oven to melt and loosen the extra caramel.*

baking dish or pan that is both taller and wider than the cake pan. Add enough hot water to the baking dish to come no more than halfway up the side of the flan pan. Crimp foil over the baking dish to completely seal.

6. STEAM THE FLAN. Transfer to the oven and steam until the edges of the flan are firm and slightly pulling away from the sides of the pan but the center still looks slightly jiggly, 45 minutes to 1 hour. Check the doneness of the flan by peeling back the foil and giving the pan a jiggle; the wobble should be about 2 inches (5 cm) across right in the center. (Alternatively, use an instant-read thermometer to check that the internal temperature is 170°F/75°C.)

7. COOL, CHILL, AND SERVE. Remove from the oven and let the flan cool completely in the water bath. Remove the cake pan, wrap tightly in plastic wrap, and refrigerate for at least 4 hours or overnight to chill. Slice the reserved orange into big wedges. Invert the flan (see tip #2) onto a serving platter right before serving. Pour the mezcal over the top. Generously sprinkle with flaky sea salt and scatter the orange segments on top. Slice into 8 wedges and serve more mezcal, if desired.

Condensed Milk

Fresh whole milk is an essential component of flan, and for that reason I make my own condensed milk, with milk that I source and purchase, rather than buying a premade product. It's a lengthy extra step, but it requires hardly any hands-on time, and the smell of gently simmering milk wafting through your home is a sweet bonus.

MAKES 2⅓ CUPS (ABOUT 775 G)

10 MINUTES ACTIVE TIME
4 HOURS INACTIVE TIME

1 quart (950 g) whole milk
2 cups (400 g) sugar
1 vanilla bean

IN A LARGE POT, combine the milk and sugar. Use a small knife to halve the vanilla bean lengthwise, pry open the halves, and use the knife to scrape the vanilla seeds out into the pot of milk. Throw in the spent pod (and any others you've been saving up) and bring to a simmer over medium heat, stirring occasionally with a spoon, until almost reduced by half, or just over 2 cups (see tip). After about 3 hours, the mixture will look glossy, feel super thick, and smell fragrant. Let cool completely.

TIP——*It's always tough to eyeball "reduced by half," especially when dealing with large quantities of liquids. Have a pitcher and scale ready when the milk is getting close; weighing the mixture will give you the most accurate results. The final condensed milk should weigh 775 g total.*

More Than Cake

CHAMOMILE PUFF CROWN

Though I've written hundreds of menus for fancy fine-dining restaurants, you'd never know that most of my dishes are permutations of no more than a dozen core recipes that I've tweaked and fine-tuned over the years. Pâte à choux is a classic example of how one core technique stretches into an infinite number of ideas, flavors, and arrangements. I can hardly take credit for this iconic pastry, as the majority of choux recipes follow the same formula of cooking butter, milk, water, and flour in equal amounts. If you're new to choux preparations, this crown is an easy place to start, because, like a daisy chain, it's a series of small individual puffs linked together, nudged into any shape you desire. This cream puff crown would be a dramatic centerpiece for a brunch, picnic, or any daytime fete (or a genius birthday cake alternative).

1. MAKE THE RYE PUFFS. In a medium pot (see tip #1), combine the butter, water, milk, sugar, vanilla, and kosher salt and bring to a simmer over medium heat, about 3 minutes. Add the all-purpose and rye flours and vigorously beat the mixture with a wooden spoon or spatula until a ball of dough forms, pressing down with the spoon to work out any lumps.

2. COOK THE FLOUR PASTE. Continue to push, smear, and move the dough ball around, releasing steam from the paste. After 3 to 4 minutes, a gummy layer of starch should form on the bottom of the pot. Do not scrape this mixture up; let it build! Lift up the side of the dough with your spatula and let it drop back into the pot; it should feel supple and emulsified and pull cleanly away from the pot. Transfer the mixture to a stand mixer fitted with the paddle. Let the mixture cool for at least 15 to 20 minutes before adding the eggs. (Ideally, the dough should be completely cool before adding the eggs, which will result in a stronger and better rise in the oven.)

3. MEANWHILE, PREHEAT THE OVEN. Preheat the oven to 400°F (200°C).

→

MAKES 36 TO 40 SMALL PUFFS, ENOUGH FOR ONE 12-INCH (30 CM) CROWN PLUS EXTRA TO SNACK ON OR FREEZE FOR FUTURE TREATS

CHOUX:
20 MINUTES ACTIVE TIME;
1 HOUR INACTIVE TIME

ASSEMBLY:
20 MINUTES ACTIVE TIME

4 tablespoons (2 ounces/60 g)
 unsalted butter, cubed
¼ cup (60 g) water
¼ cup (60 g) whole milk
2 tablespoons (25 g) sugar
1 teaspoon vanilla extract
½ teaspoon kosher salt
½ cup (60 g) all-purpose flour
2 teaspoons rye flour

(ingredients continue)

4. ADD THE EGGS. With the mixer running on medium-low speed, drop in 1 of the eggs and paddle until combined. Turn off the mixer, scrape the bottom of the bowl well, and mix again. Repeat this process with the next egg and then assess the dough. The mixture will gradually loosen and increase in shine. For the final egg, whisk it up with a fork in a small dish and add it a tablespoon at a time, as you may not need it all (see tip #2). The dough should appear glossy and spool easily around the paddle. (If you turn the mixer off, the ribbon of dough should cling to the paddle for one beat and then slowly slump away.)

5. PORTION THE CHOUX. To bake in batches, line two half-sheet pans with parchment. Transfer the dough to a piping bag or large freezer bag, cutting a ¼-inch-wide (6 mm) opening, or use a small spoon. Pipe or spoon 2-teaspoon mounds of dough, 1 inch (2.5 cm) wide and spaced 2 inches (5 cm) apart, on the prepared sheet pans. You should be able to fit 18 to 20 puffs per sheet pan. You need at least 24 puffs for the crown (see tip #3).

6. BAKE THE CHOUX. Perch a round of frozen craquelin on top of each choux. Bake until the choux are puffed and deeply golden and feel hollow when picked up, 15 to 17 minutes. Remove from the oven and use a small paring knife to prick a small hole in the bottom of each puff, to allow steam to escape, and rest them on their sides to cool.

7. FILL THE CHOUX. Use a butter knife to widen the opening in the underside of each puff. Cup an upside-down puff in your hand and use the other hand to insert the piping bag filled with chamomile cream into the puff. Squeeze gently to fill the puff, using your other hand as a "scale" to feel it get heavier. Repeat until all the puffs are filled.

8. ASSEMBLE THE PUFF CROWN. Set the ring of a 12-inch (30 cm) springform pan on a platter or cardboard cake round. Use the ring as a guide and support as you arrange the puffs. Lay down the first ring of puffs flat side up. Stick a toothpick halfway into each puff, then stick a second layer of puffs on top, flat side down. Remove the springform ring when ready to serve. Garnish with the fresh chamomile and flaky sea salt. The choux are best within 3 to 4 hours of building.

→

2 to 3 eggs (100 to 150 g)
Vanilla Craquelin (recipe follows), frozen
Chamomile Cream (recipe follows)
2 big handfuls fresh chamomile flowers, for decorating
Flaky sea salt

TIP 1 —— *Choose an enamel-coated cast-iron or stainless steel pot for cooking the puff dough. This dough needs a cooking surface with some tension so that a pasty film can form on the bottom of the pot, which indicates doneness—so avoid nonstick surfaces.*

TIP 2 ——*You can always add, but you can't take away. When in doubt, it's always better to add very gradually, and watch how the dough responds and changes, before adding more. I like using trigger-style ice cream scoops to test the choux; the dough should slightly spread into a wide coin, with a spiky hedgehog ruffle on top. If the dough spreads too much, you've added too many eggs; if it's too upright, you need to add another egg.*

TIP 3 ——*Save some unbaked choux puffs for future projects. Pipe the extra dough onto a small pan lined with parchment paper. Transfer them to the freezer to solidify completely, about 2 hours. Peel the frozen dough mounds off the parchment and transfer to an airtight container and keep frozen, for up to 2 months.*

Chamomile Cream

MAKES 3½ CUPS (ABOUT 600 G)

15 MINUTES ACTIVE TIME
1 HOUR INACTIVE TIME

1 cup (240 g) whole milk

¼ cup (about 10 g) fresh chamomile flowers or 2 tablespoons (about 5 g) chamomile tea leaves

2 tablespoons (15 g) cornstarch or tapioca starch

½ teaspoon kosher salt

2 tablespoons (25 g) sugar

1 egg (50 g)

4 tablespoons (2 ounces/60 g) unsalted butter, cubed

½ teaspoon vanilla extract

1 cup (240 g) cold heavy cream

1. MAKE THE PASTRY CREAM. In a small saucepan, heat the milk and chamomile over medium heat until hot and steaming. In a small bowl, whisk together the cornstarch, kosher salt, sugar, and egg. Add a big spoonful of the hot milk to the bowl and whisk. Stir the slurry into the saucepan and whisk well. Cook for no longer than 1 minute, whisking thoroughly and getting into the corners so the milk doesn't burn; the mixture should thicken considerably. Remove the pastry cream from the heat and whisk in the cubed butter and vanilla. Pass the mixture through a fine-mesh sieve into a small bowl. Press a small piece of plastic wrap on top and set aside to cool.

2. LIGHTEN WITH WHIPPED CREAM. In a stand mixer fitted with the whisk (or in a large bowl using a handheld mixer), whip the heavy cream until very stiff, about 3 minutes. Add the cooled chamomile cream and use a spatula to gently combine. Immediately transfer to a piping bag fitted with a plain piping tip.

Vanilla Craquelin

1. MIX THE DOUGH. In a stand mixer fitted with the paddle (or in a large bowl using a handheld mixer), cream the butter and sugar together for 2 minutes. Add the vanilla and food coloring and beat for 1 minute. Add the flour and salt and mix on low speed for about 15 seconds, or until just combined.

2. ROLL OUT THE DOUGH. Transfer the dough to a 12-by-16-inch (30 by 40 cm) sheet of parchment paper and press another piece of parchment on top. Use a rolling pin to firmly press the dough down, sandwiching it between the sheets of parchment. Roll the dough out very thin, to about the dimensions of the parchment paper. Refrigerate the parchment pack until thoroughly chilled, 30 minutes.

3. PORTION WITH A COOKIE CUTTER. Remove the dough sheet from the refrigerator. Carefully peel off the top piece of parchment. Using a 1½-inch (4 cm) round cookie cutter, punch out 36 to 40 rounds. If the craquelin dough begins to soften and smear, return to the fridge to chill before attempting to punch more. Transfer the rounds to a pan lined with parchment and freeze until solid before stacking in a container. Store frozen until ready to use.

MAKES ABOUT THIRTY-SIX 1½-INCH (4 CM) ROUNDS, ENOUGH FOR ONE CHAMOMILE PUFF CROWN WITH A FEW LEFT OVER

15 MINUTES ACTIVE TIME
1 HOUR INACTIVE TIME

4 tablespoons (2 ounces/60 g) unsalted butter, cubed, at room temperature
¼ cup plus 2 tablespoons (75 g) sugar
1 teaspoon vanilla extract
3 drops green food coloring
½ cup plus 2 tablespoons (75 g) all-purpose flour
½ teaspoon kosher salt

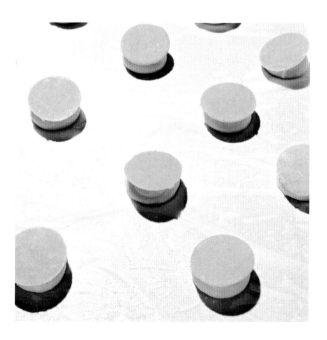

CHOCOLATE AND EARL GREY MOUSSE

When I first entered the world of fine dining, I felt so overwhelmed by the process of building "entremets," the elaborate, multilayered mousse-based cakes that usually boast shiny, lacquered finishes; sharp, clean lines; and seemingly endless components. But the trick to any fancy dish is to view it as a series of small manageable tasks—all extremely doable on their own, but when combined into a greater whole, almost shockingly professional and chic. Here, the components of a classic entremet are reimagined as an easy-to-plate bowl of chocolate mousse, layered with rich chocolate ganache, crunchy cookies, and candied Amarena cherries.

SERVES 8

30 MINUTES ACTIVE TIME
2 TO 3 HOURS INACTIVE TIME

1 cup (240 g) cold heavy cream
¼ cup plus 1 tablespoon (75 g)
    water
¼ cup (50 g) sugar
1 Earl Grey tea bag
8 ounces (225 g) dark chocolate,
    roughly chopped (about 1½ cups)
2 eggs (100 g)
1 large egg yolk (20 g)
½ teaspoon kosher salt
1 tablespoon (15 g) Cointreau
1 cup (290 g) Chocolate and Earl
    Grey Ganache (recipe follows),
    chilled
24 to 32 candied cherries (see
    Resources, page 311)
Flaky sea salt
Feuilletine (recipe follows)
1 tablespoon (5 g) unsweetened
    cocoa powder

1. WHIP THE CREAM. In a stand mixer or a large bowl, whisk the heavy cream to stiff peaks, 2 to 3 minutes. Keep chilled.

2. MAKE THE EARL GREY SYRUP. In a small pot, bring the water, sugar, and tea bag to a boil over medium heat, 2 to 3 minutes. Remove from the heat and discard the tea bag, pressing out the extra syrup inside.

3. BLEND THE CHOCOLATE BASE. In a blender, combine the chopped chocolate, whole eggs, egg yolk, kosher salt, and Cointreau. With the blender on high speed, slowly pour in the hot sugar syrup through the hole in the blender's lid and blend until the mixture appears smooth, 2 to 3 minutes. Set the mixture aside to cool; it should look bouncy and thick.

4. PORTION INTO INDIVIDUAL BOWLS. Fold half of the chocolate mixture into the chilled whipped cream until streaky, then add the rest of the mixture and fold until it looks smooth and combined. Add 2 tablespoons (36 g) each of the chilled ganache to the bottom of eight dessert bowls or cups about 4 inches (10 cm) across. Dividing it evenly, pour the mousse over the ganache (or get more decorative with a piping bag; see tip). Cover and refrigerate for at least 2 hours, and up to 24 hours.

→

TIP ——*For a different look, pour the mousse into a piping bag fitted with a star tip and refrigerate for about 30 minutes to set up slightly. Pipe squiggly piles into the bowl, on top of the ganache.*

5. ADD THE TOPPINGS. After the mousse is set (it should feel like soft taffy), remove from the fridge. Nestle 3 or 4 candied cherries on top of each mousse. Sprinkle the mousse with flaky sea salt, then press 3 or 4 shards of the feuilletine onto the surface, like shingles. Dust the feuilletine with cocoa powder. Serve immediately.

Chocolate and Earl Grey Ganache

MAKES 1¼ CUPS (365 G)

10 MINUTES ACTIVE TIME
1 HOUR INACTIVE TIME

½ cup (120 g) heavy cream
¼ (60 g) whole milk
2 tablespoons (40 g) light corn
   syrup, glucose, or rice syrup
1 Earl Grey tea bag
3½ ounces (100 g) dark chocolate
   (70% cacao or higher), roughly
   chopped (about ⅔ cup)
3 tablespoons (1½ ounces/45 g)
   unsalted butter, cubed
½ teaspoon vanilla extract
½ teaspoon kosher salt

IN A SMALL POT, gently warm the heavy cream, whole milk, syrup, and tea bag over low heat until steaming, about 5 minutes. Remove the tea bag and set aside. Add the chocolate and butter to a medium bowl and pour the hot cream over. Wait 2 minutes, then whisk the mixture by hand until smooth and emulsified. Stir in the vanilla and salt. Refrigerate for at least 1 hour.

$\longrightarrow$

At restaurants, pastry cooks keep their mise en place neatly organized so that plated desserts with many little elements—like candied cherries, crunchy cookies, and a jar of ganache—can come together in just a few minutes. Though you can set the chocolate mousse well in advance, I like to store it in pastry bags and pipe dramatic ruffles into clear glass bowls right at the last minute.

Creamy, Elegant Desserts

Feuilletine

MAKES TWELVE TO FIFTEEN 2- TO
3-INCH (5 TO 7.5 CM) SHARDS

10 MINUTES ACTIVE TIME
1 HOUR INACTIVE TIME

¼ cup (50 g) sugar
2 tablespoons (1 ounce/30 g)
   unsalted butter, melted
1 large egg white (30 g)
¼ cup (30 g) all-purpose flour
¼ teaspoon kosher salt

TIP —— *If the crunch does not crunch
even after cooling, you can "flash" the
wafer again in the oven for 10 minutes
to continue to crisp it up.*

1. MAKE THE BATTER. In a medium bowl, whisk the sugar, melted butter, and egg white together until smooth. Stir in the flour and salt. The batter should look runny and drip off the whisk. Refrigerate for at least 45 minutes to chill before baking.

2. PREHEAT THE OVEN AND PREP THE PAN. Preheat the oven to 350°F (175°C). Line a half-sheet pan with parchment paper.

3. BAKE THE FEUILLETINE. Spread the batter thin on the prepared pan. (The batter should look slightly sheer on the parchment paper; pulling the straight side of a bowl or bench scraper slowly across the parchment will give you the smoothest results.) Bake until fragrant and deeply golden, 10 to 12 minutes.

4. SNAP INTO SHARDS. Let the wafer cool completely, then peel off the parchment and snap into tortilla chip–size pieces (see tip). Store in an airtight container for up to 1 month.

ADZUKI BEAN AND BROWN BUTTER PIE

Adzuki beans, the nutty-tasting red beans grown throughout East Asia and the Himalayas, are a staple of Chinese pastry. They often appear as a creamy filling inside buns and tarts sold in dim sum teahouses or bakeries, or bobbing on the surface of light, tapioca-enriched dessert soups. As a child, during a sweltering summer in Beijing, the only treats I desired in the shimmering heat were frozen ice pops, barely sweet and dotted with chewy flecks of red bean.

Though you can easily cook red beans from scratch, there are many delicious high-quality canned varieties that already come perfectly sweetened. This pie, spiked with Chinese five-spice powder and drizzled with condensed milk, is inspired by classic Thanksgiving pies like sweet potato, pumpkin, and pecan, with their earthy, warming spices and sticky fillings. This red bean pie would be a welcome addition to any cross-cultural Thanksgiving spread—a not-too-decadent, nutty East-meets-West treat.

1. **PREHEAT THE OVEN.** Preheat the oven to 375°F (190°C).

2. **ROLL THE BRISÉE.** Remove the dough from the refrigerator and let sit at room temperature until slightly softened but still cool to the touch, 10 to 15 minutes. Sprinkle a large sheet of parchment paper with flour and place the disc of dough on top. Using firm, even pressure, roll the dough out from the middle of the round in a radius pattern, rotating the parchment like a turntable, until you have a large circular shape about 12 inches (30 cm) in diameter. Carefully drape the dough into a 9-inch (23 cm) pie dish, fitting the pastry into the corners of the dish. Trim the dough with a pair of scissors so that there is 1-inch (2.5 cm) overhang. Fold the overhang under itself on the rim of the pie dish and press the border of pastry into V-shaped crimps. Transfer the pie dish to the freezer while you prepare the pie filling. (Unbaked pie shells in aluminum pie tins can be stacked and stored frozen for up to 1 month.)

→

MAKES ONE 9-INCH (23 CM) PIE
SERVES 8

30 MINUTES ACTIVE TIME
1 HOUR INACTIVE TIME

395 g Pâte Brisée (page 164)
All-purpose flour, for rolling the
    dough
4 tablespoons (2 ounces/60 g)
    unsalted butter
3 eggs (150 g), at room temperature
One 16-ounce (455 g) can
    sweetened adzuki beans
¼ teaspoon Chinese five-spice
    powder

(ingredients continue)

3. **MAKE THE BROWN BUTTER.** In a small pot, melt the butter over medium heat, swirling as it comes up to a boil. After 2 to 3 minutes, the butter will heavily foam and bubble. As the milk solids begin to settle to the bottom of the pot, the foam will burn off. Once the milk solids are a deep mahogany hue and the air smells nutty and sweet, another 3 to 4 minutes, remove the pot from the heat. Carefully scrape the butter and milk solids into the bowl of a food processor.

4. **MIX THE PIE FILLING.** Separate one of the eggs, setting the white aside in a small bowl for brushing on the pie edges later. To the food processor or blender, add half of the sweetened adzuki beans, the yolk, the remaining 2 eggs, Chinese five-spice, heavy cream, kosher salt, maple syrup, tapioca starch, vanilla, and whiskey and buzz up until smooth. Transfer to a medium bowl, then whisk in the rest of the adzuki beans. The filling can be mixed 2 days in advance and stored in an airtight container in the refrigerator; pull it out 1 hour before baking so it comes to room temperature.

5. **BLIND-BAKE THE PIE SHELL.** Dock the bottom of the chilled pie shell by pricking it all over with a fork or small knife. Cut a piece of parchment or foil into a round slightly larger than the diameter of the pie pan. Press it into the shell and fill with pie weights (like dried beans, glass beads, or uncooked rice). Brush the crust edges with the lightly beaten reserved egg white and sprinkle with the sugar. Transfer to the oven and bake until the edges are barely golden and the parchment releases cleanly from the shell, 15 to 18 minutes. Remove the parchment and pie weights. Return the pie shell to the oven and bake until the bottom looks set and opaque (any raw dough will look greasy and translucent), another 10 to 15 minutes. Reduce the oven temperature to 350°F (175°C).

6. **BAKE THE PIE.** Pour the adzuki bean custard into the baked pie shell. Transfer to the oven and bake until the custard is puffed and set on the edges, 30 to 35 minutes (see tip #1). Let cool for at least 1 hour before serving. The pie can be stored in the refrigerator for up to 4 days.

7. **SLICE AND SERVE.** Drizzle the pie with the condensed milk. Slice the pie into 8 wedges and sprinkle with flaky sea salt.

½ cup (120 g) heavy cream, at room temperature
½ teaspoon kosher salt
2 tablespoons (30 g) maple syrup
1 tablespoon (7 g) tapioca starch or cornstarch
1 teaspoon vanilla extract
1 tablespoon (15 g) whiskey
1 tablespoon (15 g) sugar
¼ cup (75 g) Condensed Milk (page 238; see tip #2)
Flaky sea salt

TIP 1 —— *To prevent the edges of the crust from getting too dark, cover the exposed edges with strips of tented foil before baking with the custard inside.*

TIP 2 —— *Condensed milk is a classic Chinese and Vietnamese garnish for sweets, adding a zip of sugar to desserts that are otherwise mellow and subtle. Give the condensed milk a little extra twist by adding ½ teaspoon vanilla extract, a spoonful of instant espresso, or ¼ teaspoon five-spice powder.*

YEASTED

TREATS

Many home bakers approach a recipe that uses yeast with a little wariness, like eyeing the sky for rain clouds. Successfully managing yeasted doughs is a sensory skill to hone, just like rolling out dough evenly or thickening a stovetop custard. Like athletes, strong bakers develop physical skill and mental confidence through the repetition of the same task, over and over. Enriched doughs, which are raised with yeast but have a higher concentration of fat and sugar than plain white bread, have a pillowy crumb—ideal for accentuating with inventive fillings.

What's the best way to make a memorable yeasted pastry? For me, it's taking the classics and injecting them with something unexpected. The dough itself should be incredibly flavorful, with richness from eggs, good butter, honey, and whole milk. Any inclusions should be full of distinctive flavor, but not so chunky that they get in the way of each tender bite. These extras shouldn't feel predictable, either; there should be an ingredient that feels hard to pin down. The result will be a pastry that is both comforting and balanced, seemingly wholesome yet clearly, shamelessly decadent.

In the summer of 2016, months before opening Flora Bar at the Met Breuer, I was determined to elevate the American bakery classic, the sticky bun (see page 259). I slipped wildflower honey into the brioche and twisted the dough into coiled seashells lined with cinnamon and smoky black cardamom, a spice grown in Nepal and India, which reminds me of menthol cigarettes and warm embers. I baked them at high heat until they were deeply tanned, then painted the rolls with a drippy caramel glaze.

The results paid off: the plump, glassy buns—their fat ribbons of minced pecans peeking through the coiled brioche—often disappeared from the glass case within an hour of our opening the Breuer doors. I set them aside for VIPs, shipped them out of state, and topped them with ice cream for off-menu birthday celebrations. Now you can make them yourself, and so many other yeasted treats, too.

TWISTY FRUIT AND NUT BUNS

We are tactile creatures, with fingers that love untying knots or detangling hair. The same goes for baked treats; somehow, it just feels so good to run your fingers along the bumps and braids of an intricately woven, puffy parcel of bread (not to mention the increased surface area to receive deeply delicious fillings). Perhaps that's why complex, mazelike breads are found widely throughout the world, from the perfumed cardamom buns of Sweden to the serpentine curves of challah in Jewish bakeries. Here, the classic not-too-sweet pairing of currants, walnuts, and orange marmalade, gently tucked and then twisted into a honey brioche, recalls the English hot cross buns traditionally eaten on Good Friday.

MAKES 12 LARGE BUNS

45 MINUTES ACTIVE TIME
4 HOURS INACTIVE TIME

4 tablespoons (2 ounces/60 g)
   unsalted butter, melted and
   cooled
½ cup (75 g) dried currants
½ cup (75 g) walnuts
⅓ cup (70 g) dark brown sugar
3 tablespoons (30 g) fortified wine
   (like sherry, port, or Marsala)
1 teaspoon ground cinnamon
¼ teaspoon ground nutmeg
1 teaspoon kosher salt
Dough for No-Knead Honey Brioche
   (recipe follows), chilled
All-purpose flour, for dusting
¼ cup (80 g) orange marmalade
1 egg (50 g)
Flaky sea salt

1. **PREP THE FILLING.** In a food processor, combine the melted butter, currants, walnuts, dark brown sugar, 2 tablespoons (20 g) of the fortified wine, the cinnamon, nutmeg, and kosher salt and pulse until the currants and walnuts are pebbly and sticky. (This mixture can be made up to 2 weeks in advance and kept in an airtight container in the fridge.)

2. **ROLL THE DOUGH.** Remove the chilled brioche dough from the fridge and turn out onto a large piece of parchment paper well dusted with flour. Roll the dough out into a rectangle about 12 by 22 inches (30 by 56 cm).

3. **ADD THE FILLING.** With a long side facing you, sprinkle the currant and walnut mixture over the dough rectangle. To seal in the filling, fold the left third of the dough over the center. Then fold the right third of the dough over that. The "envelope" should be about 7 by 12 inches (18 by 30 cm). Transfer the envelope, on its parchment, to the freezer to chill for 1 hour.

4. **SLICE AND BRAID THE DOUGH.** With a long side facing you, slice the envelope vertically into 12 strips 1 inch (2.5 cm) wide. Pick up each end of a strip with your fingertips and gently rotate your fingertips to spiralize the strip, then coil the strip into a small circle, tucking the ends underneath it.

$\rightarrow$

5. PROOF THE BUNS. Top two half-sheet pans with parchment paper and lightly mist the paper with cooking spray. Use a bench scraper to transfer each bun to one of the prepared pans. Space the buns no fewer than 3 inches (7.5 cm) apart, 6 buns to a half-sheet pan. Gently drape the pans with plastic wrap and let proof until doubled and puffed, 1 hour to 1½ hours.

6. MEANWHILE, PREHEAT THE OVEN. Preheat the oven to 375°F (190°C).

7. MAKE THE GLAZE. While the buns are proofing, whisk together the marmalade and the remaining 1 tablespoon wine until smooth.

8. BAKE AND GLAZE. In a small bowl, whisk the egg with a fork and then brush generously on the buns. Bake until golden and fragrant, 25 to 30 minutes. Let cool for 10 minutes, then brush the marmalade glaze all over the buns. Sprinkle with flaky sea salt. Eat some buns immediately and let the rest cool completely before freezing in an airtight container for up to 2 weeks. To reheat, bake for 15 minutes in a 325°F (165°C) oven.

No-Knead Honey Brioche

MAKES 565 G DOUGH

10 MINUTES ACTIVE TIME
4 HOURS INACTIVE TIME

¼ cup plus 2 tablespoons (90 g)
    warm water
1 heaping teaspoon (4 g) active dry
    yeast
2 tablespoons (40 g) honey
2 eggs (100 g), at room temperature
6 tablespoons (3 ounces/85 g)
    unsalted butter, melted and
    still warm
2 cups (240 g) all-purpose flour,
    plus more for shaping the dough
1 teaspoon kosher salt

1. MIX THE DOUGH. In a stand mixer fitted with the paddle (or in a large bowl using a handheld mixer), combine the warm water, yeast, and honey. Let sit for 4 minutes, or until the yeast is dissolved and looks puffy. Add the eggs, melted butter, flour, and salt. Paddle until smooth and combined, about 3 minutes. The dough will look very wet and almost whipped-like in texture.

2. LET THE DOUGH RISE. Transfer the brioche to a medium bowl (no need to shape, as it will be very sticky and runny), cover with plastic wrap, and let proof until doubled in volume, 1½ to 2 hours in a warm kitchen environment.

3. CHILL THE DOUGH. Transfer the dough to the refrigerator to chill for at least 2 hours (or up to 2 days) before rolling or shaping. (It's best to make this dough at least the night before you'd like to bake it so it can firm up in the refrigerator.)

PECAN AND BLACK CARDAMOM STICKY BUNS

If I could be said to be known for a recipe, it's probably this sticky bun, which is loaded with ground pecans, brown sugar, cinnamon, and black cardamom. I'm thrilled to finally share the entire recipe, including the ratios for the perfect "bun goo," the salted caramel sauce that coats the bun with its signature stickiness.

   Both the pecan paste and the salty bun goo will hold in your refrigerator for up to 2 weeks (or in the freezer for up to 2 months), so it's worth keeping some on hand for impromptu cravings. I prefer to bake the buns in muffin tins, which keeps them from spreading in the oven and ensures a very neat, professional look.

1. **MIX THE PECAN PASTE.** In a stand mixer fitted with the paddle (or in a large bowl using a handheld mixer), cream together the softened butter and dark brown sugar on medium speed until fluffy, about 4 minutes. Add the ground pecans, black cardamom, cinnamon, and kosher salt and paddle to combine, about 2 minutes.

2. **ROLL AND FREEZE THE BRIOCHE DOUGH.** Turn out the chilled brioche dough onto a large piece of parchment paper heavily dusted with flour. Roll the brioche to a rectangle about 12 by 14 inches (30 by 35 cm). Transfer the dough rectangle, on the parchment paper, to a half-sheet pan and freeze until stiffened but still slightly pliable, 1 to 2 hours (see tip).

3. **SHAPE THE BUNS.** When the brioche feels mostly frozen, return it to your counter. Spread the pecan paste over the dough with a small offset spatula, all the way to the edges. If it begins to crack as you roll, let it sit for 5 minutes and try again. Cut the brioche in half crosswise so you have two rectangles 7 by 12 inches (18 by 30 cm). Starting on a long side of a rectangle, use the tips of your fingers to lift up the dough and roll it up into a spiral about 3 inches (7.5 cm) wide and 12 inches (30 cm) long. Repeat with the second rectangle. Use a sharp, serrated bread knife to slice each roll crosswise into 6 buns each about 2 inches (5 cm) thick, for a total of 12 buns.

$\rightarrow$

MAKES 12 LARGE STICKY BUNS

30 MINUTES ACTIVE TIME
4 HOURS INACTIVE TIME

8 tablespoons (4 ounces/115 g) unsalted butter, at room temperature
½ cup (100 g) dark brown sugar
1½ cups (200 g) finely ground pecans
2 tablespoons (16 g) powdered or finely ground black cardamom
2 teaspoons ground cinnamon
1 teaspoon kosher salt
Dough for No-Knead Honey Brioche (opposite), chilled
All-purpose flour, for dusting
1 large egg white (30 g), lightly whisked
Salty Bun Goo (recipe follows), gently rewarmed
Flaky sea salt

$4 \cdot$ **PROOF THE BUNS.** Mist two large muffin pans with cooking spray. (Alternatively, you can bake in a standard [9-by-13-inch/23 by 33 cm] baking dish, the buns placed 2 inches/5 cm apart.) Drape the pan in plastic wrap and set aside to proof until puffy, about 1½ hours.

$5 \cdot$ **PREHEAT THE OVEN.** About 30 minutes before the buns have completed their rise, preheat the oven to 375°F (190°C).

$6 \cdot$ **BAKE AND GLAZE THE BUNS.** Use a small pastry brush to gently paint the egg white on the buns. Transfer to the oven and bake until deeply golden and fragrant, 25 to 28 minutes. Pop the buns out of the muffin tins and transfer to a cooling rack or platter. Brush the bun goo all over the tops and bottoms of the buns; really slather it on. Add a generous pinch of flaky sea salt to each and serve.

TIP——*The secret to perfect-looking sticky buns is to parfreeze the rolled-out brioche dough before adding the nut filling and rolling up into a spiral. Brioche is an enriched dough, filled with fats and sugar, that is prone to stickiness, making it hard to handle. Using the freezer as a tool puts you—not the sticky brioche—in control.*

Salty Bun Goo

Season with kosher salt the way the pros do in restaurant kitchens: add a pinch of salt, and taste; another pinch of salt, and taste. Keep doing that until the goo is properly sweet-and-salty. (You've added enough salt once the goo doesn't taste that sweet anymore; that's how salt works! Pretty amazing.)

IN A SMALL POT, combine the butter and light brown sugar over medium heat until bubbling, about 4 minutes. Add the heavy cream and honey and whisk well. Simmer over medium heat until the caramel looks glossy and emulsified, about 4 minutes. Remove from the heat and stir in the vanilla. Let cool for 20 minutes, then sprinkle in the salt a little at a time, tasting as you go. Refrigerate in an airtight container until ready to use.

MAKES 1 HEAPING CUP (300 G)

15 MINUTES ACTIVE TIME
20 MINUTES INACTIVE TIME

5 tablespoons (2½ ounces/70 g) unsalted butter
3 tablespoons (38 g) light brown sugar
½ cup (120 g) heavy cream
¼ cup (80 g) honey
1 teaspoon vanilla extract
½ teaspoon kosher salt, plus more to taste

TUTTI-FRUTTI TART

If "whipped cream sandwich" sounds like your dream dessert, then this recipe is for you. It may remind you of two canonical European desserts, both of which made their way to France and Italy by way of Eastern Europe: the forever bistro staple baba au rhum, a sticky, spongy brioche saturated in boozy syrup, and the tarte tropézienne, the pearl sugar–crusted bread of the French Riviera, stuffed with sweetened cream.

Here, No-Knead Honey Brioche (page 258) is soaked with a scarlet hibiscus syrup, then filled with a silky Champagne sabayon cream. Diced tropical fruit adds acidity and a jumble of bright colors. If you're taking the tart somewhere, think of it as a giant muffuletta sandwich: wrap the tart tightly in plastic wrap and then, when serving, slice it with a serrated knife while still wrapped, which will keep the wedges tidy and sharp.

MAKES ONE 12-INCH (30 CM) TART
SERVES 8 TO 10

CREAM:
10 MINUTES ACTIVE TIME;
10 MINUTES INACTIVE TIME

TART:
45 MINUTES ACTIVE TIME;
2 HOURS INACTIVE TIME

FOR THE TART

Dough for No-Knead Honey Brioche
  (page 258), chilled
All-purpose flour, for dusting
2 tablespoons (4 g) hibiscus tea
⅓ cup (70 g) sugar
⅓ cup (80 g) water
¼ cup (60 g) rum

(ingredients continue)

1. **SHAPE THE DOUGH FOR THE TART.** Turn the chilled brioche dough out onto a lightly flour-dusted sheet of parchment. Gently shape the brioche into a ball about 4 inches (10 cm) across, then use your fingertips to roll the dough into a long rope about 1 inch (2.5 cm) wide. Gently wind and twist the rope around itself to form a tight coil 7 to 8 inches (18 to 20 cm) across. Pick up the parchment, with the dough coil on top, and transfer to a half-sheet pan. Loosely drape plastic wrap over the coil and let rise until doubled, 1 hour to 1½ hours.

2. **MEANWHILE, MAKE THE HIBISCUS SOAK.** In a small pot, combine the hibiscus tea, sugar, and water and bring to a rolling boil over medium heat. Simmer until the syrup is reduced and slightly thickened, 3 to 4 minutes. Strain the mixture into a jar or glass. Stir in the rum and set the soak aside to cool.

3. **PREP THE FRUIT TOPPING.** Remove the pits if necessary and slice the fruits into slabs ½ inch (1.25 cm) thick. Slice each slab into sticks ⅜ inch (1 cm) wide and then cut those matchsticks into ⅜-inch (1 cm) dice. (Snack on the trim or toss into sparkling water.) Transfer the diced fruit to a small bowl and add the

Whipped cream sandwich anyone? A giant snail-shaped brioche is split in half; soaked in a tangy, boozy hibiscus syrup; and topped with fluffy champagne cream and all manner of tropical fruit.

More Than Cake

lemon juice, honey, and a pinch of flaky sea salt. Gently toss with a spoon to combine. Keep covered and refrigerated until ready to use.

4. **PREHEAT THE OVEN.** About 30 minutes before the brioche coil has completed its final rise, preheat the oven to 400°F (200°C).

5. **BAKE AND GLAZE THE BRIOCHE.** When the brioche looks fully proofed, remove the plastic wrap and brush the brioche all over with the egg white. Slide into the oven and bake until golden and fragrant, 25 to 30 minutes. Remove from the oven and transfer the brioche to a cooling rack to cool completely. Slice the brioche horizontally in half with a serrated knife. Flip the top half cut side up and brush the soak all over the cut sides of the brioche, letting the pink syrup seep into the crumb.

6. **MAKE THE CHAMPAGNE SABAYON.** In a small heatproof bowl, whisk together the egg yolks, sparkling wine, sugar, and kosher salt. Set the bowl snugly over a small pot containing 1 inch (2.5 cm) of barely simmering water. The bottom of the bowl should not touch the water. Whisk constantly over low heat until the sugar has dissolved and the mixture has paled in color and feels warm to the touch. Remove the bowl from the pot and continue to whisk, off the heat, until the mixture is thick and glossy.

7. **WHIP THE CREAM AND FOLD IN THE SABAYON.** In a stand mixer fitted with the whisk (or in a large bowl with a handheld mixer), beat the cream until soft peaks begin to form, about 3 minutes. Add the cooked yolk mixture and continue to whip until the mixture is glossy yet stiff, 3 to 4 minutes. Keep chilled. (This mixture can be made 1 day in advance but will need to be re-whipped.)

8. **ASSEMBLE THE TART.** With an offset spatula, spread the cream all over the bottom brioche half. Spoon 2 cups (about 220 g) of diced fruit on top of the cream. Place the other brioche half, cut side down, on top, pressing gently to close. Refrigerate for at least 1 to 2 hours before slicing into wedges. Serve with the remaining fruit mixture on the side.

3 to 4 small colorful tropical fruits (see tip), such as yellow or green kiwi, dragon fruit, mango, or papaya

Juice of 1 lemon

1 teaspoon honey

Flaky sea salt

1 large egg white (30 g), lightly whisked

FOR THE CHAMPAGNE CREAM

4 large egg yolks (80 g), at room temperature

3 tablespoons (45 g) sparkling white wine, like Champagne or Prosecco

3 tablespoons (35 g) sugar

¼ teaspoon kosher salt

2 cups (480 g) cold heavy cream

TIP——*When selecting the fruits, look for firm medium-size fruit that will cube easily, can be eaten uncooked, and will resist oxidation (avoid bananas and apples, for example). Slightly underripe stone fruits, and small to medium tropical fruits are great choices. If all else fails, just dollop 1 cup (320 g) of your favorite tart jam, mixed with 1 tablespoon lime juice, on top of the Champagne cream.*

LEAFY DINNER ROLLS

There's a large fig tree that grows in the corner of my backyard, but the squirrels eat the budding fruits well before I can harvest them myself. Luckily, there's so much more to this plant than its jammy lobes of fruit—the flat, wide leaves, like edible sheets of wrapping paper, have plenty of uses, too. And, like banana and grape leaves, fig leaves are sturdy enough to wrap anything from sticky rice to poached fruit while also infusing the contents with their unique, dreamy scent.

When gently toasted in the oven or over an open fire, fig leaves release an intoxicating aroma—something between coconut sunscreen and vanilla buttercream. They also provide an elegant, natural lining for fluffy dinner rolls, infusing the dough with their sweetness in the oven. Think of these as Parker House rolls on a beach vacation.

You can absolutely make these rolls without fig leaves; the coconut milk in the bread dough has the same beachy notes as the fig leaves.

MAKES 12 ROLLS

30 MINUTES ACTIVE TIME
4 HOURS INACTIVE TIME

¼ cup (60 g) warm water
2 tablespoons (40 g) honey
2 teaspoons active dry yeast
1 cup (240 g) full-fat coconut milk, warmed
1 egg (50 g)
3½ cups (420 g) all-purpose flour, plus more for rolling the dough
1½ teaspoons kosher salt
8 tablespoons (4 ounces/112 g) unsalted butter, at room temperature
12 small or 6 large fresh fig leaves (see tip #1)
1 large egg white (30 g)
Flaky sea salt

1. **MIX THE DOUGH.** In a stand mixer fitted with the dough hook, combine the warm water, honey, and yeast and let sit for a few minutes, or until the yeast looks foamy and puffy. Add the coconut milk, egg, flour, and kosher salt and mix on medium-low speed until the dough begins to wind around the hook, about 5 minutes. With the mixer still running, pinch 4 tablespoons (2 ounces/ 56 g) of the butter into small pieces and add piece by piece to the dough, beating until the dough looks smooth and the butter is incorporated. (The dough will be sticky and wet; scrape the bottom of the bowl with a spatula halfway through mixing to ensure that the dough mixes evenly.)

2. **LET THE DOUGH RISE.** Transfer the dough to a medium bowl. Cover tightly with plastic wrap and let rise in a warm area until doubled and puffy, about 1½ hours. Then refrigerate the bowl of dough for at least 1 hour (or up to 24 hours) to make it easier to handle.

→

A yeasted, coconut-scented dough proofs
and bakes inside a cradle of fragrant,
edible leaves. Why buy muffin or cupcake
liners when there are fig leaves?

TIP 1 ——*To create a similar frilly skirt to dress the rolls, try substituting other flat, wide leaves like Swiss chard, beet greens, or Savoy cabbage for the fig leaves.*

TIP 2 ——*The motion of shaping dough balls by hand is a very tactile, intuitive feeling. Add too much flour to the counter, and you won't have enough grip on the table to create the tension needed to shape the balls; don't add enough flour, and the enriched, buttery dough will stick to the counter and smear. Form a protective cage over the dough ball with your palm, and don't apply any downward pressure. Just lightly move it around in a circular motion until you feel the bottom of the dough "catch" on the table and tighten up. Remember that feeling. It will also serve you for shaping the matcha buns for Buttered Cucumber Sliders (opposite).*

3. BUILD THE NESTS. Set out two large muffin tins. In a small saucepan, melt the remaining 4 tablespoons (2 ounces/56 g) butter over low heat. Lightly brush the muffin cups with half of the melted butter. Gently drape a small fig leaf into each muffin cup, pressing it into the corners to adhere to the butter; the edges of the leaf should poke up out of the top of the tin. If using large fig leaves, tear into 3- to 4-inch (7.5 to 10 cm) pieces and press them into the cups to fit.

4. SHAPE THE BUNS. Divide the chilled dough into 24 equal portions (between 30 and 35 g each). Lightly flour a clean work surface. Cup your hand into a claw position and quickly roll each portion of dough into a tight, taut ball (see tip #2). Place 2 balls side by side in each lined muffin cup. Drape plastic wrap over the muffin tins and let the dough rise again until doubled, 1½ hours.

5. PREHEAT THE OVEN. About 30 minutes before the rolls have completed their second rise, preheat the oven to 400°F (200°C).

6. EGG-WASH AND BAKE THE ROLLS. Whisk up the large egg white with a fork, then brush all over the rolls, being careful not to deflate their rise. Transfer to the oven and bake until the rolls are shiny and golden, about 20 minutes.

7. SOAK THE BUNS WITH MORE BUTTER. Remove the rolls from the oven and immediately brush with the remaining melted butter, then add a sprinkle of flaky sea salt to each. Gently pop out each roll from the pan, and admire the fig leaf pattern underneath.

BUTTERED CUCUMBER SLIDERS

A stack of crunchy cucumber coins, slathered in bright, zippy sorrel butter and topped with a nest of flowering chives, is sandwiched in your new favorite bun—a squishy milk bread with a swirled, psychedelic crumb. The matcha adds a subtle hint of grassy, sweet flavor to these tender rolls, which are so versatile on their own, they're perfectly happy without the cucumber slices and butter. (And keep a freezer bag of baked rolls in your freezer for milk bread cravings.)

1. **MAKE THE DOUGH.** In a stand mixer fitted with the dough hook, combine the sugar and warmed milk. Sprinkle the yeast on top and let sit for a minute or so, until foamy. With the mixer on medium-low speed, add one of the eggs, the flour, and salt and mix until a stiff ball of dough forms around the hook, 5 to 7 minutes. With the mixer on low speed, add the cubed butter piece by piece, beating until it is incorporated and the dough looks smooth, 4 to 5 minutes. Scrape the mixer bowl occasionally with a spatula to ensure that the ingredients are incorporated.

2. **ADD THE MATCHA.** Turn the dough out onto a surface lightly dusted with flour. Divide the dough in half with a bench scraper and put one half back in the stand mixer. Sprinkle the matcha on top and mix on low speed until combined, about 2 minutes. Gently shape each dough piece into a smooth ball on the floured surface. Transfer each ball to a separate bowl and cover with plastic wrap. Let rise in a warm area until doubled in size, about 1½ hours. (Alternatively, the dough can be chilled for 1 to 3 days before the shaping, final proof, and bake.)

3. **SWIRL THE DOUGH, SHAPE, AND PROOF.** Line a half-sheet pan with parchment paper and mist the paper with cooking spray. Turn one bowl of dough out onto the counter. Pat the dough into a roughly 9-inch (23 cm) square. Cut the dough into 12 pieces. Repeat with the second bowl of dough. For each bun, pinch together a square of each color, so you have 12 pieces of green-and-white dough. Cup your hand into a claw position and roll each piece together on the work surface until a smooth, swirled ball has formed.

→

MAKES 12 SANDWICHES

30 MINUTES ACTIVE TIME
3 TO 4 HOURS INACTIVE TIME

FOR THE MATCHA BUNS

¼ cup (50 g) sugar
¾ cup (180 g) whole milk, warmed
1 tablespoon plus 1 teaspoon (12 g) active dry yeast
2 eggs (100 g), at room temperature
3 cups (360 g) all-purpose flour, plus more for dusting
1½ teaspoons kosher salt
4 tablespoons (2 ounces/60 g) unsalted butter, cubed, at room temperature
2 tablespoons (8 g) matcha powder

FOR THE SLIDERS

¼ cup (55 g) Sorrel Butter (recipe follows), at room temperature
4 mini or Persian cucumbers, sliced into ¼-inch (6 mm) coins
Flaky sea salt
15 flowering chives (see tip #1)

Transfer the balls to the prepared sheet pan. (The shaped balls can also be refrigerated overnight, and then pulled out the next day to complete their second rise and bake.) Drape a piece of plastic wrap on top and let proof until the dough feels tender and buoyant to the touch, like a balloon, about 1½ hours.

4. PREHEAT THE OVEN. About 30 minutes before the buns have completed their second rise, preheat the oven to 400°F (200°C).

5. EGG-WASH AND BAKE THE BUNS. Whisk up the remaining egg and brush generously on the buns (see tip #2). Bake until the buns are golden and feel hollow to the touch, 16 to 18 minutes. Remove from the oven and let the buns cool completely.

6. ASSEMBLE THE SLIDERS. Slice each bun in half horizontally. Spread 1 teaspoon of sorrel butter on the bottom half of each and top with some sliced cucumber and a pinch of flaky sea salt. Roughly chop the flowering chives and add a spoonful on top of each. Place the bun lids on top to close and skewer a toothpick through each one. Arrange on a platter and serve.

→

TIP 1——*Plain chives or dark green scallion tops, cut into 2-inch-long (5 cm) batons, are a good substitute for the flowering chives.*

TIP 2——*To avoid a visible, scraggly egg wash line on the finished buns—caused by applying egg wash unevenly—brush the wash generously around the base of the buns, even painting the parchment.*

Sorrel Butter

MAKES ½ CUP (130 G)

10 MINUTES ACTIVE TIME

10 to 15 green sorrel leaves
(about 15 g)
8 tablespoons (4 ounces/115 g)
unsalted butter, at room
temperature
1 teaspoon flaky sea salt

SET UP A BOWL filled with ice and water. Bring a small pot of water to a boil. Drop the sorrel leaves and blanch until just tender, about 5 seconds (see tip). Remove with tongs and immediately drop into the ice bath. Wring the excess water from the blanched sorrel and roughly chop the leaves. Transfer to a food processor and add the softened butter. Puree until the sorrel has stained the butter green. Add the flaky sea salt and pulse to combine. Scrape the butter out and store in an airtight container in the refrigerator for up to 2 weeks or in the freezer for up to 3 months.

TIP —— *Blanching or steaming the sorrel leaves sets their bright-green hue and makes it easier to puree them into a smooth paste, so don't skip this step!*

DATE-SWIRLED BROWN BRIOCHE

If I had to pick a favorite bread, one that I could eat plain and never tire of, I'd go for the sour, full-flavored black breads and coarse pumpernickel loaves found in Eastern European and German bakeries, which derive their complexity from unexpected inclusions like melted chocolate and coffee grounds. These sturdy dark loaves, often scented with caraway or coriander, epitomize coziness and comfort.

This brown loaf starts with flat beer and honey, and the flavor keeps building from there: you add cocoa powder, fennel seeds, caraway seeds, and instant coffee. Because I try to build little surprises into all of my baked goods, each slice reveals a swirl of softened dates and dark chocolate.

1. **MIX THE DOUGH.** In a stand mixer, combine the beer, yeast, sugar, and honey. Let sit for several minutes, or until foamy. Snap on the dough hook, add one of the eggs, the bread flour, bran flakes, dark rye flour, whole wheat flour, salt, cocoa powder, caraway seeds, fennel seeds, and instant coffee and mix together on low speed. Beat on medium-low speed until a smooth dough has formed around the hook, 5 to 7 minutes. With the mixer running, add the butter piece by piece until it has disappeared into the dough, another 5 minutes. Scrape the bowl often with a spatula.

2. **PROOF AND REFRIGERATE THE DOUGH.** Transfer the dough to a work surface sprinkled with water and gently shape into a ball. Transfer the dough to a medium bowl, cover with plastic wrap, and let rise until doubled, 1½ to 2 hours. Transfer to the refrigerator for at least 6 hours, and up to 48 hours, to chill.

3. **ROLL, FILL, AND SHAPE THE DOUGH.** Divide the dough into 3 equal portions (each weighing about 300 g). On a large piece of parchment paper sprinkled with flour, roll each portion into an oval about 10 inches (25 cm) long and 5 inches (12.5 cm) wide. Use a small offset spatula to spread ⅓ cup (80 g) of the date and chocolate paste over the oval. With a long side of the oval facing you, fold the top third of the dough over the middle third and press to seal. Fold the bottom third of the dough to cover

MAKES ONE 10-INCH (25 CM) LOAF
SERVES 8 TO 10

30 MINUTES ACTIVE TIME
10 HOURS INACTIVE TIME

1 cup (250 g) flat beer
1 tablespoon plus 1 teaspoon (16 g)
  active dry yeast
2 tablespoons (25 g) sugar
1 tablespoon (20 g) honey
2 eggs (100 g), at room temperature
2¾ cups (320 g) white bread flour,
  plus more for rolling the dough
½ cup (40 g) bran flakes, any kind
½ cup (60 g) dark rye flour
½ cup (60 g) whole wheat flour
2 teaspoons kosher salt
1 tablespoon (5 g) cocoa powder
1 tablespoon (4 g) caraway seeds
1 teaspoon fennel seeds
1 tablespoon (5 g) instant coffee or
  finely ground espresso

(ingredients continue)

the middle third and press to seal. You should have a long, skinny rectangle about 10 inches (25 cm) long and 3 inches (7.5 cm) wide. Starting from the left edge, roll up the rectangle like you would roll up a sleeping bag; the roll should measure about 3 inches (7.5 cm) across. Repeat with the remaining dough and date paste.

4. PROOF THE LOAF IN THE PAN. Mist a 10-inch (25 cm) loaf pan with cooking spray. Nestle the three rolls, seam side down, in the pan. Cover with plastic wrap and let proof until puffed and the tops of the rolls are slightly visible above the sides of the pan, about 2 hours (see tip).

5. PREHEAT THE OVEN. About 30 minutes before the bread has finished proofing, preheat the oven to 375°F (190°C).

6. EGG-WASH AND BAKE THE BREAD. Whisk up the remaining egg and use a pastry brush to paint it all over the surface of the bread. Transfer to the oven and bake until the loaf is cooked all the way through, 50 to 60 minutes. (You can skewer the bread to check for doneness; the internal temperature of the bread should be between 190° and 200°F/90° and 95°C). Remove from the oven and let rest in the pan for 10 minutes, then slide the bread out of the pan and cool completely on a drying rack.

8 tablespoons (4 ounces/115 g) unsalted butter, cubed, at room temperature
Sticky Date and Chocolate Paste (recipe follows), at room temperature

TIP——*Let bread work for your schedule, not the other way around. After you have assembled the rolls in the loaf pan, you can wrap the shaped loaf tightly in plastic wrap and refrigerate for up to 2 days before the second proofing and bake.*

Sticky Date and Chocolate Paste

IN A HEATPROOF BOWL set over a small pot of gently simmering water, combine the dark chocolate, dates, butter, cocoa powder, and salt. Stir with a spatula until a paste forms, 3 to 4 minutes. Transfer to an airtight container and refrigerate until ready to use.

MAKES 1 CUP (300 G)

10 MINUTES ACTIVE TIME

1 ounce (28 g) dark chocolate, chopped (about 2½ tablespoons)
1 cup (150 g) pitted dates, chopped
8 tablespoons (4 ounces/115 g) unsalted butter
2 tablespoons (10 g) cocoa powder
1 teaspoon kosher salt

FIRST-LIGHT
BAKES

My version of counting sheep: While tucked into bed, I like to mentally run through the next morning's hypothetical breakfast menus. Will it be some seedy toast and jam? Or a scone decked out with butter and honey? Is it a griddled whole-grain muffin and some wilted greens? Black coffee or oolong? Reviewing the endless, tempting choices relaxes me, filling me with a Zen-like readiness for the next day.

Though my neighborhood is packed with great bakeries and bodegas, I prefer to start the day at home, still in slippers and with my cat. But while I appreciate a freshly baked scone or muffin, I do not love mixing anything that early in the morning and try my hardest to avoid pulling out my stand mixer and scale. If this sounds familiar, you'll be happy to hear that it is possible to transform your freezer and fridge into a mini bakery so that mornings are about as complicated as turning your oven on and waiting.

Over the years, I've spent countless mornings perfecting ambitious "bake-offs" for different restaurants, and understanding how pastries should be stored and handled was critical in my success. The trick is to stock up on ready-to-go items, like batters that keep well in the refrigerator (muffins and corn bread), unbaked shaped pastries (biscuits, scones, and choux), and fully baked treats that ask for little more than a quick thaw or toasting (seeded breads, rolls, and loaves). Doesn't that sound nicer than bland grocery store waffles or disappointing frozen croissants?

Many restaurants and bakeries you love already utilize similar strategies for maximizing the fleeting early hours and tight oven space. Organizing your own morning bake-off is like solving a little riddle—how many pastries can I bake in an hour, in what order, and in what quantity? I love that this strategy allows me the gift of flexibility and scale. Bake one scone, or two, or twelve. One batch can be stretched into days, weeks, even a month.

Once the bake-off is complete, you'll be able to dive into your handiwork. Depending on my mood, I'll reheat some braised beans and spoon them over a biscuit, or dunk a muffin cap into thick yogurt and sprinkle crunchy granola on top. Often we save our showiest dishes for nighttime, but to my mind there is nothing more graceful and enduring than a simple homemade pastry, hot coffee, and some fresh fruit.

More Than Cake

SPICED RUTABAGA LOAF

We accept carrots and zucchini into our baked goods, but knotted, unglamorous root vegetables like rutabaga are often overlooked, despite their appealing nutritional benefits, inexpensive price point, and sweet, distinctive insides. Take a chance on these mottled root vegetables to refresh your morning pastry repertoire—you'll be thrilled at how well rutabaga plays with zesty warming spices, earthy whole-grain flours, and sticky brown sugar.

MAKES ONE 10-INCH (25 CM) LOAF
SERVES 8 TO 10

25 MINUTES ACTIVE TIME
1 HOUR INACTIVE TIME

2 medium rutabagas (at least
   17½ ounces/500 g total; see tip)
2 eggs (100 g)
½ cup (100 g) granulated sugar
½ cup (105 g) dark brown sugar
⅔ cup (150 g) grapeseed oil
1 teaspoon vanilla extract
1½ cups (180 g) all-purpose flour
⅓ cup (60 g) whole wheat flour
1 teaspoon baking powder
2 teaspoons baking soda
½ teaspoon ground cinnamon
⅛ teaspoon ground nutmeg
1 teaspoon kosher salt
1½ cups (150 g) pecans, toasted and
   roughly chopped
¾ cup (60 g) unsweetened coconut
   flakes
2 tablespoons (30 g) turbinado
   sugar

1. **PREHEAT THE OVEN AND PREP THE PAN.** Preheat the oven to 350°F (175°C). Drape a saddle of parchment paper into a 10-inch (25 cm) loaf pan.

2. **PREP THE RUTABAGA.** Peel off the outer skin of the rutabaga, then cut each one into quarters for easier handling. Grate the rutabaga on the largest holes of a box grater. Measure out 3 cups (400 g) of shreds and set aside.

3. **WHISK THE WET INGREDIENTS.** In a stand mixer fitted with the whisk (or in a large bowl using a handheld mixer), whip the eggs on medium speed until frothy, about 15 seconds. With the mixer on medium-high speed, gradually stream in the granulated and dark brown sugars until the mixture is doubled in size, about 5 minutes. Add the grapeseed oil and vanilla and whip to combine. Remove the bowl from the mixer stand.

4. **ADD THE DRY INGREDIENTS.** In a small bowl, whisk together the all-purpose flour, whole wheat flour, baking powder, baking soda, cinnamon, nutmeg, and salt. Tip the dry ingredients into the wet ingredients and stir with a spatula until the ingredients are halfway combined and the batter is streaky.

5. **FINISH THE BATTER AND BAKE.** Add the grated rutabaga, pecans, and coconut flakes and gently fold into the batter. Pour the batter into the loaf pan. Scatter the turbinado sugar on top. Transfer to the oven and bake until a cake tester comes out dry, about 1 hour.

6. COOL AND SERVE. Let the loaf rest in the pan for 10 minutes, then tug the parchment liner out and transfer the loaf to a cooling rack. Let cool completely before slicing. Store leftovers at room temperature in an airtight container for up to 5 days or tightly wrapped in plastic wrap in the freezer for up to 3 weeks.

TIP —— *Need to clean out your vegetable drawer? A dappled root vegetable medley featuring parsnips, celery root, beets, and/or sunchokes could also be added in concert with the rutabaga.*

MILLET, PARSNIP, AND CHOCOLATE CHUNK MUFFINS

We expect muffins to perform the tricky double act of being both scrumptious *and* healthy, but it's not as simple as reducing the fat and sugar, which can leave muffins tough, monotonous, and all-around dreadful. Muffins *can* feel like a treat; if the base batter is rich in moisture and intensely flavored, you can confidently sprinkle in your favorite crunchy textures, bright flavors, and a few sneaky treats like chocolate chips, too.

Shreds of grated parsnip offer nutty, earthy moisture and a shaggy texture. A coating of millet seeds cloaks the muffins with a satisfying crunch, a texture our palates crave. A handful of chopped dark chocolate suggests decadence, in moderation.

MAKES 12 MUFFINS

25 MINUTES ACTIVE TIME
25 MINUTES INACTIVE TIME

½ cup (100 g) millet
4 to 5 small parsnips (about
    10½ ounces/300 g total)
8 tablespoons (4 ounces/115 g)
    unsalted butter, at room
    temperature
½ cup (100 g) sugar
2 tablespoons (40 g) honey
1 egg (50 g), at room temperature
1 teaspoon vanilla extract
⅓ cup (80 g) applesauce or Apple
    Butter (page 169)
⅓ cup (80 g) buttermilk, at room
    temperature
⅓ cup (80 g) plain yogurt, at room
    temperature
1 cup (120 g) all-purpose flour
¾ cup (112 g) whole wheat flour
¼ cup (30 g) oat or wheat bran
1 teaspoon baking powder

1. **PREHEAT THE OVEN AND PREP THE MUFFIN TIN.** Preheat the oven to 350°F (175°C). Thoroughly mist 12 cups of a muffin tin with cooking spray. Add 1 teaspoon of millet to each cup and gently swish the pan around to coat. Tip out any extra millet that doesn't stick and set aside.

2. **PREP THE PARSNIPS.** Peel the parsnips and grate on the large holes of a box grater. Measure out 2 cups (220 g) and set aside.

3. **CREAM THE WET INGREDIENTS.** In a stand mixer fitted with the paddle (or in a large bowl using a handheld mixer), cream the butter, sugar, and honey on medium speed until fluffy and aerated, about 5 minutes. Add the egg and vanilla and paddle to combine, about 1 minute. Scrape the bowl well with a spatula. Add the applesauce, buttermilk, and yogurt and paddle until combined.

4. **ADD THE DRY INGREDIENTS.** In a small bowl, whisk together the all-purpose flour, whole wheat flour, bran, baking powder, baking soda, ground ginger and kosher salt. Tip this mixture into the mixer bowl and paddle on very low speed until halfway combined, about 10 seconds. Remove the bowl from the stand mixer and stir in the grated parsnips and chocolate chunks by hand (see tip #1). If not baking right away, store in the fridge; see tip #2.

5. PORTION AND BAKE THE MUFFINS. Using a large spoon or an ice cream scoop, fill each muffin cup three-quarters full with batter. Sprinkle 1 teaspoon of the remaining millet and a small pinch of flaky sea salt on the top of each muffin. Bake until the muffins are domed and spring back after a gentle poke, 26 to 28 minutes. Serve warm. Store cooled leftover muffins in an airtight container in the freezer for up to 1 month.

1 teaspoon baking soda

1 teaspoon ground ginger

1 teaspoon kosher salt

6 ounces (170 g) dark chocolate, roughly chopped (about 1¼ cups)

Flaky sea salt

TIP 1 —— *Unlike thinner, oil-based batters, a butter-based muffin batter is thick enough to support the addition of diced fresh or dried fruit, like 1 cup (150 g) blueberries, diced rhubarb, or dried cranberries, which won't sink to the bottom of your muffin—so feel free to add some fruit, if you wish.*

TIP 2 —— *For fresh muffins at any given moment, mix the batter up to 3 days in advance and store it in your fridge until you're ready to bake.*

First-Light Bakes

TERRAZZO BREAD

If you love starting your mornings with crunchy toast but yearn for something more substantial, you'll go crazy for this easy seeded loaf, which is endlessly customizable and deeply nourishing, and tastes so, so good. And if you're a visual baker, as I am, you'll be tickled by this loaf's speckled cross section, which recalls the mosaic terrazzo floors of fifteenth-century Venetian palaces.

Because the bread is so moist, it tastes extra wonderful toasted in a buttered skillet and plated as an open-faced tartine. Or feature this bread in your next breakfast snack plate: cut slices into chubby batons, broil until crisp, and serve with crunchy radishes and apple slices, salty cheese, and soft-boiled eggs.

1. **PREP THE LOAF PAN.** Lightly mist an 8-inch (20 cm) loaf pan with cooking spray.

2. **MIX THE DOUGH.** In a large bowl, combine the oats, millet, hazelnuts, sunflower seeds, sliced almonds, pumpkin seeds, flaxseeds, psyllium seed husks, chia seeds, and salt. Add the water, maple syrup, and olive oil and massage the mixture with your hands. The mixture will be squishy and porridge-like. Sprinkle in the candied watermelon rind. Transfer to the bread pan and use the backs of your knuckles to press the mixture in evenly. Wrap the pan tightly in plastic wrap and refrigerate for at least 8 hours, or up to 3 days.

3. **PREHEAT THE OVEN.** Preheat the oven to 375°F (190°C).

4. **BAKE THE LOAF.** The mixture should look considerably drier and stiff. Transfer the pan to the oven and bake until the top is browned, the sides are beginning to pull away from the pan, and a cake tester inserted comes out clean, 45 to 55 minutes. Remove from the oven.

5. **COOL AND SERVE.** Let the loaf cool completely, about 2 hours, before slicing. Store the bread whole in the refrigerator for up to 1 week, or freeze slices, wrapped well, for up to 1 month.

→

MAKES ONE 8-INCH (20 CM) LOAF
SERVES 8 TO 10

15 MINUTES ACTIVE TIME
8 TO 12 HOURS INACTIVE TIME

1 cup plus 3 tablespoons (100 g) rolled oats

¼ cup plus 1 tablespoon (60 g) millet

1 cup (120 g) hazelnuts, toasted

⅓ cup (45 g) sunflower seeds, toasted

½ cup (45 g) sliced almonds, toasted

¼ cup (40 g) pumpkin seeds, toasted

⅓ cup (60 g) flaxseeds, toasted

2 tablespoons (10 g) psyllium seed husks

1 tablespoon plus 2 teaspoons (15 g) chia seeds

1 teaspoon kosher salt

1¼ cups (300 g) water

2 tablespoons (30 g) maple syrup

2 tablespoons (30 g) olive oil

1 cup (about 130 g) diced Candied Watermelon Rind (recipe follows), drained of syrup

Candied Watermelon Rind

For a sweet, chewy accent that tastes more unexpected than the ubiquitous raisin, delicate cubes of sheer, ombré watermelon rind are pressed into the loaf before baking. Here, summer's leftover melon rinds are cooked into a glossy, sweet-and-sour candy that can be scattered on everything from ice cream to pork chops.

MAKES 2 QUARTS (ABOUT 2 KG)

20 MINUTES ACTIVE TIME
1 HOUR INACTIVE TIME

About 14 ounces (400 g)
   watermelon rind (see tip)
2½ cups (590 g) water
2½ cups (590 g) white vinegar
3 cups (600 g) sugar

TIP —— *Mini watermelons, in addition to their honeyed flavor and crisp texture, possess a thin green rind perfect for candying, so keep an eye out for them at the store and at the farmers' market.*

1. PREP THE RIND. Remove the tough outer green skin of the watermelon with a vegetable peeler. Remove most traces of the red flesh with a spoon, leaving a thin, sheer red layer attached. Cut the rind into strips ½ inch (1.25 cm) thick. Cut the strips into small dice.

2. CANDY GENTLY. In a medium pot, bring the water and vinegar to a simmer. Add the diced rind and cook over a low simmer until just tender, about 20 minutes. The rind should still feel firm. Add the sugar, stir to incorporate, and bring back up to a low simmer. Continue to cook until the syrup has reduced by one-third and the rind looks candied and glossy, about 40 minutes. Let cool completely in the syrup and store in an airtight container, chilled, until ready to use, for up to 1 month.

CORN HUSK MUFFINS

Dried corn husks, fragrant and sturdy, are the indispensable casing for traditional Mexican tamales. In the summer, when corn is fresh, plentiful, and cheap, the fresh husks can double as natural muffin liners, providing just enough structure to support this coconut-scented corn batter.

    Three distinct expressions of coconut—milk, oil, and sugar—convey a tropical, energetic sunniness no matter the time of the year. Unlike most muffin batters, this mix starts with cooking a thick, sludgy porridge made from rich coconut milk and corn flour (coarser meals may be substituted for a nubbier texture). Inspired by classic Italian polenta technique, a precooked porridge adds moisture and tenderness to the muffin, a job usually left to sugar and vegetable oil.

1. **PREHEAT THE OVEN AND PREP THE MUFFIN TIN.** Preheat the oven to 350°F (175°C). Lightly mist 12 cups of a muffin tin with cooking spray.

2. **HUSK THE CORN.** Pull off the corn husks and set them in a bowl of hot water to soak for 15 minutes. (Strip the corn off the cobs and freeze the kernels for future fried rice.) Remove the soaked husks from the water and pat dry. Wind a husk around your index finger to form a loose cigar shape. Place it inside a muffin tin cup and use your fingers to open it to fit. This is your muffin "liner." Repeat with 11 more husks.

3. **COOK THE CORN PORRIDGE.** In a small pot, combine the coconut milk and ½ cup (60 g) of the corn flour. Whisk well over medium-low heat until the mixture has thickened into a paste, about 2 minutes. Remove the porridge from the heat and whisk in the coconut oil until smooth. Whisk in the coconut sugar, yogurt, egg, and vanilla.

4. **MIX THE BATTER.** In a medium bowl, whisk together the remaining ½ cup plus 2 tablespoons (80 g) corn flour, the all-purpose flour, baking powder, baking soda, and salt. Add the

MAKES 12 MUFFINS

30 MINUTES ACTIVE TIME
30 MINUTES INACTIVE TIME

2 ears unshucked corn (see tip)
½ cup plus 2 tablespoons (150 g) canned full-fat coconut milk
1 cup plus 2 tablespoons (140 g) corn flour
¼ cup (60 g) coconut oil
2 tablespoons (40 g) coconut sugar
½ cup (120 g) unsweetened coconut yogurt, at room temperature
1 egg (50 g), at room temperature
1 teaspoon vanilla extract
½ cup (60 g) all-purpose flour
1 teaspoon baking powder
¼ teaspoon baking soda
1 teaspoon kosher salt
Coco-Corn Crumble (recipe follows)

TIP ——*In lieu of fresh corn husks, you can purchase dried corn husks at larger grocery stores, tortilla factories, or online.*

warm corn porridge to the dry ingredients and stir with a spatula to combine. The mixture will feel super thick.

5. **PORTION AND BAKE.** Using a large spoon or an ice cream scoop, spoon 2 tablespoons of batter into the center of each husk nest. Add 1 tablespoon of the corn crumble, then cover with 2 more tablespoons of muffin batter. Add 1 more tablespoon of crumble to the top. Place the pan in the oven and bake until the muffins are domed and spring back when pressed, 25 to 30 minutes.

6. **SERVE AND STORE.** Serve warm. Store cooled leftover muffins in an airtight container in the freezer for up to 1 month. Toast split muffins under a broiler or reheat whole for 5 minutes in a 350°F (175°C) oven (discard the husks first!).

Coco-Corn Crumble

This corn crumble is enough for two dozen muffins, but you can use the leftovers on just about everything. For adding a little crunch and lots of corn flavor, bake a sheet pan of the corn crumble at 350°F (175°C) for 10 to 12 minutes. Let cool, then sprinkle over cold wedges of melon, scoops of ice cream, or the Rose Water and Mezcal Flan (page 235).

MAKES A SCANT 1 CUP (145 G)

10 MINUTES ACTIVE TIME

½ cup (60 g) corn flour
¼ cup (50 g) coconut sugar
½ teaspoon kosher salt
1½ tablespoons (35 g) coconut oil

IN A SMALL BOWL, mix the corn flour, coconut sugar, and salt with your fingertips. Drizzle in the coconut oil and lightly combine with the tips of your fingers. Try not to compress the crumb too tightly. Store in an airtight container in the refrigerator until ready to use.

PEACH COCKTAIL SKILLET

There's a large, spindly peach tree at my parents' house that erupts into fuchsia blooms in the early spring, transforming into heavy fruits in the summer. In Chinese culture, I was taught, the peach is a beloved, enduring symbol of longevity, immortality, and unity. It appears in ancient poetry, ceramics, paintings, and textiles, where depictions of the peach's magical, life-extending properties accompany blushing brides, young love, supernatural myths, and natural vistas.

A fresh peach is worthy of fervent worship. Is there a more immediate pleasure than biting into a waiting peach, its juices streaming down your hand? Even better, peaches lead to irresistible bakes, as in this simple creation, which lies somewhere between a whole wheat muffin, a tender one-layer cake, and a summery fruit crisp.

Fragrant peaches are poached in a syrup spiked with lemon verbena, and can be prepared days in advance. (These can be enjoyed in their own ambrosial syrup or with buttered toast if you aren't making the "skillet.") Once the peaches are cooled and their fuzzy skins tugged off, the slippery segments are tucked into a buttermilk batter, which puffs and rises around the fruit as it bakes.

MAKES ONE 10-INCH (25 CM) PAN
SERVES 8

30 MINUTES ACTIVE TIME
45 MINUTES INACTIVE TIME

3 large ripe peaches, with their
    leaves (see tip #1)
4 to 5 sprigs lemon verbena
    (see tip #2)
1 cup (200 g) granulated sugar
1 cup (240 g) water
Juice of 1 lemon
2 tablespoons (25 g) light brown
    sugar
2 tablespoons (40 g) honey

(ingredients continue)

1. **PREHEAT THE OVEN AND PREP THE PAN.** Preheat the oven to 350°F (175°C). Mist a 10-inch (25 cm) cast-iron skillet (or a large baking dish or cake pan with similar dimensions) with cooking spray. Line with a generous round of parchment paper with edges that ruffle beyond the top of the skillet. Set aside.

2. **POACH THE PEACHES.** Slice the peaches in half lengthwise and pop out the pits (do not discard). In a small deep pot, combine the peach pits, lemon verbena, granulated sugar, and water and bring to a simmer, stirring briefly to dissolve the sugar. Drop the peach halves into the syrup. Poach over very low heat until cooked through (see tip #3)—a small kitchen knife slid into the flesh should enter smoothly—about 12 minutes. Let the peaches cool for 30 minutes, then carefully peel off the skin and slice the peaches into wedges 3/8 inch (1 cm) wide. In a small bowl, toss the sliced peaches with the lemon juice; set aside.

$\rightarrow$

More Than Cake

2 tablespoons (30 g) grapeseed oil
½ cup (120 g) buttermilk, at room
    temperature
¼ cup (60 g) yogurt, at room
    temperature
1 egg (50 g), at room temperature
1 teaspoon vanilla extract
¾ cup (90 g) all-purpose flour
¼ cup plus 2 tablespoons (45 g)
    graham flour
½ teaspoon baking powder
¼ teaspoon baking soda
1 teaspoon kosher salt
Honey Graham Crisp (recipe follows)
Flaky sea salt

TIP 1 ——*If you are fortunate enough
to source fresh peaches with their
green leaves still attached, add them
to the poaching liquid, where they
will impart a subtle almond perfume.
Before baking the cake, rinse the
leaves, pat dry, and tuck them around
the ruffles of the parchment edges, to
form a wreath within the skillet.*

TIP 2 ——*If you aren't able to
source fresh lemon verbena, poach
the peaches in a syrup steeped with
jasmine or oolong tea.*

TIP 3 ——*If the peaches bob to the
surface and refuse to stay submerged,
cut a round of parchment just larger
than your pot and press it on the
surface. For larger batches, a small
dessert plate on top of the parchment
will add enough weight to keep the
fruit under the liquid.*

3. MIX THE BATTER. In a large bowl, whisk together the light brown sugar, honey, grapeseed oil, buttermilk, yogurt, egg, and vanilla. In a second bowl, whisk together the all-purpose flour, graham flour, baking powder, baking soda, and kosher salt. Scrape the wet mixture into the dry ingredients and gently stir with a spatula until just barely combined. Spread the batter in the prepared pan.

4. ADD THE FRUIT AND BAKE. Dot the poached peach slices all over the top, nudging them into the batter. Sprinkle the graham crisp over the cake batter, leaving the peaches mostly exposed. Bake until the cake is slightly pulling away from the parchment ruffle and is set in the center, 30 to 40 minutes. Let cool briefly, then sprinkle with flaky sea salt and slice into wedges. Store leftovers well wrapped in plastic in the refrigerator for up to 4 days.

More Than Cake

Honey Graham Crisp

IN A SMALL POT, melt the butter over low heat. Whisk in the honey and vanilla. Remove from the heat. In a small bowl, mix the graham flour, all-purpose flour, light brown sugar, cinnamon, and salt with your fingertips. Drizzle the honey butter mixture over the dry ingredients. Gently toss together with your fingertips, trying not to compress the crumb too much. Spread out on a pan and refrigerate until the crumbs feel firm to the touch, about 15 minutes. Store in an airtight container in the refrigerator for up to 2 weeks.

MAKES 1 CUP (180 G)

10 MINUTES ACTIVE TIME
15 MINUTES INACTIVE TIME

2 tablespoons (1 ounce/30 g) unsalted butter
1 tablespoon (20 g) honey
1 teaspoon vanilla extract
¼ cup plus 2 tablespoons (45 g) graham or whole wheat flour
¼ cup (30 g) all-purpose flour
¼ cup (50 g) light brown sugar
½ teaspoon ground cinnamon
¼ teaspoon kosher salt

BIG GREEN SALAD SCONES

This savory scone packs an entire salad into its tender, buttery insides. Flush with fresh vegetables, fruits, and cheese, it feels light and bursts with bright flavor. It doesn't have flaky layers, like the Scallion Pancake Biscuits (page 297). Instead, it has a crumbly, puffy texture, with just enough dough to knit together the generous amounts of kale, zucchini, blueberries, and olives.

Unassuming breakfast pastries like scones and muffins are a great way to clean out the fridge, or reinvent last night's leftovers. Rely on the natural moisture and big flavor of raw and cooked produce to add tenderness and character to traditional baked goods. You want every bite to be interesting and full of delicious surprises.

Here, swap out the fresh kale for leftover sautéed, blanched, or roasted greens like broccoli, spinach, or Swiss chard. The grated zucchini can be swapped out for chopped roasted vegetables that are high in moisture, like sweet potatoes, pumpkin, or beets.

1. **PREP THE FILLING.** Bring a few inches (about 8 cm) of water to a boil in a pot. Add the kale and simmer until tender, about 2 minutes. Drain and let cool. Wring out the excess water with your hands and finely chop. Shred the zucchini on the largest holes of a box grater set in a bowl. Wring out the excess water with your hands and weigh out 250 grams of the zucchini (about 1½ cups). In a bowl, combine the kale, zucchini, blueberries, chopped olives, and parsley. Add the olive oil and feta and fluff up with your fingers to combine. Place your "big salad" in the fridge to chill.

2. **START MIXING THE SCONE DOUGH.** In a stand mixer fitted with the paddle, combine the all-purpose flour, whole wheat pastry flour, baking powder, sugar, kosher salt, and pepper. Mix on low speed to combine, about 20 seconds. Add the cold cubed butter and paddle until the butter is the size of small peas, with a few larger chunks, about 3 minutes. With the mixer running on low speed, stream in ½ cup (125 g) of the buttermilk, mixing until combined, about 10 seconds. The mixture will start to look damp,

MAKES 15 SCONES

30 MINUTES ACTIVE TIME
30 MINUTES INACTIVE TIME

1 bunch lacinato (Tuscan) kale, midribs removed, leaves roughly chopped (about 100 g)
2 small zucchini
1 cup (150 g) fresh blueberries (see tip #1)
½ cup (60 g) green olives, pitted and finely chopped
½ cup (15 g) finely chopped fresh parsley
2 tablespoons (30 g) olive oil
8 ounces (225 g) feta cheese, crumbled (about 1½ cups)

(ingredients continue)

3 cups (360 g) all-purpose flour,
    plus more for rolling the dough
½ cup (60 g) whole wheat pastry
    flour
1 tablespoon plus 2 teaspoons
    (25 g) baking powder
2 tablespoons (25 g) sugar
1 teaspoon kosher salt
½ teaspoon freshly ground black
    pepper, plus more for garnish
8 ounces (225 g) unsalted butter,
    cut into ½-inch (1.25 cm) cubes,
    very cold
1 cup (250 g) cold buttermilk
Flaky sea salt

TIP 1 ——*Fresh, frozen, and dried blueberries all work here but require different methods of handling. Frozen blueberries should stay in the freezer until the moment you are ready to add them, so they don't thaw and release additional liquid into the dough. Dried blueberries are also delicious but can get tough and chewy in the oven; reconstitute the berries in 1/2 cup (120 g) boiling water for 10 minutes, and then drain and lightly pat dry.*

TIP 2 ——*If you'd like to make the scones ahead, portion the full batch and then freeze them completely on the pan. Peel the scones off the parchment once frozen and store in freezer bags. Brush buttermilk on them right before they go in the oven.*

with wet dough clinging around the paddle, and drier-looking dough in the bottom of the bowl.

3. FINISH MIXING BY HAND. Turn the dough out onto a clean work surface. Use your fingers to lightly break apart the larger curd-size pieces of dough. Add the zucchini/kale/blueberry mixture. Imagine your hands are salad tongs and gently fluff and fold the ingredients into the flour and butter mixture. Do not compress the crumb with your fingers; let the floury curds drift through your fingertips as you toss the mixture. Use a very light touch and add additional buttermilk 1 tablespoon at a time until the mixture just comes together; it should feel like a wet wool sweater. You will not need all the buttermilk (the rest will be used for a wash); the moisture from the vegetables should assist in binding the dough together.

4. PREHEAT THE OVEN AND PREP THE PANS. Preheat the oven to 400°F (200°C). To bake in batches, cover two half-sheet pans with parchment paper and lightly mist the paper with cooking spray.

5. PORTION AND BAKE. Using the sides of your hands and a bench scraper, pat the dough into a flat rectangle about 6 by 10 inches (15 by 25 cm) and 2 inches (5 cm) thick. Sprinkle on some flour and use a few strokes of a rolling pin to smooth the surface. Use a knife to portion the scones into fifteen 2-inch (5 cm) squares. Transfer 7 or 8 scones to each prepared sheet pan, giving at least 3 inches (7.5 cm) of space between them (see tip #2). Brush the surface of each scone with the remaining buttermilk and transfer to the oven. Bake until the surfaces are deeply golden and the tops spring back when lightly prodded, 25 to 30 minutes. Sprinkle the tops with flaky sea salt and extra black pepper. Serve within 4 to 5 hours of baking.

SCALLION PANCAKE BISCUITS

Growing up, I knew the meal would be special if my mother unearthed her rolling pin to make cong you bing, or scallion pancakes. She rolled, shaped, and pan-fried stack after stack of the flaky unleavened pastries, which were often paired with a hot-pot feast and cold beers. The aroma of these crisp, golden pancakes sizzling in a pan is one of the most indelible scents of my childhood.

The all-American biscuit, too, carries sentimental meaning for so many, whether made from scratch or sprung from a cardboard can. These biscuits incorporate the savory flavors of allium and toasted sesame, sandwiched between layers of tender, yeasted dough.

1. **SHRED THE FROZEN BUTTER** on the largest holes of a box grater. Gather it into a small bowl and return it to the freezer. In another small bowl, combine the sesame oil, chopped scallions, and ½ teaspoon of the kosher salt. Set aside.

2. **MIX THE DOUGH.** In a large bowl, combine the flour, baking powder, baking soda, yeast, sugar, and remaining 1 teaspoon kosher salt and whisk to combine. Add the frozen grated butter all at once and toss and pinch with your fingertips to coat the butter. The mixture will look dry but feel damp.

3. **ADD THE BUTTERMILK.** Form a small well in the center of the flour mixture and drizzle in half of the buttermilk. Using your hands as salad tongs, very gently lift the liquid into the flour mixture, fluffing and folding to combine. Do not compress the crumb with your fingers; let the floury curds fall through your fingertips as you toss the mixture. Use a very light touch and add additional buttermilk 1 tablespoon at a time until the mixture just comes together, like a wet wool sweater. (You should have between 2 and 4 tablespoons buttermilk left over.)

4. **ROLL AND FOLD THE DOUGH.** Using the sides of your hands and a bench scraper, pat the dough into a flat 9-inch (23 cm) square that's ½ inch (1.25 cm) thick. Cut the square vertically into 3 equal columns. Sprinkle the far-left column with

MAKES 8 BIG BISCUITS

30 MINUTES ACTIVE TIME
8 TO 10 HOURS INACTIVE TIME

12 tablespoons (6 ounces/170 g) unsalted butter, frozen
1 tablespoon (15 g) toasted sesame oil
½ cup (50 g) finely chopped scallions (about 4 scallions)
1½ teaspoons kosher salt
3 cups minus 2 tablespoons (345 g) all-purpose flour
½ teaspoon baking powder
½ teaspoon baking soda
1 teaspoon active dry yeast
¼ cup (50 g) sugar
1¼ cups (300 g) cold buttermilk
Flaky sea salt and freshly cracked black pepper

half of the sesame oil/scallion mixture. Gently lift up the middle column and place it on top of the left column. Scatter the remaining scallions on the surface of this stack. Gently lift the far-right column and place it on top of the stack. Use a rolling pin to press this tower down, flattening and shaping the dough to a rectangle 8 by 4 inches (20 by 10 cm) and 2 inches (5 cm) thick.

5. **PORTION THE BISCUITS.** Top a half-sheet pan with a piece of parchment paper and lightly mist with cooking spray. Use a large knife to portion the dough into eight 2-inch (5 cm) squares. Wipe the knife clean after every cut for the cleanest results. Carefully transfer the biscuits to the lined sheet pan, spacing them at least 3 inches (7.5 cm) apart. Drape the pan with plastic wrap and let rest at room temperature for 2 hours (see tip #1). The biscuits will look puffy and feel light and tender to the touch. (Take care not to overproof; see tip #2).

6. **PREHEAT THE OVEN.** About 30 minutes before the biscuits have finished proofing, preheat the oven to 400°F (200°C).

7. **BAKE THE BISCUITS.** Gently brush the remaining buttermilk on the surface of the biscuits and transfer to the oven. Bake until golden, about 20 minutes. Remove from the oven and sprinkle with flaky sea salt and black pepper.

TIP 1 —*The biscuits can also rest, covered, overnight in the fridge. When ready to bake, pull from the fridge and let come to temperature for an hour.*

TIP 2 —*Overproofing yeast results in a dense, short biscuit, as the gluten has been stretched to its limit and can no longer support the gases building inside. If you spot small holes on the surface of the biscuits before baking, that's an indicator that the biscuits are beginning to overproof and may collapse in the oven.*

SWEET ONION AND SESAME GOUGÈRES

These cheese puffs, known as gougères, are a symphony of contrasting textures, temperatures, and intense, piquant flavor. The foundation of this essential savory pastry is the silky, golden dough known as pâte à choux.

Traditionally, bite-size gougères are served as a snack or an appetizer with wine and cocktails, a salty morsel intended to stimulate the palate before dinner. But for breakfast, or a midmorning pick-me-up, a gougère, dotted with sweet caramelized onions, feels surprisingly substantial.

Bake these puffs for longer than you might think; the shell should look deeply burnished, and the inside hollow and light. A thick paste made with sesame seeds and rice flour adds structure and crunch, similar to the buttery cookie topping called craquelin (see page 243).

MAKES 40 TO 50 TWO-BITE GOUGÈRES

45 MINUTES ACTIVE TIME
35 MINUTES INACTIVE TIME

¼ cup (40 g) rice flour
¼ cup (35 g) white or black sesame seeds
2 teaspoons light brown sugar
2 teaspoons toasted sesame oil
¾ cup (180 g) water, plus more if needed
1 tablespoon (15 g) olive oil
1 medium yellow or white onion, halved lengthwise and cut into ½-inch (1.25 cm) half-moons
8 tablespoons (4 ounces/115 g) unsalted butter
½ cup (120 g) whole milk
1 tablespoon (15 g) sugar

(ingredients continue)

1. **MIX THE SEED TOPPING.** In a small bowl, whisk together the rice flour, sesame seeds, light brown sugar, sesame oil, and ¼ cup (60 g) of the water. The mixture should look like a runny, drippy paste.

2. **COOK THE ONIONS.** In a medium pot (see tip #1 on page 241), heat the olive oil over low heat. Add the onions and cook, stirring occasionally, until the onions are yielding and caramelized, 30 to 35 minutes. (Splash in an extra tablespoon of water if the onions are sticking.) Scrape the onions out of the pot and onto a cutting board. Finely chop and set aside.

3. **START TO MAKE THE DOUGH.** In the same pot, combine the remaining ½ cup (120 g) water, the butter, milk, sugar, and salt and bring to a simmer over medium-high heat, about 3 minutes. Add the all-purpose flour and vigorously beat the mixture with a wooden spoon or spatula until a ball of dough forms, pressing down with the spoon to work out any lumps.

4. **COOK THE FLOUR PASTE.** Continue to push, smear, and move the dough ball around, releasing steam from the

1 teaspoon kosher salt

1⅓ cups (160 g) all-purpose flour

5 eggs (250 g), whisked together

½ cup (55 g) coarsely grated melty cheese, such as cheddar or Gruyère

TIP —— *Choux bakes tall and sturdy from frozen, not to mention it's so much easier to move the small frozen pucks of dough around on a baking sheet. Place the sheet pans of piped dough in the freezer until completely solid, then peel the discs off the parchment and transfer to a sealed container or freezer bag. The sesame paste can be frozen in a small airtight container and thawed overnight before baking.*

paste. After 3 to 4 minutes, a gummy layer of starch should form on the bottom of the pot. Do not scrape this mixture up; let it build! Lift up the side of the dough with your spatula and let it drop back into the pot; it should feel supple and emulsified and pull cleanly away from the pot. Remove from the heat and immediately transfer the mixture to a stand mixer fitted with the paddle. (If using a handheld mixer, transfer to a medium bowl.) Let the mixture cool for at least 15 to 20 minutes. (Ideally, the batter should be completely cool before adding the eggs, which will result in a stronger and better rise in the oven.)

5. MEANWHILE, PREHEAT THE OVEN. Preheat the oven to 425°F (220°C).

6. STREAM IN THE EGGS. With the mixer running on medium-low speed, stream in ⅓ cup of whisked egg and paddle until combined. Turn off the mixer, scrape the bottom of the bowl, and mix again. Add another ⅓ cup of whisked egg and repeat. The mixture will gradually loosen and increase in shine. When you have ⅓ cup of whisked egg left, stream in a tablespoon at a time, until the dough appears golden and glossy and spools easily around the paddle. (If you turn the mixer off, the ribbon of dough should cling to the paddle for one beat and then slowly slump away.) You may not need all of the whisked egg. Add the chopped caramelized onions and the grated cheese and stir to combine.

7. PORTION THE GOUGÈRES. To bake in batches, top two half-sheet pans with parchment paper. Transfer the dough to a piping bag or plastic storage bag, cut an opening ½ inch (1.25 cm) wide in the tip or a bottom corner, and portion 1½ tablespoons of dough onto the parchment-lined pans. (Alternatively, use a spoon to portion the dough.) Aim for gougères about 1 inch (2.5 cm) wide and space them 2 inches (5 cm) apart; you should be able to fit 20 to 25 on each pan. (If you want to save some, or all, to bake later, see tip.)

8. TOP THE GOUGÈRES AND BAKE. Spoon ½ teaspoon of the sesame seed paste on top of each choux. Bake until puffed, fragrant, and deeply golden and the gougères feel hollow when picked up, about 20 minutes. Remove from the oven, tilt each one on its side, and use a small paring knife or cake tester to prick a small hole in the base of each puff, allowing the steam to escape. Serve warm or let cool.

MOCHA LATTE PUFFS

For a recipe that triples as a breakfast treat, an afternoon snack, or an elegant dessert, pâte à choux is the perfect place to start. I love these puffs for breakfast, as the buckwheat's earthy scent snuggles right up to the warming, roasted fragrance of coffee, maple syrup, and pecans.

1. **START TO MAKE THE DOUGH.** In a medium pot (see tip #1 on page 241), combine the butter, water, milk, vanilla, maple sugar, and salt and bring to a simmer over medium-high heat, about 3 minutes. Add the all-purpose and buckwheat flours and vigorously beat the mixture with a wooden spoon or spatula until a ball of dough forms, pressing down with the spoon to work out any lumps.

2. **COOK THE FLOUR PASTE.** Continue to push, smear, and move the dough ball around, releasing steam from the paste. After 3 to 4 minutes, a gummy layer of starch should form on the bottom of the pot. Do not scrape this mixture up; let it build! Lift up the side of the dough with your spatula and let it drop back into the pot; it should feel supple and emulsified and pull cleanly away from the pot. Remove from the heat and transfer the mixture to a stand mixer fitted with the paddle (or to a large bowl if using a handheld mixer). Let the mixture cool for at least 15 to 20 minutes. (Ideally, the batter should be completely cool before adding the eggs, which will result in a stronger and better rise in the oven.)

3. **MEANWHILE, PREHEAT THE OVEN.** Preheat the oven to 425°F (220°C).

4. **STREAM IN THE EGGS.** In a small bowl, whisk together the eggs. With the mixer running on medium-low speed, stream in 3 tablespoons of the whisked egg and paddle until combined. Turn off the mixer, scrape the bottom of the bowl well, and mix again. Add another 3 tablespoons of whisked egg and repeat. The mixture will gradually loosen and increase in shine. Stream in the remaining whisked egg just a tablespoon at a time, until the dough appears golden and glossy and spools easily around the

MAKES 12 TO 15 PUFFS

30 MINUTES ACTIVE TIME
30 MINUTES INACTIVE TIME

4 tablespoons (2 ounces/60 g)
   unsalted butter
¼ cup (60 g) water
¼ cup (60 g) whole milk
1 teaspoon vanilla extract
2 tablespoons (25 g) maple sugar
½ teaspoon kosher salt
½ cup (60 g) all-purpose flour
2 teaspoons buckwheat flour
3 eggs (150 g), whisked together
Mocha Craquelin (recipe follows),
   frozen
1½ cups (360 g) cold heavy cream
½ cup (110 g) mascarpone, well
   chilled
1 tablespoon (6 g) instant coffee
1 tablespoon (7 g) powdered sugar,
   plus more for dusting
½ cup (65 g) Maple Pecans (recipe
   follows), roughly chopped

paddle. (If you turn the mixer off, the ribbon of dough should cling to the paddle for one beat and then slowly slump away.) You may not need all of the whisked egg.

5. **PORTION THE PUFFS.** To bake in batches, top two half-sheet pans with parchment paper. Transfer the dough to a piping bag or zip-seal bag, cut an opening ½ inch (1.25 cm) wide in the tip or a bottom corner, and portion 2 heaping tablespoons of dough onto the prepared sheet pans, staggering the puffs 3 inches (7.5 cm) apart. (Or use a spoon to portion the dough.) You should be able to fit 6 to 8 puffs on each half-sheet pan.

6. **TOP WITH CRAQUELIN AND BAKE.** Place a frozen round of craquelin on top of each puff. Bake for 20 minutes, then rotate the pans front to back and reduce the oven temperature to 375°F (190°C). Bake until the puffs feel hollow when picked up and have crisp bottoms, 8 to 10 minutes. Remove from the oven and use a small paring knife or cake tester to prick a small hole on the base of each puff, allowing the steam to escape. Lean each puff on the rim of the baking sheet and let cool completely.

7. **MEANWHILE, MAKE THE CREAM FILLING.** In a stand mixer fitted with the whisk (or in a large bowl using a handheld mixer), whip the chilled heavy cream, mascarpone, instant coffee, and powdered sugar on high speed until stiff, glossy peaks form, about 5 minutes. Transfer the mixture to a piping bag fitted with a star tip.

8. **FILL THE PUFFS.** Slice the puffs in half crosswise, like you'd slice a hamburger bun, and pipe a thick ring of cream on each bottom half. Sprinkle the maple pecan pieces in the center and place the top halves of the choux on top, like a jaunty hat. Serve immediately.

→

Mocha Craquelin

Versions of a crunchy cookie topping—called *craquelin* in France, where it is paired with eclairs, cream puffs, and more—appear in pastries all around the world, where they inspire descriptive titles. In Mexico, the sandy topping on concha buns is scored to resemble a seashell. On tijgerbrood, a Dutch bread with a mottled crust, it recalls a tiger's stripes. For the Chinese yeasted bun bo lo bao, the cookie cap resembles the knobby skin of a pineapple, while in Japan, a similar bun is called *melonpan*, due to the cookie crust's similarity to the scaly exterior of a cantaloupe.

MAKES 12 ROUNDS

15 MINUTES ACTIVE TIME
1 HOUR INACTIVE TIME

4 tablespoons (2 ounces/60 g) unsalted butter, cubed, at room temperature
¼ cup plus 2 tablespoons (75 g) sugar
1 teaspoon vanilla extract
½ cup plus 2 tablespoons (75 g) all-purpose flour
1 tablespoon (5 g) unsweetened cocoa powder
½ teaspoon ground cinnamon
1 tablespoon (6 g) ground espresso or instant coffee
½ teaspoon kosher salt

1. MIX THE CRAQUELIN. In a stand mixer fitted with the paddle (or in a large bowl using a handheld mixer), cream the butter and sugar together for 2 minutes. Scrape the bowl well. Add the vanilla and paddle to combine, about 5 seconds. Add the all-purpose flour, cocoa powder, cinnamon, ground espresso, and salt and paddle on low speed until just combined, about 15 seconds.

2. ROLL OUT THE CRAQUELIN. Transfer the dough to a 12-by-16-inch (30 by 40 cm) sheet of parchment paper and press another piece of parchment on top. Use a rolling pin to firmly press the dough down, sandwiching it between the sheets of parchment. Roll the dough out very thin, to about the dimensions of the parchment paper. Transfer the parchment pack to the fridge for at least 30 minutes.

3. PORTION THE CRAQUELIN. Remove the dough sheet from the refrigerator. Carefully peel the top piece of parchment off. Using a 3-inch (7.5 cm) round cookie cutter, punch out 12 rounds. If the craquelin begins to smear, return to the fridge before attempting to punch more. Let the rounds freeze fully on a parchment-lined sheet before stacking in a container. Store frozen until ready to use.

Maple Pecans

IN A SMALL BOWL, combine the maple sugar and a big pinch of flaky salt. In a small pot, bring the maple syrup, butter, rum, and vanilla to a boil over medium-high heat. Whisk well. Let reduce by half, swirling the pot occasionally, 3 to 4 minutes. The sauce should look thick and golden brown and bubble evenly (see tip). Add the pecans and reduce the heat to medium-low. Continue to simmer until the syrup tightly clings to the nuts and the pot is beginning to dry out, another 4 to 5 minutes. Transfer the hot nuts to the bowl of maple sugar and toss to coat. Spread the nuts on a sheet pan covered in parchment paper and let cool completely. Store in an airtight container in the refrigerator for up to 2 weeks.

MAKES 1 CUP (130 G)

10 MINUTES ACTIVE TIME

2 tablespoons (25 g) maple sugar
Flaky sea salt
2 tablespoons (40 g) maple syrup
1 tablespoon (½ ounce/15 g) unsalted butter
1 teaspoon rum or bourbon
½ teaspoon vanilla extract
¾ cup (75 g) pecan pieces, toasted

TIP ——*If your caramel sauce ever breaks (the butter will separate from the sugar and it will look greasy), you can recover it by removing it from the heat, adding 1 tablespoon cold butter, and whisking well until it looks smooth again.*

RESOURCES

To purchase the ingredients I use to make these recipes, refer to this guide to plan your shopping for some of the more hard-to-find ingredients. If you don't have access to these types of stores where you live, a quick search on the internet will give you plenty of options for shipping ingredients right to your door.

Specialty Cake and Restaurant Supplies

Online stores like NY Cake or JB Prince stock essential kitchen tools as well as more obscure cake-related ingredients, such as these:

Doughnut sugar (also called snow sugar)
Flavor extracts, like almond and rose water
Food coloring
Hazelnut praline
Invert sugars (like glucose, Golden Syrup, and
    Trimoline)

Asian Supermarkets

I shop at markets like H Mart, Mitsuwa, 99 Ranch Market, and Katagiri for the following ingredients, but check your own neighborhood for similar Asian groceries.

Barley tea (mugicha)
Black sesame paste
Miso paste
Roasted peanuts, skin-on
Shoyu
Sweetened adzuki bean paste
Toasted sesame oil
Wakame seaweed
White rice flour

Stores That Specialize in Bulk

For spices, extracts, oils, coffees, and nuts, specialty stores that sell in bulk are a great place to look (in New York City, I go to Kalustyan's or SOS Chefs).

Cooking wines
Fruit purees (I love Boiron brand)
Ground sumac
Hard-to-find dried fruits, nuts, and seeds
Verjus

Italian Markets

Imported European ingredients are easily found online, but I love in-person shopping, from the big stores like Eataly to the compact shelves of Archestratus Books + Foods in Brooklyn, where you can find the following:

Amarena or candied cherries (my favorite brands are
    Toschi and Luxardo)
Calabrian chiles in oil
Finishing olive oil
Fruit and wine vinegars
Italian cheeses like Taleggio, caciocavallo, and
    fontina
Mortadella
Pistachio paste (look for Italian brands, like Vincente
    Delicacies or Marco Colzani)

Neighborhood Stores and Online

Here are some of my very favorite and most trustworthy brands that I find online and in stores.

Burlap & Barrel: spices, like cinnamon and
    black peppercorns, as well as poppy seeds
    and finishing salt
Guittard: chocolate bars, chocolate chunks, and
    cocoa powder
Heilala Vanilla: vanilla extract and whole beans
King Arthur Flour, Flourist, and Anson Mills: whole-
    grain and freshly milled flours
Supernatural Kitchen: sprinkles and coconut sugar
Tart Vinegar: Delicate, raw vinegars
Valrhona: white chocolate and gianduja

ACKNOWLEDGMENTS

I still can't believe it—we made a book! The completion of this project simply would not have been possible without the unique contributions of so many people I love and respect.

Thank you to my wise, all-knowing editor, Judy Pray; publisher Lia Ronnen; publicist Theresa Collier; and all the incredible women at Artisan Books, including Sibylle Kazeroid, Suet Chong, Nina Simoneaux, and Nancy Murray, who brought this book to life. To my indispensable agent, Kitty Cowles, I would have crumbled from the beginning without you. To my book designer, Giulia Garbin, I've admired your work for so long, I still can't believe your hand is in these pages.

Almost every photo in this book was shot either at my parents' home in La Jolla or in my home, in Greenpoint, Brooklyn. I owe so much to the extraordinary team of people who convened to make these shoots some of the most memorable and intense experiences of my life. To photographers Nikole Herriott and Michael Graydon, you are true artists. It was an honor to work with you. Emily Eisen, peerless creative director and prop stylist, your vision, stubbornness, and dedication make me weep with gratitude. Audrey Chin, Audrey Snyder, and Kate Steffy—thank you for doing literally everything and anything. To Claudette Zepeda and Crystal White, thank you for your generosity (and speed racks and stand mixers).

Thank you to the Chino family, of the beloved Vegetable Shop at Chino Farm, for your generosity and faith in this project.

I'm deeply indebted to three spectacular women who shared their kitchens so I could bake every recipe in the book. Thank you, Farideh Sadeghin and Munchies. Thank you, Doris Hồ-Kane and your perfect bakery, Ban Bè. Thank you, Paige Lipari and Archestratus Books + Foods.

To the New York Public Library system, thank you for your big, quiet rooms and nice staff. I wrote most of my book in these sacred spaces.

Thank you to all of my dedicated recipe testers: Sophie Jenkins, Jake Stavis, Monica Stolbach, Becky Waddell, Lauren Schofield, Chantal Nguyen, Salley Koo, Simone Steinicke, Maggie Helmick, Ayano Elson, Elayna Smith, Hannah Borghi, Ida Fung Rifkin, Anya Kurennaya, Felicity Spector, Shirine Sajjadi, Kirsten Lee, Caroline Tisdale, Jessica Sbarsky, Christine Foote, Nikki Metzgar, Anais Hawkins, and Maggie Be.

So many terrific businesses supported the making of this book. Thank you, All-Clad, Guittard Chocolate Company, Handsome Brook Farms, Madre Mezcal, Supernatural Kitchen, Material, Waka Waka, Caron Callahan, Vermont Creamery, Tart Vinegar, Sanzo, Zev Rovine Selections, Heilala Vanilla, Burlap & Barrel, Susan Alexandra, and Natoora.

To my irreplaceable, implacable, outrageous friends. Thank you, Alison Leiby, Al Culliton, Zoë Mowat, Lindsey Peckham, Erina Angelucci, Mindy Cardozo, Georgia Hilmer, Cynthia Leung, Sierra Echegaray, Adinah Dancyger, and Judy Kim.

And to my fellow pastry pals, who dispensed advice and friendship. Thank you, Michelle Marek, Camilla Wynne, Jen Monroe, Agatha Kulaga, Kerry Diamond, Ana Ortiz, and Zoë Kanan. They say you should never meet your heroes, but I'm so glad I did; thank you, Claudia Fleming, Liz Prueitt, Carla Lalli Music, Claire Saffitz, Dorie Greenspan, Brooks Headley, Antoni Porowski, and Kristina Cho.

To Steven Reker, who cooked me so many delicious meals and played me so much good music but mostly was there, unflinching, through uncertainty and anxiety: thank you and I love you.

My parents, Paul and Lee, became artists and scholars, which led them to each other, and then they had me: thank you and I love you. Everything that I am in this world would not be possible without your love and guidance. I hold gratitude especially for my mom, who created the artwork for every single one of my pop-ups, and now, this book.

And thank you, reader, for taking a chance on this book; all of me is in it.

INDEX

Natasha Pickowicz is a New York City–based chef and writer. She is a three-time James Beard Foundation Award finalist.

Much of her pastry work explores the relationship between baking and social justice, including ongoing collaborations with seminal New York City institutions like Lenox Hill Neighborhood House and God's Love We Deliver. Her bake sales for the Brigid Alliance and Planned Parenthood of Greater New York raised more than $180,000 between 2017 and 2022.

Currently, Pickowicz runs the pastry pop-up called Never Ending Taste, which has been held at NYC's Superiority Burger, Brooklyn's the Four Horsemen, the American-Vietnamese bakery Bạn Bè, the Taiwanese tearoom Té Company, Los Angeles's Kismet, and the legendary Chino Farm in Rancho Santa Fe, California.

Pickowicz's recipes and writing have been published in the *New York Times*, the *Wall Street Journal*, *Bon Appétit*, *Saveur*, *Food & Wine*, *New York* magazine, *Cherry Bombe*, and many other publications. Follow her on Instagram at @natashapickowicz.